MATERIAL DIFFERENCES: ART AND IDENTITY IN AFRICA

MATERIAL DIFFERENCES is published in conjunction with an exhibition of the same title organized by the Museum for African Art, New York. The exhibition and this catalogue have been made possible in part through the generous support of the National Endowment for the Arts and Hennessy Privilège V.S.O.P.

Deputy Director of Exhibitions and Publications: Frank Herreman
Curator: Laurie Farrell
Text editors: David Frankel (H. Cole, P. Foss, P. Girshick, M. Jordan, J. Vogel); Stephen Robert Frankel
(M. Chadeisson, W. Dewey, C. Roy); Kathleen Mills (C. Petridis).
Translation: Alger D. Buat from Dutch for H. Burssens essay

Library of Congress Control Number. 2003103198
Paper bound ISBN 0-945802-34-X
Cloth bound ISBN 90-5349-458-8

Front cover: cat. 64. Figure representing Ogun or Gu. Fon peoples, Republic of Benin; cat. 26. Ivory head. Lega peoples, Dem. Rep. of Congo; cat. 1. Brass head. Benin, Nigeria; cat. 42. Stone head. Guinea; cat. 126. Power figure. Songye peoples, Dem. Rep. of Congo; cat. 85. Ceramic in the shape of a vessel by Madeleine Odundo, 2001;

Back cover: cat. 57. Currency(?). Lobi (?)peoples, Burkina Faso; cat. 74. Terracotta head. Akan peoples, Ghana; cat. 89. Helmet. Koma-Builsa peoples, Ghana; cat. 103. Ceremonial swords. Ashanti peoples, Ghana; cat. 20. Mask. Bwa peoples, Burkina Faso .

Designed, printed, and bound in Belgium by Snoeck-Ducaju & Zoon.

Photo credits: All catalogue objects by Jerry L. Thompson except for the following catalogue numbers:
Roger Asselberghs, 26, 28-31, 34, 36-38; Dick Beaulieux, 9, 27, 40, 48, 66, 94, 111, 124; Michael Cavanaugh/Kevin Montague, 72, 73; Jennifer Chiappardi, 95; Judy Cooper, 4, 13, 21, 74, 76, 96, 97, 104-109, 116; Charles Davis, 115; Hughes Dubois, Brussels, 118; courtesy Etnografisch Museum, Antwerpen, 10, 63; Lynton Gardiner, 49, 55, 56, 65; Bart Herreman, 42-46, 79, 114; Jonathan Lynch, 85; Hugo Maertens, 113; Scott McCue, 8, 52; Winston M. Rodney, 82; H. Schneebeli, London, 89; Gregory Staley, 41, 90, 92; Gary Van Wyk, 83; Wettstein und Kauf, Zurich, 88. Illustration photographs credited in accompanying captions.

NATIONAL ENDOWMENT FOR THE ARTS   Hennessy Privilège V.S.O.P

Material Differences

Art and Identity in Africa

Edited by
Frank Herreman

with contributions by
Herman Burssens
Michelle Chadeisson
Herbert M. Cole
William J. Dewey
Perkins Foss
Paula Ben-Amos Girshick
Manuel A. Jordán
Constantine Petridis
Christopher D. Roy
Jerome Vogel

MUSEUM OF AFRICAN ART, New York

SNOECK-DUCAJU & ZOON, Gent

Preface

Photo: Phillip Lasansky, in the home / studio of Mauricio and Emilio Lasansky May 2001.

This exhibition is dedicated to Roy Sieber, a remarkable African art scholar, whose notes, printed here, remind us of the extraordinary degree to which he discovered and analyzed subjects not previously considered, and of how his great knowledge of historical sources allowed him to put together and make sense of seemingly unrelated facts.

There is probably no other scholarly field in which one person's lifework formed such an amazing percentage of the teachers and scholars as Roy did for African Art History. Because of his extraordinary generosity of spirit, virtually everyone in the field considered themselves his "student." Indeed we all benefited from his invaluable advice and, in doing so, became part of his enormous extended family. Even institutions like the Museum for African Art, to which he had no formal link, benefited from his encouragement, wisdom and the stimulation of his constant flow of ideas. We had hoped that he would be able to take a more active role in this project as he did with our exhibition *Hair in African Art and Culture*. Sadly, this was not possible. As with everyone connected to African art, we realize that no one will ever fill his special place.

He will be greatly missed.

The Board of Trustees of the Museum for African Art

ELSIE McCABE
President

FRANK HERREMAN
Deputy Director for Exhibitions

Acknowledgments

It is a great pleasure for me to acknowledge the people involved in the making of the exhibition **Material Differences: Art and Identity in Africa**. Over the last three years I worked with several scholars who provided me with precious information and support. Therefore, I would especially like to thank the essayists in this catalogue: Herman Burssens, Michelle Chadeisson, Herbert M. Cole, William Dewey, Perkins Foss, Paula Ben-Amos Girshick, Manuel Jordán, Constantine Petridis, Christopher Roy, and Jerome Vogel.

I also would like to thank Jan Van Alphen, Director, and Els De Palmenaer, Curator for African Art, Etnografisch Museum - Antwerpen; and David E. Chesebrough, Director and Elizabeth Peña, Curator - Buffalo Museum of Science, Buffalo.

No exhibition is possible without the willingness of the many collectors, public and private, to lend their artworks. The lenders are: Buffalo Museum of Science, Buffalo; Corice Canton Arman and Arman, Myrna and Ira Brind, Mr. and Mrs. Carrie-Vacher, Dr. and Mrs. James Christensen, John Crawford, Gerald and Lila Dannenberg, Charles and Kent Davis, Walt Disney Imagineering, Drs. Jean and Noble Endicott, Etnografisch Museum, Antwerpen, Galerie Jacques Germain, Montreal, Marc and Denyse Ginzberg, Toby and Barry Hecht, W. and U. Horstmann, William Itter, Leonard and Judith Kahan, Mr. and Mrs. J. Thomas Lewis, Adam M. Lindemann, Drs. Daniel and Marian Malcolm, Charles D. Miller III, Michael Oliver, Pace Primitive Gallery - New York, Françoise Billion Richardson, Laura and James J. Ross, Richard H. Scheller, Simmons Collection, Anthony Slayter-Ralph, Cecilia S. Smiley, Gary van Wyk and Lisa Brittan/ Axis Gallery - New York, Jerome Vogel, Stewart J. Warkow, James Willis Tribal Arts, and those who wish to remain anonymous.

I wish to thank the Board of Trustees at the Museum for African Art, and Elsie Crum McCabe, President. My gratitude goes to all staff members and volunteers of the Museum. I would especially like to thank Jerome Vogel, Senior Advisor; for his precious suggestions. Finally, I would like to thank the curatorial staff, Laurie Farrell, Curator; Giacomo Mirabella, Registrar; Carol Braide, Publications Manager; and Alisa McCusker, Curatorial Assistant.

FRANK HERREMAN
Curator and Deputy Director for Exhibitions

Contributors

Herman Burssens is Professor Emeritus of African Arts and Cultures, University of Ghent, Belgium. He is author of several books and essays on the sculpture of Northern Congo.

Michelle Chadeisson is a French independent scholar of Sub-Saharan African aesthetics who has published a book and articles on the function and meaning of religious imagery in African art. Forthcoming is a chronicle of the evolving perceptions of African art.

Herbert M. Cole is Professor Emeritus of African Art at the University of California, Santa Barbara. Considered the preeminent scholar on the Igbo peoples of Nigeria, he has written, co-authored or edited eight books on African art, and is the recipient of the ACASA Leadership award at the 2001 Triennial Symposium.

William J. Dewey teaches African Art History in The School of Art at the University of Tennessee. Since 1983, when he conducted dissertation fieldwork in Zimbabwe focusing on Shona blacksmiths, he has visited and interviewed blacksmiths in Zaire (now Democratic Republic of the Congo), Zambia, Mozambique, Uganda, Tanzania, Zanzibar and Madagascar. A recreation of traditional Shona iron smelting is featured in his 1990 video, *Weapons for the Ancestors.*

Perkins Foss has taught the History of Art at Dartmouth College and Plymouth State College. Currently curating an exhibition on the Urhobo of southeastern Nigeria at the Museum for African Art, he has documented this culture since the 1960s first as an ethnographer for the Nigerian Department of Antiquities and subsequently on trips to this region, accumulating a lifetime of scholarship on the Urhobo.

Paula Ben-Amos Girshick is Professor of Anthropology and African Studies at Indiana University, Bloomington. After years of fieldwork and research conducted in Africa, Europe, and the U.S., she is considered an expert on the culture and art of the Edo people and the Benin Kingdom of Nigeria and has written several books and publications on this and related subjects.

Frank Herreman, the Deputy Director for Exhibitions and Publications at the Museum for African Art since 1995. He has curated the exhibition *Face of the Spirits: Masks from the Zaire Basin*, 1994, which premiered in Belgium and traveled to the United States. He also curated *Liberated Voices: Contemporary Art from South Africa, Hair in African Art,* co-curated with Roy Sieber; *In the Presence of Spirits,* and *Facing the Mask.*

Manuel A. Jordán is Curator of the Arts of Africa, Oceania, and the Americas at the Iris & B. Gerald Cantor Center for Visual Arts, Stanford University. He is considered a leading authority on the arts and culture of Angolan and Zambian peoples, having conducted fieldwork and research among them as a graduate student and later as curator of a major exhibition on the Chokwe peoples.

Constantine Petridis is Assistant Curator of African Art at the Cleveland Museum of Art and Assistant Professor of Art History at Case Western Reserve University in Cleveland, Ohio. He is the editor and main author of *Frans M. Olbrechts (1899-1958): In Search of Art in Africa*, which appeared in conjunction with an exhibition at the Ethnographic Museum Antwerp, Belgium, in 2001.

Christopher D. Roy teaches African Art History at the University of Iowa. He has been conducting research in Africa since 1966, focusing on the peoples of Burkina Faso where he was director of the National Art Center while serving as a Peace Corps volunteer. He has published three books and collaborated on the creation of a CD-ROM on African Art funded by the National Endowment for the Humanities and the US Department of Education.

Jerome Vogel teaches a course on African ceramics as part of the Drew University West Africa Program. He has been conducting research on Baule potters with special emphasis on the changes caused by their shifting client base. His long-time relationship with the Baule dates from 1968 when he was director of Crossroads Africa and continues to the present.

Contents

CAT. 1

Head

Benin, Nigeria
Brass. H. 28 cm.
Laura and James J. Ross

CAT. 2

Head

Bini peoples, Nigeria
Wood and copper sheet. H. 45.1 cm.
Private Collection

CAT. 3

Head

Benin, Nigeria
Terracotta. H. 35.6 cm.
Drs. Daniel and Marian Malcolm
Private Collection

Different materials are used for the making of these three heads from the Kingdom of Benin. All three are used to honor ancestors. The Brass heads are placed on royal altars. The commemorative heads of wood are placed on the altars of the chiefs. The terracotta heads are placed on the altars of the brasscasters to honor their ancestors. The use of different materials indicates different levels of social stratification. (F.H.)
(Ezra 1992:47).

Introduction

FRANK HERREMAN

'*Material Differences; Art and Identity in Africa*' assembles a series of artworks executed in different media to uncover the meaning in these materials. Most of the selected objects were used in ancestor, initiation, and agrarian rituals or were used in ceremonies that strengthened leadership or fostered social cohesion. This exhibition however, does not focus mainly on their ritual function. First, it intends to demonstrate that in many cases each of the materials that are chosen to create a work of art, have an intrinsic symbolic meaning which contributes to a major extent to the metaphorical significance of the artwork as a ritual object. Secondly, the nature of these materials demonstrates that each of them may lead to different formal solutions in the way African artists create figural sculptures.

The Medium as an Animated Substance

The belief that certain materials have a metaphorical meaning is universal. Among many sub-Saharan cultures, this belief places great importance on the materials used in different ritual and secular contexts. Many mineral and organic materials are believed to contain supernatural properties that are associated with protection and healing or with leadership. The symbolic meaning of a specific raw material may differ from people to people, often depending on its availability or its control by individuals within the group.

African sculptures are functional objects. Many of them are considered to provide a link with the world of gods, ancestors and nature spirits. They serve as containers of supernatural powers that can be manipulated or as the earthly residence of ancestor spirits. Through these sculptures, individuals or the community are believed to solicit and receive help. African artists do not choose the materials they will use to make these sculptures randomly. They are carefully selected before they are to be transformed into a specific tool of communication with the supernatural. For sculptors, these raw materials are already inhabited by spiritual forces. They show respect for the wood, ivory, iron or brass to be used by asking permission before transforming them into ritual objects. Throughout the process of creation, the artist continues to maintain contact with the supernatural world through prayers and sacrifices and will abstain from sexual intercourse. It is believed that observing these rules will assure a successful result.

In *African Accumulative Sculpture: Power and Display*, Arnold Rubin sorts materials that are used to make sculptures into two functional categories: the first category consists of display materials that are primarily oriented toward enhancement of the splendor of the objects to which they are attached. The second category consists of materials connected with the organization and exploitation of spiritual power. Both should be considered as active or 'animated' components of the work of art. Arnold Rubin connects these categories to objects that are made by accumulated materials. However, separately, each of these materials must be considered as animated. He also mentions that both power and display can also be associated in the same material. Rubin's categories continue to apply today. The concepts display and power run like a red thread throughout the entire exhibition.

Transforming Materials into Works of Art

The wide variety of materials used to create works of art requires the mastering of different techniques. Subtraction, applied to wood, ivory or stone, contrasts with techniques that involve modeling or building up in clay or wax, or blacksmithing that consists of the bending of glowing iron. Each of these techniques leads to different ways of figural representation. Often, the technique affects the look of the finished piece.

The vast majority of wooden sculptures in Africa encourage the stereotype that African art is static, symmetrical and frontal. Two of the contributors, William Dewey and Jerome Vogel, mention that this notion does not apply to materials such as iron and clay. Indeed, many of the sculptural objects in these materials demonstrate that a sense of movement can be obtained through the modeling of asymmetric poses. Clay and wax, the latter modeled in a similar way to the first, are soft substances that are molded directly by the artists without the use of tools. When fresh, they can constantly be modified or reshaped. Sculpting in wood, ivory or stone is more definitive and excludes major modifications. This diversity in the representational possibilities for each of the materials indicates that different formal traditions have been developed simultaneously over a long period of time.

While many artists may master different techniques like woodcarving and blacksmithing, it should be mentioned that the technique of casting in lost wax that is used for copper alloys and gold requires specialization that would lead to the creation of guilds as in the Kingdom of Benin. Women generally model vessels in clay. Some figural sculptures in terracotta are also attributed to women artists. The creation of works in wood, iron or copper alloys, by women is in traditional sub-Saharan cultures uncommon.

The Exhibition

'Material Differences; Art and Identity in Africa' is organized in a sequence of sections that give information about the techniques that are applied to the transformation of raw materials into works of art. Simultaneously, an attempt is made to underscore the symbolic meaning of these materials in relation to the function of the art works they are used for. The first section of the exhibition deals with techniques of subtraction that reveal the forms contained in materials such as wood, ivory and stone. Transforming through fire is the second section that assembles the materials iron, clay, copper alloys and gold. It is followed by a selection of works made of ephemeral and 'un-transportable' materials. The exhibition concludes with a discussion of various materials that are applied to create works of art that accumulate supernatural powers or may enhance the prestige of their owners.

In our society materials are considered inanimate substances that are chosen for practical reasons. They are valued according to a balance that shifts between usefulness and rarity, reasons that bring them also into the realm of economic activities. Sub-Saharan African cultures share many of the values we associate with particular materials. But most of all, they believe that a number of them contain spiritual powers that when used properly may provide protection and prosperity.

CAT. 4

Mask with costume
Dan peoples, Ivory Coast
Wood, animal hair, horn, feathers, woven cotton cloth, cowrie shells, leather, aluminum, pigment.
H. 83.8 cm.
Charles and Kent Davis

This facemask, *sagbwe*, still has the upper part of the costume. It consists of a blue and white colored fabric, one checkered and the other striped. The mask also has parts of its red and white head gear with feathers. Most important are amulets and cowry shells that are attached to the costume. The face of the mask and part of the costume are covered with remains of sacrificial substances. (F.H.)

Material Differences

Art and Identity in Africa

Revealing Forms Through Subtraction

14

Sculpting
in Wood, Ivory and Stone

HERMAN BURSSENS

T *his essay brings together a number of data concerning what is usually termed the traditional sculptor, and investigates which raw-materials he uses for carving his sculptures,
masks and figuratively decorated utensils, as well as the techniques he employs for this[1]. As will
become evident below, there are eminently practical reasons why wood is the material of first
choice, with ivory and stone then trailing well behind. My intention here does not extend
beyond sketching a general picture, illustrated here and there with some specific examples
which, indeed, are sometimes chosen rather arbitrarily, but are nevertheless apt in shedding
some light on the subject as a whole. The fact that the reality is always more complex and diverse
than can be fully reflected, and that for every rule an exception can be found, should be taken
as given.*

Materials Employed in the Aggregate of African Sculpture

Among peoples who are strongly dependent on their own local natural environments, it is
only logical that they first and foremost make use of those materials which are most easily
accessible and which may be worked with the limited technical means available to them.
By preference it is the immediate environs which are exploited. The raw materials are used
alone, or in a combination where the underlying ratio can be quite unequal. Some of the
materials used may to us seem unusual and, similarly, the objects so-made can also come
over as rather strange, particularly on our initial encounter with them. This will be all the
more true according to the degree of deviation from what is taken as "usual" in our own
cultures for the making of art works. Seeing that over the last decades some Western artists
have also come to use more unusual and even quite inexpensive materials, the average contemporary viewer has to some extent gotten over this estrangement, particularly when it is
only a matter of additions made to a sculpture. This said, the tendency remains for many
among us to retain a distinction with regard to materials, putting the "precious" ones in
one category and non-precious (or totally worthless) ones in another, and this view no
doubt, exercises some influence on the appreciation one assigns to the object concerned.

Gold, silver, bronze, ivory and rare kinds of stone are not only expensive; they also
stand the test of time. Originally it was thought that in sub-Saharan Africa these sorts of
precious raw-materials were not used, that they were either not available or else unable to
be processed and worked. This was the prevailing view up to 1897, when - to the surprise
of many - a great number of so-called "antique" art objects in bronze and ivory were discovered in the royal palace at Benin in Nigeria. Since then many other objects have been
found in other African locations. These too were made from costly and/or durable materials and, moreover, could boast of having a quite considerable age. Notwithstanding this
fact, it should be stated that to a very considerable extent use was, and still is, made of
everyday - and very often extremely perishable - raw materials. In the local context, how-

CAT. 5

Figure
Mumuye peoples, Nigeria
Wood. H. 133.4 cm.
Corice Canton Arman and Arman

Most African sculpture in wood is made of one piece.
The shape of the figure often stays within the cylindrical volume of the wood from which it is made, as can
be seen on this figure. Most sculptures are frontal and
symmetrical. Mumuye sculptors tend to create a negative space between the arms and the trunk, and do not
attach the hands to the hips. (F.H.)

ever, this last point is perhaps of less dramatic consequence, for considerable numbers of sculptures are made for temporary or even one-time use. They might be termed unique disposable objects. In other cases, the clear intention and practice is to provide them a longer life, and their makers go out of their way to accomplish this.

Vegetal components, with wood by-far leading the way, are the most prevalent constituents in the making of statues, masks and other figurative or ornamented objects. Furthermore one finds earthenware (dried in the sun, or oven-baked, yielding terracotta), copper, brass (or perhaps another copper-based alloy) and, more exceptionally still, a few other metals, and finally ivory and stone, as we will see below.

Raffia and other fibers are used to make braided cap masks in West Africa among the Duyla, the Dogon, and the Senufo, and in the Democratic Republic of the Congo among the Pende, the Chokwe and the Salampasu. Colorful disguises of cotton material, provided with beads, are encountered among the Bamileke in Cameroon, and masks fashioned from sheets of beaten tree bark are found among the Komo in the northeastern part of the Democratic Republic of the Congo. The Afo of Nigeria elaborate small figures with the help of bundles of grass; while the Bobo and the Bwa of Burkina Faso decorate their dancers - for but a single day - with leaves, branches and other savanna vegetation, rendering them into what can be seen as veritable living works of art. And hard fruits, too, are not ignored. The Shilluk of East Africa are known to have masks carved from a piece of dried gourd, and the Pende have been known to make small schematic figures out of the hard nuts (*kulu*) of the raffia palm tree, just as they do with the grains of the *muhafu*. The Luba, the Chokwe and the Lwena on occasion also carve miniscule figures or heads from solid pits. Likewise, it is known that sculptors in the ancient kingdom of Benin also decorated coconuts with figurative images carved in low-relief.

A look at the pieces in this volume equally shows - and certainly not by chance - that the vast majority is fashioned from wood, and so it is fitting that we first direct our attention to this particular material.

WOOD

Why is it that wood is the basic material of choice? The reasons are quite simple. It is sufficiently plentiful in most areas, it is resistant to immediate breakage, it is not too difficult to work with and a wide variety of results can be achieved. For purely practical reasons as well as those which may be termed magic-religious, not all varieties of wood come under consideration. Practical reasons: is the wood indeed sound enough for sculpting? Is it appropriate for the specific object that one wishes to carve? Does it offer sufficient resistance to climatic conditions and insects? Is it amenable to working with, considering the few simple tools that one has available? Would it not be too heavy to serve for a large mask which must be danced for an appreciable period of time and without respite?

Magical-religious reasons: trees normally occupy a rank in the hierarchy of the forces and powers from out of which the universe exists. For quite a number of peoples there are tree species with a particular religious content, and these must be employed in particular circumstances. In this way, the Bamileke sculptors are required to use a specimen from the sacred forest when they make pieces intended for cults (Lecoq 1953:202). Some trees have a symbolic meaning, or bring one into contact with ancestors and spirits. The Kalabari of Nigeria, writes Horton (1966:30 & 35), associate the *odumdum* tree (*Newbouldia laevis*) with heroes and the dead, and the *emo* (*Rhizophera alata*) with water spirits. According to Hersak (1986: 30 & 126), the Songye (D.R. Congo) use wood of the *kicipicipi* tree (*Erythrina abyssinica*) for specific, protecting power-figures (*mankishi*), because herbalists employ this tree's bark to treat coughs and it stands in direct relation with the ancestors. This last point likewise holds true for a number of sacred trees among the Chokwe of Angola (Bastin 1982:64). Some trees serve exclusively for ritual objects, and chopping them down requires prayers and offerings so that the spirit of the tree may be appeased, and not bring injury, accident or subsequent disease to the sculptor.

Among the Grassland-peoples of Cameroon as well, writes Harter (1986:20), a ritual takes place prior to felling a tree, but the author does not precisely tell us of what this consists. Among the Dogon, as noted by Griaule (1938:405), the tree from which a mask will be carved must be purchased with a symbolic gift from the *yeban*, supernatural anthropomorphic spirit-beings. The sculptor will bring such offerings to prevent the tree's "life force" (*nyama*) from damaging his own *nyama*. In choosing the variety of tree, the Yoruba take into account the spirits and divinities which must be induced to take up residence in the object, or at least be connected with it, and thus one or another type of wood is or is not appropriate for one or another particular figure. For example, the felling of the *iroko* tree requires considerable gift offerings (Cordwell 1952:327). This is also apparently the case among the Eastern Kongo. Once the variety of tree (and it is always a living tree) is chosen for making the sculpted image, offerings are brought to propitiate the spirit of the tree so as to assure that no accidents will occur during the sculpting process itself (Lehuard 1989:89).

Indeed there are still many other examples that could be cited of similar ideas, and some will be treated below.

In practice, often the types of wood chosen have an average or, more preferably, a low density. This presents the double advantage of being easier to carve as well as easier to wear or carry. The fact that these woods are more susceptible to attack by wood-eating insects (mainly termites), and that they split or burst more easily and are generally more perishable, is something well known to sculptors and users alike. In many cases, and particularly with respect to masks, this has little importance since they are intentionally begot to have but a short lifespan. Within the framework of boys' initiations, these objects must be continually re-made. Often it is the initiates themselves, and not the adults, who are responsible for their making.

By way of example, here follows some wood varieties which are well known and much used:
-   *Crossopterix febrifuga*. In Congo it is one of the most often used varieties because the wood is not too hard, it can be sculpted in all directions, and is not prone to cracking and splitting. The renowned Kuba royal statues (*ndop*) were made from this wood, and also a large number of sculpted figures from the Luba, the Tabwa and other peoples.

-   *Alstonia congensis*. This tree is prevalent to the West- and Central African rainforests; its wood is light, but does not easily split. In Nigeria its users include the Yoruba and the Urhobo, and in Congo the Lega people choose it for making their figures and masks (Biebuyck 2002:56).

-   *Bombax*. Various eligible types. The Nafana (Ghana) use it to carve their very large masks, owing to the wood's lightness, and the Bamana (Mali) use it for the same reason.

-   *Ricinodendron*. Here, too, there are many sub-species. These are light wood varieties which harden upon drying. The Yaka speak of *m'tsenga* and they sculpt their *kakuungu* masks from it. The Songye designate it by the term *mulele* and use the wood for their *kifwebe* masks. The Kuba, too, often employ it, as do the Luba.

-   *Butyrospermum barkii*. A relatively soft wood type, used by the Lobi sculptors, is that obtained from the *barr* tree (*Butyrospermum barkii*). When the wood has become too hard from drying, it is soaked in water before work commences (Meyer 1981:124).

- *Chlorophora excelsa.* This yields a durable type of wood, and the tree is known as the *iroko* in Nigeria and other parts of West Africa. Given its extreme hardness, this material is not easy to work with, but it does offer considerable resistance to deterioration, even in open-air conditions. The Yoruba make their *ifa* dishes and other weather-resistant objects from it, and in the Congo it is employed by the Luba and other peoples.

- *Afzelia africana.* This is another very dense wood. The Mbembe (Nigeria) use it for their very large, figuratively conceived drums, and the Lobi - who call this wood *khoo* - also sculpt it. They also use other hardwood types for their sculpted works, such as that yielded from the *thuo* bush (*Gardenia perniflora*) and the *sankolo* tree (*Prosopis africana*). This last-named variety is extremely hard, and one of its uses is to fashion supporting roof-pillars. When a sculptured figure is meant to endure, the wood chosen must be as dense as possible and also as resistant as possible to termite infestation. Meyer (1981:124) adds that a Lobi sculptor would normally use five to six different varieties of wood and that in the environs of Wourbira alone there are some twenty sorts of wood employed in making sculpted images. The wood-carvers make a further distinction between smooth varieties such as the *sankolo* and the *gie* (*Pterocarpus eraneceus*), and un-smooth ones like the *sii* (*Diospyros mespiliformis*). Their preference is for the former.

- *Funtumia africana* or *elastica.* This is a rubber tree with fine texture, and quite resistant to deterioration when the requisite care is taken. The Yoruba call it *ira*, employing it for carving *ibeji* statues as well as figuratively executed support pillars.

- *Lannea acida.* The Bamana name for this is *mpeku*; it is a kind of wild grapevine and is taken for a symbol of fertility. For some crest masks this same people use the *toro* (*Ficus gnaphalocapus*) because it symbolizes life.
- *Cordia millinii bak.* The Grassland-groups of peoples use this wood (called *m'be*), among others, to make larger-size statues which are more exposed to the weather. *Polyscias ferrugina* (locally called *lemdje*) is similarly employed[2].

Ever the most resistant woods have a life-expectancy of only a limited number of decades if kept in tropical climate. It follows that the majority of wood statues and masks encountered *in situ* are seldom as old as some may contend. From the middle of the nineteenth century on, nonetheless, a great many such specimens were brought to Europe. In a few cases, this even sporadically occurred as far back as the 15th century, though wider Western interest in African art is indeed a relatively recent phenomenon[3].

In quite particular circumstances, for instance in water or in dry caves, wood may be preserved considerably longer. One example of this described by Van Noten (1972), comes from Angola. This was an animal head - possibly a mask - discovered in 1922 and which had for centuries lain in a riverbed. Carbon-dating carried out in 1972 placed it between the eighth and ninth centuries. Other wood objects, originating from the vanished Tellem and the Dogon in the Bandiagara caves of Mali, are even older. Recent dating has put some examples at ca. 100, 530 and 570 A.D. Certain pre-Dogon and Dogon specimens were presumably made in ca. 790, 930, 1060 and 1155[4]. Others would have been elaborated between the tenth to eighteenth centuries. The large figure from the the Mboye, Nigeria (Cat. 6) was presumably made in the fourteenth century A.D. Such data, however, remain the exception with regard to African wood sculpture taken as a whole.

CAT. 6

Figure
Mboye peoples, Nigeria, 14th Century A.D. (?)
Wood. H. 133 cm
Museum for African Art, Gift of Corice Canton Arman and Arman

Tools and Working Methods

The first thing a sculptor must do is to search for the appropriate tree. Wherever found, far off in the forest or close by the village, and whether growing wild or the property of some-one - who then must be reimbursed - in any case, the tree must be felled and chopped into pieces. This is done with an axe, a machete, or a large adze. A ritual of appeasement may take place first, for example by laying an offering around the trunk, for reasons mentioned above. Among sculptors of the Dan people, even before setting out to look for the appro-priate tree, offerings must be made to the ancestors, without whose help and support no success is possible. Shortly after the tree is felled, the piece intended for use is sought out. Given that fresh wood is more easily worked, not much time passes before actual sculpting begins. Among the Anang an interval of around six months is the maximum; after this, carving is rendered significantly more difficult. The Bamileke begin almost immediately once the tree is chopped down. First the trunk is stripped of bark; next it is divided into the desired sections. It is only seldom that a sculptor uses wood from a tree which had long previous been felled (Lecoq 1953:202).

Not all parts of the chosen block of wood are equally desirable for a particular sculpt-ed work. Normally the heartwood is avoided for, once dry, it is prone to splitting.

The marked cylindrical form of the trunk or thick branch can have a direct influence upon the work's ultimate outcome. Thus, some peoples carve typical pole-figures from long, thin pieces of wood. It also happens that a sculptor, if he has an innovative set of mind, will incorporate one or another specific particularity of the tree into the finished work, for instance by intentionally choosing a deformity or a forked branch. Such is not the rule among traditional sculptors, especially in the case of objects of religious signifi-cance, where the practice is to stick closely to the design proper to his own group and to observe other prescriptions which can act as limits to imaginative freedom (Cat. 7).

Before any actual carving commences, the sculptor already has a precise idea of what he wants to make. Here he can be led by the example of an old statue or mask that he sets up beside him while working, or he can base himself on a detailed description given by the person commissioning the object.

Among the Kongo, Lehuard notes [trans.]: "... the sculptor, facing his piece of wood - generally a cylindrical block - traces the main sections constituative of the personage to be portrayed: the head, the body and the lower limbs." (1989:89)[5].

There are other peoples, too, who take the same approach. Dexterous wood-carvers work the block of wood with an amazing rapidity, and this without prior line-sketching on the piece in question. They pause only now and then to assess their work and to consider how to proceed.

The transformation from wood block into a sculpted work is always carried out by means of direct hewing where one or more adzes play the main role, with perhaps a few other instruments in support. In any case the tools are of simple form and manufacture. They are made either by the sculptor himself or else by the local smith.

The most important as well as the most common tool is undoubtedly the adze. There are two distinctive categories: the tang-adze, where a piece of iron (flat underneath and with a cutting-plane, pointed above) goes through a wooden handle (figs. 1a & b); and the mantled-adze, where an iron sleeve is clamped over a handle (figs. 1c & d). The first type is found more in savanna-areas, the other in forested territories. Vandenhoute (1945:912 seq.) remarks that the mantled-adze used by Dan sculptors has a less acute angle between handle and blade.

Among the Kalabari it is the large, flat machete and not the adze which is the tool of choice in fashioning head-shapes from the block of wood. Horton (1965:41-42) believes

CAT. 7

Figure
Dogon peoples, Mali
Wood. H. 43.2 cm.
Jerome Vogel

Some Dogon sculptors purposely incorporate the bent shape of the trunk to give a suggestion of movement to the figure. (F.H.)

that this tool itself is the possible cause for the angular design in their sculpted works, a contention not easily proved. The Bangwa (Cameroon) also prefer, according to data provided by Brain & Pollock (1971:49), a similar sort of machete, at least in the early stages of their work.

In subsequent stages, knives are generally used which may be straight or curved, and single- or double-sided (figs. 1e & f). Equally, gouges (hollow chisels) and awls may also be utilized. Smoothening is accomplished with the aid of fresh, "sanding" leaves - from a particular type of liana - or, alternatively, the surface may be lightly carbonized.

The Dan, among others, maintain that their tools in themselves already possess a certain potency, and women and the non-initiated are forbidden to cast their glance upon them.

Lecoq (1953:202) emphasizes that among the Bamileke the sculptor's tools (kam'jue) are quite rudimentary. They are limited to adze, axe, scissors, hammer (made from an old axe-blade), a curved scraper and an imported machete.

Ottenberg (1975:76-77) noted that among the Afikpo the following tools were formally used in the making of a mask: a machete for cutting the block of wood and for the rough work; a small adze for the general shaping and further wood-working; a kind of U-shared blade with a wooden handle on each side for removing the interior of the mask; a long chisel without handle - struck with a stone or piece of wood - for creating details like the eyes and mouth; a long thin rod of iron for boring holes and the pyrogravure of small sections; a broad and flat piece of iron or a machete for the carbonizing of larger surfaces; a fresh, sanding leaf for smoothing. Finally, the sculptor made use of an iron needle for the fastening of raffia fibers around the mask once carving was complete.

For the Songye, Hersak (1986:57) relates that the most important tools for the making of a kifwebe mask are a few adzes of different dimensions, where the largest is used for hewing the rough form and the smallest serves to fashion the actual traits. Further, use is made of a chisel for facial forms and especially to render angular planes. To eliminate facets caused by chiseling and to round-off concave or convex planes, the sculptor uses a curved gouge. Next he will carve angles, sharp edges and grooved striations with the aid of a knife. Finally, the surface is polished with the coarse textured leaves of the luhela tree.

Lega sculptors, according to Biebuyck (2002:58), make use of an axe (isaga), an adze (nkondo), a knife (kene), a small iron tool to apply the typical circle-dot designs (kapiga), small iron blades which are made red-hot to render incisions, a small drill and, finally, sandpaper leaves for smoothing.

Among a considerable number of peoples, sculptors do not have an extensive array of tools and instruments at their disposal. Sometimes only one or two adzes and/or a few knives are available to them. The question may be posed as to whether this paucity of means has presented a real hindrance in terms of aesthetic sculptural expression. Although personal dexterity and artistry are important factors, it is obvious that the limited assortment of material and technical possibilities works restrictively as regards just what and how something can be made. Nonetheless, a gifted sculptor will succeed to bring forth superior work, albeit within the framework of said limitations. Cole & Aniankor (1984:114) have the following to say with respect to Igbo:

> ...even though (the carver) is fashioning a known type of mask
> with 'expected' features, he has considerable latitude to exercise
> his artistry and imagination (...) The competitive components of
> masking also contribute to new and highly inventive solutions.
> Mask makers are often called upon to exceed existing models, to
> create something 'different, larger, or better'. Carvers who can
> repeatedly produce unusual new masks are sought after, and
> many achieve considerable fame.

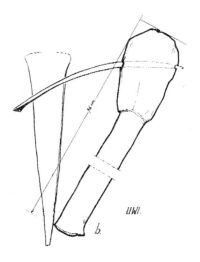

Fig. 1 a
Tang-adze used by the Dan sculptor Uwi. Village of Flanpleu, Upper Cavally region, Ivory Coast (Drawing P.J.Vandenhoute)

Fig. 1 b
Dan artist working with a tang-adze, Upper Cavally region, Ivory Coast.
(Photo P. J. Vandenhoute 1938-39)

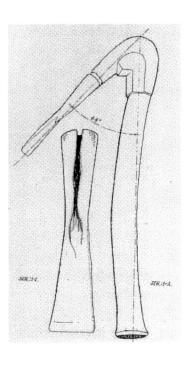

Fig. 1 c.
Mantled-adze used by the Dan sculptor Yomi of Flampleu, Upper Cavally region, Ivory Coast (Drawing P.J.Vandenhoute)

Fig. 1 d.
The sculptor Mwane from the village Benge, Lower Uele - Democratic Republic of the Congo, working with a mantled-adze. (Burssens 1962, pl. XX).

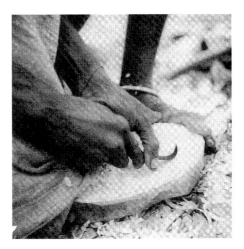

Fig. 1 e
Gouging the inside of a face mask with a bent knife. Dan peoples, Upper Cavally region, Ivory Coast. (Photo P.J. Vandenhoute)

Fig. 1 f
Further finishing of a mask with a small knife. Dan (sub-group Uame), Ivory Coast. (Photo P.J. Vandenhoute)

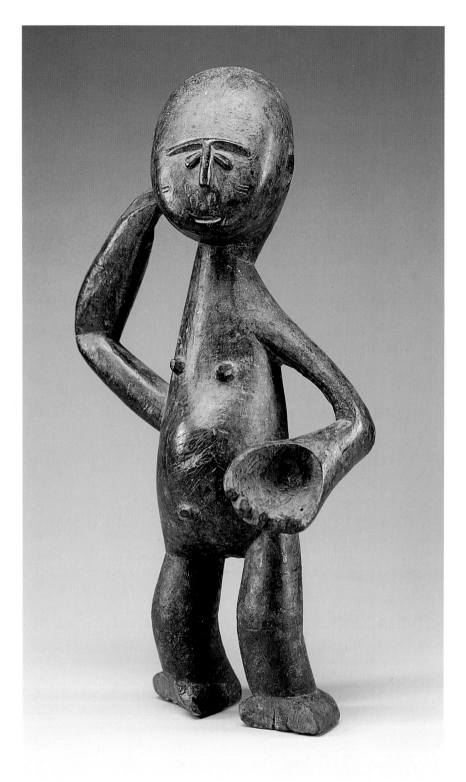

Figure

Lega peoples, Dem. Rep. of the Congo
Wood, pigment. H. 26.5 cm.
Private Collection

Both figures are asymmetrical and therefore atypical for African wood sculptures. No specific meaning can be given to the standing Fanti female figure with its open left hand in front of the left hip and the right arm that is raised. Lega figures with one or two raised arms represent Kasungalala, a high initiate of the *bwami* society who is an arbitrator, a moderator, and a peacemaker. (F.H.)
(Biebuyck 1986: 79)

Figure

Fanti peoples, Ghana
Wood. H. 35.6 cm.
Richard H. Scheller

CAT. 11

Mask: sowo-wui

Mende peoples, Sierra Leone
Wood, natural pigment, metal. H. 38.1 cm.
Gerald and Lila Dannenberg

Most *sowo-wui* masks are repeatedly painted until the
wood is saturated and the color becomes deep and even
black. They are then rubbed with palm oil or shoe polish to make the surface sleek and luminous. (F.H.)
(Boone 1986:158)

CAT. 10

Bell

Azande peoples, Dem. Rep. of the Congo
In sub-Saharan Africa, sculptures are mostly made out
of one piece of wood. This bell however, has two cylindrical sticks that serve as clappers and simultaneously
represent the legs of the anthropomorphic figure.
(F.H.)

So it comes as no surprise that also among the Igbo the names of some sculptors have remained renowned. For the Senufo, on the other hand, Förster's research (1997:475) tells us that the personal "artistic" room for manoeuvre on the sculptor's part - as well as the wishes of the commissioner of the piece - is severely limited, given that strict prescriptions must be adhered to in the case of carving a mask for their Poro-association.

It is quite apparent that most statues and masks are made from a single piece of wood and thus monoxylic. It is no easy matter to create complicated constructions this way, and yet such examples are not seldom encountered among peoples including the Yoruba. Others limit themselves to the addition of one or another protruding part once the main part is finished. True polyxylic conceived sculptures are exceptional, but a number of them are found with the Ibibio of Nigeria, among the lagoon-peoples of Ivory Coast, and also with the Lengola of Congo. Consistently these are sculpted figures with moveable limbs attached with pins. Furthermore, some crest masks in figure-form from groups along the Cross River are likewise conceived. The same holds to an even greater extent for the marionettes that are seen among the Bamana and the Marka, as well as for the moveable figures found on a number Yoruba *gelede* masks.

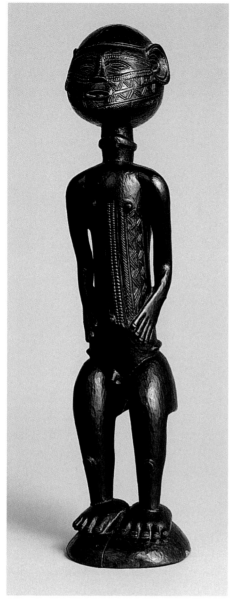

CAT. 12 (ABOVE)

Figure
Tabwa or Bwile peoples, DR Congo or Zambia
Wood. H. 39 cm
Museum for African Art, Gift of Richard Faletti

CAT. 13

Kneeling bowl figure
Yoruba peoples, Nigeria
Wood, pigment. H. 54 cm.
Charles and Kent Davis

Figures are often decorated with geometric patterns. The Tabwa and the neighboring Bwile peoples mostly make use of symmetrical scarification patterns. The Tabwa relate them to the ordering of their geographical and political universe. It is possible that through representing asymmetric body scarifications on this figure the sculptor intended to represent a territorial spirit, *ngulu*. The body of the kneeling bowl figure is completely covered with decorative geometric patterns. The incisions covering the cheeks are scarification marks. (F.H.) (Roberts and Roberts 1998: 40 and 129)

CAT. 15

Figure
Ashanti peoples, Ghana
Wood, fiber, metal. H. 36.8 cm.
Stewart J. Warkow

Both figures are covered with sacrificial patina that
may consist of a mixture of dried liquids such as blood
from sacrificial animals such as a chicken or a goat; or
beer and palm wine. Other sacrificial ingredients may
different kinds of food including eggs, millet gruel,
palm oil, and palm wine. (F.H.)

CAT. 14

Monkey figure
Baule peoples, Ivory Coast
Wood with sacrificial residue. H. 63.5 cm.
Jerome Vogel

A good many sculpted objects remain uncolored or, more properly stated, mono-chrome. Others, and then mainly masks, are painted with a variety of colors. Even when a carved object is not really painted, it can still acquire a patina in a number of ways. It can be specially applied or be the consequence of ritual handling or general use. The result is a form of sublimation of the original material. It is not only Westerners who are struck by a beautiful and preferably deep-shining patina; many African makers and viewers are also appreciative of this quality (Cat. 11).

There are many ways to arrive at a patina. An object may be massaged-in with oils such as palm and ricinus, or with fat such as that derived from the karite tree *(Vitellia paradoxa)*, or with the saps of certain shrubs or trees, or even with the red wood-powder of the *Pterocarpus*. After an initial treatment with red tree-root sap, a mask may be plunged into swampy mud and so achieve a dark color. This is practiced by the Dan and the Guro. Others obtain the same effect by smoking the piece, for instance by holding it above or close to a fire. Coating with gum or resin is another technique, as is oral spraying with chewed leaves as practiced by the Chokwe or with chewed kola-nuts as do the Dan. Further, there is also sprinkling with chicken or goat blood, with millet gruel or a com-posite porridge (Cat. 14 and 15). And there are a great many other techniques still. In the last-mentioned cases this clearly relates to giving offerings, the purpose perhaps being to amplify the inherent power of the sculpted object concerned. The result is a crusty coating, sometimes millimeters thick. Well known examples of these are the Tellem figures of Mali.

As for the Grassland-peoples, Harter (1992:20-21) writes that the patina is mostly the result of manipulation and surface treatment. Masks and statues often have a reddish or black-like patina caused by the act of holding it and regularly rubbing it in with palm oil and red wood-powder, respectively, or with soot. In this last case, a glossy lacquered aspect is achieved, with brown or red reflections on protuberances. Large royal statues, masks and drums are never or seldom touched, and thus retain their natural wood color; only occa-sionally is there a superficial layer of red earth. Memorial statues of ancestors, which stand in the open, are inevitably deteriorated by rainfall, their original form gradually disap-pearing. Sculpted figures kept by the Bangwa in their attic spaces progressively acquire a thick, grainy layer of soot and tar owing to exposure to smoke, and this eventually obscures the statue's details.

In all this discussion it should be kept in mind, as Lehuard (1989:100-101) correctly remarks with respect to the Congo peoples, that one must distinguish between the patina intended as a decorative, definitive addition to the object's surface, and the patina result-ing from anointment, offerings and placating manipulations, to which must be added unpleasant environmental effects: hardening, contamination, erosion. The true traditional patina, according to Lehuard, is that which the sculptor himself applies to his new object. According to the region and the function of the sculptor, the surface will be glossy or remain natural, or else receive an ashen or reddish tint. In the case of ancestor figures in wood, the sculptor then usually uses color-yielding bark ground with palm oil, and he coats the figure with a glaze-like layer. Rubbing-in a statue gives it a shine which can lead one to think that it has been varnished. Something similar is practiced by the Chokwe. As a function of the greater or lesser density of the obtained tint, and according to the type of wood used, the gradation of the glossy patina of objects from the Kongo peoples will vary from yellow-orange to all possible browns and brown-reds. This also holds for small, cost-ly sculpted objects like flutes, handles, small slitdrums, where the original patina is further enhanced by the multitude of manipulations, through ritual use and via temporal deteri-oration.

A few other examples of patina-concoction are the following. The sculpted *akuaba* images of the Asante (Ghana), relates Antubam (1963), are rubbed with raw egg-white,

CAT. 16

Figure

Igbo peoples, Nigeria
Wood, pigment. H. 139.7 cm.
Paul and Ruth Tishman Collection of African Art,
Walt Disney Imagineering

CAT. 17

Figure

Mumuye peoples, Nigeria
Wood, pigment. H. 96.5 cm
Private Collection

Among the Igbo, ancestor figures are sculpted by men and painted by women. The choice of colors and the design motives that covers the body of this figure probably is more likely decorative than symbolic. The application of the red and white pigment on the Mumuye figure may have a symbolic meaning. It may relate to the social structure of Mumuye society which is symbolized by the colors white and red. Red is asso-ciated with the *tjokwa* or people of blood and fire; white is associated with the *tjozoza* or people of water. Each group is complimentary to the other and the col-ors symbolizing them are often painted on masks and sometimes on sculptures to mark this social division. (F.H.) (Cole personal communication)

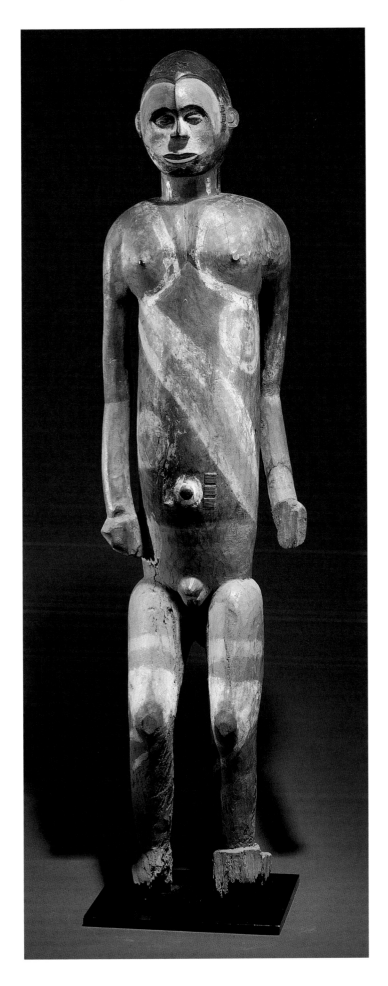

soot from the bottom of a pot, and "alkaline from the potash of plantain peels, in which had been kept small pieces of iron." The final result is glossy black or dark brown. The *yanda* figures of the Zande (Congo) sometimes receive a coating made from palm oil, resins, liver, blood, plants and spices, this activates the power lying dormant within the piece (Burssens 1962:88 seq.). According to Williams (1968), the *bedu* masks of the Nafana are covered in red and white clay mixed with fat and the black of charcoal. During the month of their performance, they receive a bath of water, egg yolk and egg white, and are rubbed-in with oil.

The Lega attach great importance to a fine patina. Biebuyck (2002:58 sqt) tells us that the wood figures, even those which are coated with kaolin, exhibit splendid glossy brown and dark patinas on the un-whitened parts. These objects are always oiled and whitened each time a *mwami* is invited for a new initiation.

The patina can also be of practical use: it offers some protection against premature decay, and - if fat or oil are used - splits and bursts are to some extent prevented. Some of the applied products repel insects, something seen with the Senufo among other groups. They coat their sculpted images with karite fat, which also results in a deep shining patina.

If the figurative and otherwise-decorated ornamental objects and the majority of sculpted works are monochrome - a notable exception here are, for example, the brightly colored figures of the Igbo - when it comes to masks the reverse is usually the case (Cat. 16). The colors employed are in the main limited to the triad red-white-black. In past times, other tints were little used. The chosen dyes may be of mineral, vegetal or animal origin. As for minerals, white is obtained from river lime, kaolin clay and aluminum silicate. Red is yielded from sandy earth or from stone, and black from various kinds of silt. From the plant category, used are the red sap of trees such as the *Bixa orellama* and the *Batida nitida*, and black is derived from certain lianae and from charcoal. Blue, to the extent that it is used, comes from the indigo plant, and yellow is obtained from the tree named *odo* by the Yoruba. Animal-derived dyes are more rarely employed: black from carbonized bones and white from reptile excrement. Halftones may be obtained by mixing, but usually one keeps to primary colors. These paints are applied with the aid of feathers, sticks (thin, and frayed at the tip), rags, with a kind of pallet knife (like the Nafana do), or simply with the fingers. Often it is the user who paints the piece, and many masks are painted anew prior to making an appearance.

The colors have, or originally had, a symbolic importance. Below are some examples.

Among a variety of peoples (in Cameroon and elsewhere), white is the color of the spirits, of the dead. Red symbolizes life and black suffering, that is to say, the dialectic connection between Life and Death (Mveng 1975:77-78). For the Igbo, light colors on their *mbari* shrines (or houses) stand for the beautiful and/or the good, while darker tones relay the bleak, the frightful and the ugly. They refer to supernatural forces and the world of the spirits. According to Ben-Amos (1980:46;49), in Benin white stands for coolness, peace,

CAT. 18 (RIGHT)

Mask

Tsogo peoples, Gabon
Wood, pigment. H. 32 cm.
Paul and Ruth Tishman Collection of African Art,
Walt Disney Imagineering

CAT. 19

Mask, mbangu

Pende peoples, Dem. Rep. of the Congo
Wood, pigment. H. 30.5 cm
Private Collection

The face of the Tsogo mask is covered with an asymmetric design that is painted in white and blue and that does not follow the symmetry of facial features. The use of color is probably more decorative than symbolic. The mask of the Pende peoples is also painted black and white. Like the facial features, the placing of the colors is asymmetric and relates to the story of *mbangu*, the character that is represented. The Pende believe that *mbangu* was a victim of sorcery that was inflicted with a disease that caused facial paralysis and who by falling in a fire burnt his face. The black color represents the burnt part of the face. (F.H.)
(Strother 1998: 141)

CAT. 20

Mask

Bwa peoples, Burkina Faso
Wood, pigment. H. 182.9 cm
Private Collection

Materials Used by Voltaic Artists

A personal note by Christopher Roy

The Voltaic artist carves masks exclusively of the wood of the Ceiba tree (*Ceiba pintandra*), which is also called the silk cotton tree, the *faux kapokier*, and the ceiba. This is the same tree that is so important in Pre-Columbian and contemporary Maya thought as the tree of life. Ceiba wood is fine grained, light, durable, and easy to carve, very much like white pine. It is obtained in the valleys of the Mouhoun and Nakambe Rivers (formerly the Volta Rivers) in game reserves where cutting wood is forbidden to all but artists, who are provided with special permits by the ministry of *Eaux et Forets* which allow them to cut ceibas for their artwork. No other wood will do. Voltaic artists most certainly never use the wood of the baobab or of the kapok tree. Both are coarse and fibrous and totally unsuitable for carving. The only other wood artists use for carving is the wood of the Shea nut (*Butyrospermum parkii*), which is hard, dense and resistant to rot. This wood is used exclusively for carving figures, for it is too heavy to be used for large masks. The artist first roughs out the shape of the mask, carefully looking at it to make sure the proportions will be correct and that it will be symmetrical. When the carving has proceeded to the point where the final shape and size are exactly as the artist desires, the last step of carving is to apply the graphic patterns, which are called scars. The carver marks these out on the surface of the mask using the blade of his adze, removed from the handles, and held in his right hand, haft in his fist with the blade opposite his thumb. Once the patterns have been traced in the surface of the wood, the blade is used as a knife to remove the wood that defines the patterns. The goal is to leave very deep depressions where the wood will be painted red or white, and much higher surfaces where it will be painted black. Among most peoples an important measure of the artists skill is the depth of the carving of these scars.

When all of the patterns have been carved the artist scorches all of the surfaces of the wood with the flat side of his adze blade heated red-hot. The Bwa artist Poboye Konate (1985) and the Mossi artist Yili Wango (1976) explained to me that this prevents the wood from cracking as it dries. In most cases the artist who carved the mask paints it red, white and black, but in the case of the Konate family of blacksmiths in the village of Ouri, there are members of the family who specialize in preparing and applying the paints. The paints are made of mineral and vegetable materials. Red is simply iron-rich stone, which is rubbed vigorously in a shallow stone bowl to pulverize it. White has traditionally been the excrement of the sun lizards that are called *margouyas* in French and which live in small burrows in the ground. Boys are sent out to collect this material, which is a brilliant white. I admit to a certain skepticism on my part about this material the first dozen or so times I was given this information, but now, after thirty years of hearing the same information from fifty-odd artists and other informants I am convinced it is true. The black is the most interesting material in terms of the way it is obtained. It consists of the dried seed pods of the Acacia tree (*Acacia nilotica*) which are stuffed in a pot with water and boiled for weeks until reduced to a thick, tarry black material that is not only glossy black when it dries, but is the only one the three materials that is completely water-proof (Hutchinson and Dalziel 1936). In all cases the binder used to apply the pigments to the mask is Gum Arabic, which has been an important export from West Africa for centuries and which literally grows on trees. In 1976 when my wife Nora and I were watching Yili Wango carve Mossi masks, he ran out of gum Arabic and we spent a pleasant hour or two wandering through the "bush" in the hills of Boubalou picking this material as lumps off the trunks of Acacia trees.

It is important to know that the red and white pigments are water soluble, while the black is not. Each year in January and February all masks are removed from the mask house and are sunk in the shallow ponds formed by the previous season's rains. They are weighted with rocks and left for two to four weeks. The soaking destroys insects that may have invaded the wood. The soaking also washes off the red and white pigment, but not the black, and when the masks are repainted just before the first performances the red and white remain thin while the black builds up a very thick layer over several years.

Finally the masks are always worn with thick costume made of hemp (*hibiscus cannabinus*) fibers. These fibers are very durable, but over a season of performances the costumes become worn and threadbare and the young men of the initiation class must remake the costumes each year. Because the process of making the costume requires that the hemp plants be soaked, a great deal of water is required, and years of severe drought there may not be enough water to make new costumes and the masks may not perform.

long life, prosperity, health and ritual purity. Black stands for the night, for mourning, for bad omens and ritual pollution. Red embodies and expresses the nature of the divinities Ogun and Osun. Both are associated with sudden and violent action, rage, fire and blood. For the Urhobo, white chalk means peace and purity. The white of the masks is connected with the spirits. Red is a symbol of nobility and dignity. Sculpted images of important ancestors bear this color (Otite 1971:50 and Foss 1973:23).

The *kakuungu* masks used by the Yaka within the framework of their *nkanda* institution are colored red and white. Here red symbolizes blood, revenge and evil, while white refers to blessings and health. The meaning of white for this same people, but in the context of *ndunga* symbolism, stands for luck, help and healing (Bourgeois 1981:43). For the peoples of the Lower-Congo, red - a morally neutral color - embodies predictability and "female qualities" such as sensitivity and sentimentality. For them white refers to goodness on a social level and expresses happiness and communicativeness; this color is also an expression of peace. Black refers to bad intentions, aggression, disobedience, revolt, and everything that runs counter to social order.

Coating of Wood

Once a wooden object is made it can be coated in a variety of ways, and may even be entirely cloaked so that the original raw material is no longer visible. The Grassland-peoples of Cameroon like to completely bedeck their statues and masks, and sometimes thrones and other objects as well, with colored glass beads affixed beforehand to cloth (Cat. 21). It is placed over the entire object, so imparting a quite surprising effect. Imported beads are signs of wealth, and thus prestige. The Kuba and other Congolese peoples, too, sometimes use beads on their masks, but then sparingly and without obscuring its structure. Here cowrie shells are also used. These originate in the Indian Ocean and were formerly used as currency in sub-Saharan Africa. They thus symbolize wealth and, given their particular form, even fertility. Among the Bamana one also encounters masks which are fully covered by such shells.

The application of skins or hides to wood is a practice specific to peoples from the area of the Cross River (border region of Nigeria and Cameroon) such as the Ejagham, Efik, Keaka, Boki, Anyang, Bifanka and others still which are often, and imprecisely, grouped together under the designation "Ekoi." They are the only groups in the world who do this. In the first place heads - in fact, crest masks are so covered. The covering is usually done with antelope hide; the technique requires a specialist's knowledge and craftsmanship.

Masks or figures may be furnished with a complete or near-complete covering of metal sheets or wound around with metal wire. Brass or copper are used, as are gold and silver. Only a limited number of peoples cover their wood sculpture this way. Metal is usually synonymous with wealth and influence given its original scarcity; this formerly held for brass and copper, and still does for the precious metals. Among the Marka, masks covered with brass and copper are fairly numerous. With the Bamana and the Senufo such examples are more rare. In Congo one finds specimens provided with copper sheets among the Kuba, the Songye and especially the Salampasu. With this last group, the metal is attached with semi-spherical nails after it has been hammered on the wood. In particular the diverse "Kota groups" (like the Mahongwe, Obamba and Shamaye) of Gabon are known for their flat figures covered with sheets or strips of brass. Usually this is affixed with staples from the same material. There are few known examples where silver sheets are used. Some may be found among the Fon, where this material's employ seems limited to court art made in Abomey. Here the metal is applied to the sculpted object in small, thin plates, and these are

CAT. 21

Mask
Grassland Region, Cameroon
Wood, woven jute, glass beads, cowrie shells. H. 45.7 cm.
Charles and Kent Davis

CAT. 22

Figural group (staff ornament)
Ashanti peoples, Ghana
Gilded wood. H. 26 cm.
Charles D. Miller III

hammered onto the wood so that all the details of the carving work remain visible. Here, too, staples and/or small rivets are used to firmly attach the metal.

The coating with gold foil or gilding is more frequent. It is especially with the Akan of Ivory Coast and Ghana that this process is widely used for the decoration of status symbols and prestige objects of the rulers (Cat. 22). The gilded regalia of the Asante, and of the Baule as well, are richly ornamented with a wide variety of motifs. These pieces are applied-sculpture in the form of figurative or geometrically designed speakers' staffs, sword handles and other weapons, flywhisks (an authority symbol), tips of parasols, and other accoutrements, which the chiefs possess in the dozens. At first sight theses objects appear to be made of solid gold. Freestanding statues which are subsequently gilded are much rarer. There are a number of known examples, however, from the hand of Baule sculptors. The technique they use employing gold foil to cover all manner of carved objects and figures has been described in some detail by Fischer and Himmelheber (1975:22-24). The broad lines of this process are given below.

Once gold powder has been melted in a small crucible, the resulting small lump of gold is laid on a miniscule anvil and hammered with the aid of a second, iron anvil. After some twenty strikes the piece is re-warmed and then suddenly cooled ("quenched") with palm wine. Hammering follows anew until the desired size of a small coin attained. At this stage one switches to a real hammer with which the gold disc is worked spirally or radially from inside to out, constantly shifting it to prevent hammer tracks. Using tongs the piece is then flamed and submerged in palm oil before it is more equalized and further flattened. Finally one arrives at a thin foil which is then halved and the procedure begins again. This is repeated several times until the desired thinness is achieved. For as long as the leaf is being worked, it is lain in a bowl of palm wine during pauses in the procedure.

In former times relatively thick pieces of gold were used to clothe wooden objects, using staples or clamps of the same metal material for attachment. For this, holes were first made in the wood using a thin stylus and then the U-shaped gold tacks were pressed in manually. For quite some time now glue has replaced tacks or nails to affix metal foil to wood. Before commencing this operation, the wooden object is closely examined for any cracks. Small splits, caused by desiccation, are filled with tree-resin; larger ones are filled with splinters of wood dipped in resin. A knife is then used to again smooth the surface. Next a hard cube of glue with a stick stuck in it is held in warm water and a thin, even layer is applied to the wood. With moistened finger tips, the foil is pressed onto a particular section, and then impressed into the wood's grooves using the thumbs. Many small leaves of foil are necessary to gild a figure or a utensil, for it is not feasible to perform this treatment on the whole object at once. To economize on gold, there is no overlapping. The small gold-leaves are cut to the correct size with a razor blade beforehand, and laid at the ready on the work board. Even the tiniest pieces are used.

IVORY

In times past we know that many elephants roamed through the east, west and center of the African continent. They were killed for their meat, but more often it was for their tusks. The hunting of the *Loxodonta africana* or the *Loxodonta cyclotis*, the scientific names for the African elephant - respectively in the savanna and in the forest - was an extremely dangerous pursuit prior to the introduction of powerful firearms. It required courage, considerable skill and organization to be able to kill the colossal animal, as well as an equal amount of ritual protection, as noted by Alpers (1992:353). With the vast majority of peoples, elephant hunting was a job for specialists. Harter (1996:101) writes that in past cen-

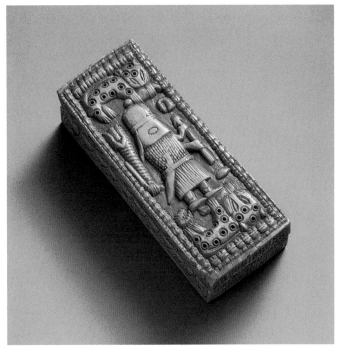

CAT. 24

Cup or lid for a box
Benin, Nigeria
Ivory rubbed with palm oil. D. 11.4 cm.
Drs. Daniel and Marian Malcolm

CAT. 25

Box with lid
Bini peoples, Nigeria
Ivory rubbed with palm oil. L. 20.8 cm.
Gerald and Lila Dannenberg

Lidded boxes with figural decoration are used to contain kola-nuts. In the Benin Kingdom, they are carved by members of the *igbesanmwan*, the ivory carver's guild. The motifs often resemble the motifs that are carved on the royal altar tusks or other ivory objects. This lid is decorated with relief carvings representing an anthropomorphic figure and two leopards. Some symbols of authority and musical instruments are also represented. (F.H.)

turies in the Grasslands of Cameroon, such hunters were organized into veritable small armies. They established a great number of chieftancies there and, as chiefs, appropriated all tusks of culled elephants. In this way ivory objects became the exclusive attributes of the rulers and dignitaries of royal blood.

In the kingdom of Benin, too, the possession of ivory was mainly the privilege of the ruler (*Oba*), just as was the case among a number of other peoples. Leading dignitaries also had the right to commission certain objects in ivory. Blackmun (1992:163) relates that ivory already occupied an important place in the economic, political and conceptual life of the people of Benin when the Portuguese first encountered them in 1472. In the time of *oba* Ewuare, ivory played a major role in art of the court. This ruler was the patron of Eghoghomaghan II who, according to Egharevba (1968:17), was a master-artist who is thought to have introduced the ivory design which was to remain in use for generations to follow (Cat. 23-25).

For the Lega, use of ivory was exclusively reserved for the members of the Bwami association and, more particularly, for those of the highest order, the *kindi*-rank (Biebuyck 1986:39-40). The fact that ivory has a special significance in the culture of so many peoples is not surprising given the animal from which it originates. Indeed, the elephant itself occupies - if possible - an even larger place, thanks to its extraordinary size and strength, not to mention its long life-expectancy and other qualities. The elephant, Alpers (1992:349) remarks, inspires fear and respect. It is the symbol of power and wisdom in the traditional lore. As for the Lega, Biebuyck (1986:40) further informs us that the *kindi* are inspired by the elephant's majestic power, "which turns into awesome destructiveness when the animal is disturbed. They are also impressed by the elephant's keen sense of smell (...) and its retentive memory (...)". The Yoruba, for their part, consider the elephant (along with the ram) their most important totem. This animal is a sign of "preeminent power" (Drewal 1992:199). Among the Kuba (Congo) there is a relationship between the elephant and its tusks and the king (*nyim*).

The material that one calls ivory primarily comes from the tusks of elephants[vi]. But other animals, too, have this creamy-white dentine, and the teeth of the hippopotamus and the tusks of the warthog are additional sources from which small anthropomorphic or

CAT. 23 (LEFT PAGE)

Pendant
Benin, Nigeria. Probably 18th century
Ivory. H. 25.4 cm
Buffalo Museum of Science

The pendant shows the *Oba*, or king with two supporters.

zoomorphic images are fashioned[vii]. Some animal bones, such as the elephant's, can equally serve as substitutes, and such is the case with the Lega and a few other forest peoples. The Chagga (Kenya) even use elephant toes for making armbands. Among the Lega the authorities and local chiefs imposed restrictions on the possession of ivory. By way of replacement in the making of figures and masks from this material, use is made of elephant bones, and for masks sometimes its skin and even foot-soles are employed. Examples of the latter are extremely rare (Biebuyck 2002:115). Moreover, the Lega also carve large heads from bone and ivory (idem:129).

The Lega seem to make no apparent distinction between ivory and bone. According to Biebuyck (1973:304), both materials are mutually exchangeable[8]. With other peoples, however, bone enjoys a lower social status. It has a very porous structure and is thus more perishable than ivory. Teeth of the hippopotamus, covered in a thick enamel, is difficult to carve with the tools which were available at the time (Shayt 1992:369), something that also holds for warthog teeth albeit to a lesser degree. On the other hand, elephant ivory is more easily carved and has other outstanding characteristics. As a labor-intensive material, the same author tells us, it has no equal. By virtue of its physical advantages it is in a class of its own:

> *The fine crosshatched microstructure of the grain, so apparent in*
> *the swirling surface finishes achieved, allows ivory to be cut in*
> *almost any direction without severe splintering. While harder*
> *than most woods, ivory does not dull cutting tools as quickly,*
> *due in part to the gelatinous lubricant found in the network of*
> *tiny vascular tubes interlacing the material and that gives ivory*
> *its characteristic shine. (Shayt 1992:368-369)*

The material further possesses a very good cross-sectional strength, and has the quality of being able to take color-pigments (idem:369). Sunlight, on the other hand, bleaches ivory. In contrast to bone and animal skin, which degrade after heavy continual rubbing, it generally retains its "overall form and finish even under constant usage" (idem:373). The ambient temperature and the changeable degree of humidity will cause ivory to crack after some decades, a consequence of the pores' expansion and shrinking (LaFontaine & Wood 1982; ap. Shayt 1992:367). Important disadvantages, if one likes, are the limited dimensions of an elephant tusk and the hollow canal found in its upper third. But as Shayt (1992:369) remarks, this limitation has only been marginal in the long and complicated history of ivory carving. In Europe as well as in Africa, from quite early on ivory was seen as a special substance, one to be reserved for highly decorative, political or spiritual use (idem:370). Adams (1989 ap. Ross 1992:348)) puts it this way: "Curiously symbolizing profligate luxury as well as purity, ivory has for uncounted millennia been procured from vast distances and masterfully carved into objects of rare beauty."

In the ancient kingdom of Benin the white smoothness of ivory was taken as "cool," same as the white kaolin clay (*orhue*) which is so fundamental in the life and thought of Benin (Blackmun 1992:184) and which, according to Duchâteau (1990:113), symbolizes joy, purity, peace and prosperity. This purity came to expression in the required obligation of cleaning the carved tusk of blood and food remains after each offering made to it. Given that the object in question is elephant-derived, the same author goes on to say that it is by extension brought into relation with this animal's physical strength.

> *Although the elephant also often symbolizes powerful and rebellious chiefs,*
> *here it is mainly its qualities as royal animal that are at the fore: leadership*
> *qualities, wisdom and venerable age - characteristics which are also ttributed to*

the Oba. The ivory tusk, with its complex symbolism, became a royal material par excellence: hard, strong and enduring, it lent itself ideally as a material for the recording of historic events and symbols for subsequent generations. [trans.] (Duchâteau 1990:113)[9]

The originally much sought after and symbolically charged white tint of ivory was, in Benin, of precarious longevity. Duchâteau (1990:118) relates that the carved tusks have a light-red color, "from very fine laterite dust, probably fallen from the palace roof, and over the course of time becoming fixed to the weathered surface of the tusk." A bit further the same author adds that:

The dark discoloration of the tusks ca. 60 to 70 cm. from below to above might originate from the action of sacrificial blood that would be smeared on the tusks, despite the fact that it would be washed off afterwards. The discoloration might also be attributable to manual handling of the tusks when these were lifted up, as it is mainly the raised parts which are dark, while the deeper parts exhibit a lighter color. [trans.] (1990:118)[10]

It is clear that both the elephant and the ivory in the form of its tusks have occupied a central role in the iconography and history of Benin. "As a symbol," writes Blackmun (1992:180), "ivory evokes associations of permanence and fulfillment; as an economic commodity ivory once brought unprecedented eminence to the kingdom." Even when ivory was not that scarce in Benin, it was as difficult to come by as copper. Ivory, and especially brass, were in those times more important than gold. Both of these materials came over land from far away. The guild of the ivory carvers (*Igbesanmwan*) was in competition for prestige and royal patronage with that of the brass-casters. According to the elders, the first-named guild was founded back in mythical times by the first rulers of Benin (the *Ogiso*), long prior to the establishment of the second. Both guilds worked mainly for the *oba*, but members of the rich upper-class were also permitted to commission them to make ornaments and insignia in ivory and brass (Blackmun 1992:163-164). The name *Igbesanmwan* approximately means, according to Duchâteau (1990:118), "those who write (carve) on ivory". Each time the *oba* called on the knowledge and know-how of the ivory carvers they would be summoned to the ruler's palace.

The guild's leader accepted the commission and would relegate the various aspects of the work to different carvers according to their special competences. Some carved the rough outline of the figures in the tusk, others worked out the band-motifs, while others still were needed to hold the ivory absolutely still for the carvers or to sharpen tools. The master carvers executed the finer details and finishing. (idem:118)

In the era of *oba* Adolo (1848-1888) the *Igbesanmwan* still carved all manner of ivory objects. The raw-material came from the ruler, as all tusks were his property. (On some small unworked teeth one finds his identifying mark). The *oba* ordered several ivory objects at once and these would then be made within the same period. Prayers to the ancestors would take place prior to commencing work and at its completion. The ivory-carvers received a cow as a gift, while the most senior among them were given a wife by the sovereign. In contrast to the case of wood sculpture, ivory was only carved by fully trained and experienced craftsmen (Dark 1973:56-57). Dark (1962:21-22) elsewhere relates that the ivory-carvers used the same tools as the wood-sculptors, namely adzes and knives "with, at least latterly, chisels of his choice made by locally by the blacksmith". In some ivory objects, copper wire or pieces of hammered brass were inlaid. Such operations were then entrusted to the brass-smiths.

With regard to the sculpted tusks, Roth Ling (1903/1968:196) relates the testimony of a certain Mr. C. Punch, "who saw some tusks half completed," and contended that "no training or drawing was applied first; the carver, who was a court official, a Ukoba, made his first design as he went on, using no model; and the only implements he saw were jack-knives and hammers." Roth Ling also discusses two ivory (belt) masks which "show elaborate care in the chiseling." He refers directly to the metal inlay of the eyes and on the forehead. Also the respective beards of the masks "... have at some period been adorned with strips of metal..." (p. 199). Roth's admiration equally extends to:

> ... two armlets, one being carved inside the other, out of the
> same piece of ivory, with only the space of a knife-blade
> thickness between them. When moved, the armlets rattle against
> each other (...). The whole shows rather fertility on the part of
> the artist in planning a difficult piece and consummate skill in its
> elaboration than any beauty in design; it is, nevertheless, a piece
> of work, which, for the ingenuity displayed in its production,
> cannot fail to be admired. (1903/1968:205)

The two well-known freestanding ivory leopards - royal animals *par excellence* - from the collection of the British queen were made at the time from five separate tusks. The eyes are encrusted with small mirrors and the flecks on the body with small brass plates (Ben-Amos 1980:64).

So far as is known, working with ivory in Nigeria dates back prior to the tenth century, namely in the location of Igbo-Ukwu. Excavations by Thurstan Shaw turned up, among other items, three (possibly) decorated tusks. Among the present-day Igbo, it is said that the Nri men of the Agbandana lineage have for long been carvers of ivory. The vast majority of elephant tusks encountered in this region, however, have no carved decoration. Cole, who discusses this subject, also relates the following about this material's symbolic significance:

> The pristine whiteness of ivory also signifies purity, sanctity, and
> coolness ascribed to Ozo and other titled men, who often wear
> white gowns as well as white eagle feathers and sometimes ivory
> bracelets to signify these revered states. (1992:214)

Not all peoples have this fixation with the color white that was present in the ancient kingdom of Benin or found among the Igbo. For the Lega, writes Biebuyck (2002:60), smoothness and a shiny patina stand as central qualities among the high ranks in the Bwami association. During initiation in the initiation house, ivory objects are oiled and polished. This process is repeated each time a *mwami* is invited for a new initiation. Elsewhere the same author adds that the small masks made from ivory and from elephant bone (which are usually smaller than the palm of a hand and, for that, matter, not worn) are regularly rubbed-in with oil and pigment, so imparting a rich, yellowish or reddish patina (2002:87). The masks and the figurines are not only rubbed with oil, they are perfumed as well. Frequent use can itself provide the patina by which it also receives, as Biebuyck puts it (1976:338), "a power of heaviness" (*masengo*). Another practice of the Lega is to polish the small figures with sandpaper, so obtaining small quantities of powder with medicinal properties (idem 1992:56) (Cat. 26-31).

CAT. 26

Head
Lega peoples, Dem. Rep. of the Congo
Ivory rubbed with palm oil. H. 18.5 cm.
Private Collection. Former collection of Henry Pareyn, Antwerp, and Bela Heim, Paris, 1910-1931

Figural ivory sculptures of human heads and figures and animals are associated with the *kindi,* or highest grade of the *bwami* society. Most of the sculptures are small and show a great stylistic variety in the representation of the human figure. (F.H.)

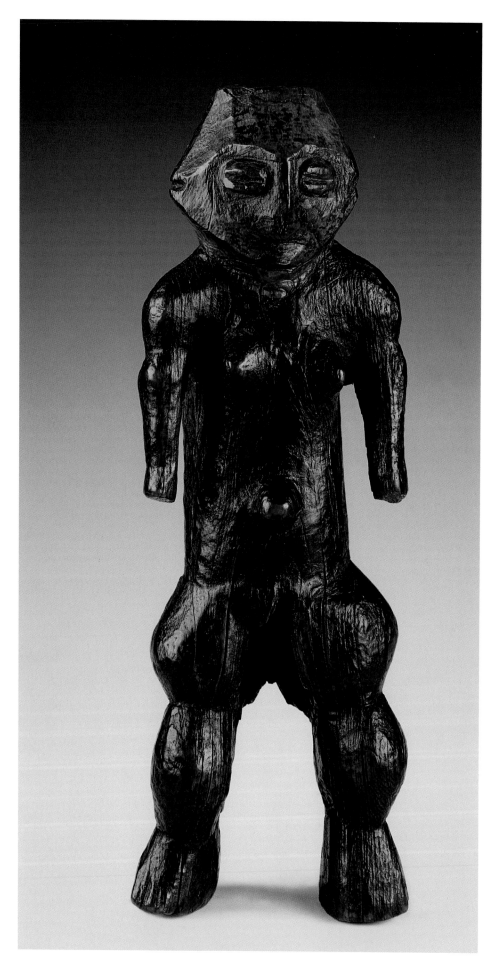

Figure
Lega peoples, Dem. Rep. of the Congo
Ivory rubbed with palm oil. H. 28 cm
Private Collection

CAT. 28

Figure
Lega peoples, Dem. Rep. of the Congo
Ivory rubbed with palm oil, beads. H. 13.5 cm.
Private Collection. Former collection of Henry Pareyn,
Antwerp, and Bela Heim, Paris, 1910-1931

CAT. 29

Figure
Lega peoples, Dem. Rep. of the Congo
Ivory rubbed with palm oil. H. 10.5 cm.
Private Collection. Former collection of Henry Pareyn,
Antwerp, and Bela Heim, Paris, 1910-1931

CAT. 30

Figure
Lega peoples, Dem. Rep. of the Congo
Ivory rubbed with palm oil. H. 12.8 cm.
Private Collection. Former collection of Henry Pareyn,
Antwerp, and Bela Heim, Paris, 1910-1931

CAT. 31

Bird's head
Lega peoples, Dem. Rep. of the Congo
Ivory rubbed with palm oil. L. 1.2 cm
Private Collection. Former collection of Henry Pareyn,
Antwerp, and Bela Heim, Paris, 1910-1931

In both the Grasslands and the forest regions of Cameroon, Harter informs us (1986:98) that over the course of time a considerable number of ivory objects have been made for ritual and prestige purposes. In past days - in contrast to today - elephants were present in large numbers. Many of the tusks are richly provided with anthropomorphic and zoomorphic motifs. Some small carved teeth (30 to 40 cm.) have become nearly black, but most have a red-brown patina (1986:101). Among the Bamileke and Bali peoples of the Grasslands, one finds small carved figures of between 7 and 12 cm. They have a bore-hole and may be hung from the neck or arm. Even smaller examples are components of neck-strings worn by magicians (1986:102). These various small ivory images are rudimentary or realistic in appearance, finely designed and well proportioned. Harter also adds that there exist extremely rare anthropomorphically conceived flutes, where the largest measure some 21 cm. in length. More numerous are the ivory armbands for both men and women. Certain chiefs wear a whole series of these, carved from a single tusk and thus of differing diameters. The armbands intended for the women of the Fumban chieftancy are more elaborated than those of the men; some even take zoomorphic motifs (1986:103). The cylindrical or flat handles of sabers may also be fashioned from ivory. Those of the royal weapons may sometimes have anthropomorphic ornamentation. The ceremonial pipes belonging to the chiefs are provided with human representations and carved bovine heads on their ivory stems. Harter claims that these have the most beautiful patina of all, having become red-brown from frequent handling. The downside of this is that the details of the carved representations have thus become largely lost (1986:103).

Practically no details have been published regarding the technique used for ivory carving, or the carvers themselves, in the Grasslands. Harter relates the name of a single ivory-carver, Umbe Massangong, who in around 1920 precisely chiseled tusks with human and animal representations, commissioned by various chiefs (1986:101). Gebauer (1979), who spent many years in the Grasslands of Cameroon, gives the names of two sculptors of whom one worked in ivory, namely Tita Yuefainji. Gebauer initially met him in Tungo in 1932, and he describes him as a man of average size, about forty years-of-age, and a specialist in the sculpting of horn:

> *While traveling he carried a bag with his fine tools and an*
> *unfinished cup to be worked on. At home he made the out-of-*
> *doors his workshop because his fine carving required good light.*
> *His media were horn, ivory, ebony and other hard woods. The*
> *largest pieces made by him were elephant tusks for the chiefs...*
> *(1979:117).*

Tita was born in around 1882 and he learned his craft from his father, a maker of pipe bowls in clay and of small figures, who would later carve objects in horn. He related how he acquired his skills:

> *I observed my father as long I can recall. When I was able to*
> *hold a tool, he persuaded me to imitate his work. As I grew*
> *older, I helped in roughing out the outlines of pie bowls and*
> *horns. Later I made my own objects under father's direction.*
> *We worked as a family. We worked because of the honor*
> *involved. The best craftsmen were close to the chief. They had*
> *privileges. They were recognized by the public on account of*
> *the 'sense' God had given them. (1979:118)*

Gebauer adds in a footnote: "It is a generally accepted assumption that talent is of supernatural origin" (1979:368). Tita Yuefainji was at one time called upon to carve an elephant tusk with low-relief motifs in connection with a visit by Queen Elisabeth II to Cameroon, something that Gebauer states he executed with brio. Tita first divided the tusk into sections by tying grass stalks around it and then shifting it until the tusk was separated "into pleasing proportions that allowed for large motifs and restful border designs. Since he was a true temperamental artist, he worked only when the spirit moved him - and the spirit needed occasional prodding" (1979:118).

Geary (1992:232) tells us about a second ivory-carver from the Babanki-Tungo region (not the only center for ivory carving in the Grasslands, but the most important one). His name was Bobe Ngincho, active in the second-half of the nineteenth century, and we know of some tusks sculpted by his hand. The Duala, too, consider such objects with great esteem. Dignitaries and their wives wore ivory wrist rings, and horns made from this material are also known (Wilcox 1992:263).

As is the case with so-many other peoples, the Mangbetu likewise use same kind of blow-horn. Originally they were made without figurative decoration, though sometimes a wooden extension piece would be attached to the narrower side in order to produce more impressive sounds. These were used, alone or together with drums, to assemble the group for festivities or to announce communal hunting or fishing outings. Burrows (1898) writes that these horns were also utilized during battle to indicate troop positions, warn of danger, or to signal retreat. He adds that such large elephant horns are quite difficult to blow. We also know that they were usually carved by smiths. Czekanowski (1924), who worked as ethnographer with the von Mecklenburg expedition in 1907-1908, saw a famous ivory-carver make this instrument in Gomban. For this he used only two tools: a toothed knife that served as a primitive saw, and a sharply honed adze. "The adze was handled with such dexterity and the strikes so finely executed, that after hewing the polishing with abrasive-leaves could immediately commence" (1924:131). Moreover, this carver's skill was such that even with such limited means he could also elaborate a serpentine motif in relief all along the instrument's surface.

In an article from 1918, Lang provides further details on ivory-working. He writes that in addition to an adze and various other tools, sculptors also used a small hatchet in preparatory work on the tusk or other piece of ivory. They also employed an indented blade that "serves as a saw to cut the deeper moldings," and they went about this in the same way as done with a piece of hardwood. The finer ornamentations "are carefully carved by variously shaped tools". Finally, the entire object is smoothed with the sharp edge of a knife and then polished with moistened tree-leaves containing fine crystals of silica. In rather high-blown style, Lang relates his obvious admiration for the ivory-carver's work:

> ... bent over the immaculate, white substance, often holding the
> object with his feet to have his hands free, industriously hewing,
> carving, scraping, and polishing, while surrounded by a group of
> enthusiastic friends who spur on his desire for greater
> accomplishments. (1918:531)

In a footnote, Lang provides an interesting glimpse of how a piece of ivory is prepared. He says that the Mangbetu neither soak it nor otherwise treat it prior to or during carving:

> The straightening of small curved pieces, however, causes no
> perplexity. In the core of the juicy banana trunk they place the ivory
> to be bent. The succulent cylinder, nearly a foot in diameter,

CAT. 32

Figural staff finial: *mvwala*

Kongo peoples, Dem. Rep. of the Congo
Ivory rubbed with palm oil. H. 14 cm.
Private Collection

Both figures are insignia of leadership that are fixed on top of a chief's staff. The kneeling woman incarnates the progenitor of the clan. The standing man represents a chief. (F.H.)

CAT. 33

Staff finial: *mvwala*

Kongo peoples, Dem. Rep. of the Congo
Ivory rubbed with palm oil, metal. H. 14.3 cm.
Cecilia S. Smiley

CAT. 34

Anthropomorphic pendant

Luba peoples, Dem. Rep. of the Congo
Ivory rubbed with palm oil. H. 10 cm.
Private Collection

These figures are made of ivory or bone. They are considered portraits that are made in honor of ancestors and are anointed with oil in their honor. (F.H.)
(Roberts and Nooter 1995: 108)

CAT. 35

Pendant, *Ikhoko*

Pende peoples, Dem. Rep. of the Congo
Ivory. H. 5.7 cm.
Cecilia S. Smiley

The *Ikhoko* is a miniature replica of a mask of the *mbuya* type. It serves as a protective device for its owner. Full ivory figures among the Pende are rare. The facial features of this example resemble those of an *Ikhoko* miniature mask but the body does not resemble the costume of an *mbuya* mask. (F.H.)

CAT. 36

Figure

Pende peoples, Dem. Rep. of the Congo
Ivory rubbed with palm oil. H. 7.6 cm.
Private Collection

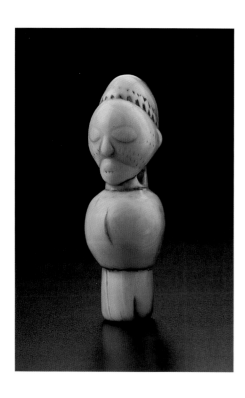

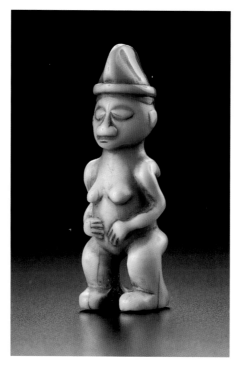

CAT. 37

Whistle

Mbala peoples, Dem. Rep. of the Congo
Ivory rubbed with palm oil. L. 9.3 cm.
Private Collection

Figural whistles serve both as musical instruments and as protective devices. (F.H.)

CAT. 38

Figure

Yaka peoples, Dem. Rep. of the Congo
Ivory rubbed with palm oil. H. 7.3 cm.
Private Collection

discharges steam from the centre as it is turned over the fire until the exterior is completely charred. The ivory, thus exposed to a moist, intense heat, and yet well protected from the flames, is removed so hot that it can hardly be touched. Water is poured over the straightened piece which is then pressed between two logs. (Lang 1918:531, note 1)

The Mangbetu are likewise known for their ivory hatpins and hairclips. Here they utilize the massive upper-ends of elephant tusks, from which a small disc is cut to serve as crowning element of a gossamer-thin pin. This requires a steady hand and a high degree of craftsmanship in general. "Bent ivory hatpins are easily straightened if put into a section of the fruit stalk of plantains and treated in the same manner." In any case, only men of means were able to acquire such exceptional examples. These objects were an outward sign of their wealth and high social position.

Sculpted objects in ivory are seen relatively more commonly among the Kongo. These usually are elaborated as applied-sculptures in the form of handles for staves, flywhisks and other chiefly insignia. Here, as well, the finished object is often given a patina, arrived at by rubbing-in a vegetal oil to which red wood-powder *(tukula)* or other dye is added (Cat. 32-33).

According to the frequency of coatings, the assiduity with which the Master's assistants apply the oily concoction and the manner of the sculpture's utilization, the translucence of the pigment allows us still today to admire the tones running from light yellow to purplish-brown, while passing through the entire range of orange tints. [trans.] (Lehuard 1989:100)[11]

Towards the end of the nineteenth century, the bulk of ivory used in East Africa came from the region known as "Lado," located to the south of the Bahr-el-Ghazal river and to the north of Lake Albert. Today this area comprises Uganda, northeast Congo and the Equatoria province of Sudan. In and around the "Lado enclave," Kasfir (1992:310) tells us, ivory was the symbol of political power and likewise the most important resource for existence. Here and with the neighboring Zande, as well as in the Buganda and Bunyoro kingdoms, the ivory trade went hand-in-hand with the slave trade. These activities brought the acquisition of arms and luxury goods. In both the kingdoms mentioned, ivory carving and elephant hunting were the domains of specialists. Due to the demand for decorative objects in ivory, ivory-carvers were already practicing prior to the arrival of Arab traders in the nineteenth century, though apparently in lesser numbers than later on. Most of them were in the employ of the king, who was also the owner of the bulk of this material. Among the favorite objects were armbands of around 7.5 cm. in thickness for women and children. Kasfir (1992:317), from whom this information comes, also tells us how these craftsmen set about their task:

The ivory carver first soaked the ivory in water until it was soft enough to cut. He used a double handled saw with a thin iron blade to cut pieces from the tusk. After this a short adze was used to shape the bracelet and to cut away the inside to the right thickness. The final carving was done with a knife, then polished with an abrasive leaf.

Ivory ornaments and armbands were, according to Jackson (1977, ap. Kasfir 1992:323), much prized among the Akamba elephant hunters as status symbols. In their extensive sys-

CAT. 39

Mask

Ngbaka (?) or Mbanja (?), Dem. Rep. of the Congo
Ivory rubbed with palm oil and red earth. H. 24.8 cm.
Private Collection

Masks in ivory of this size are exceptional. The eyebrows, nose, mouth and teeth are slightly carved in low relief. The shape of the face follows the natural shape of the part of the ivory tusk that is used. (F.H.)

tem of body decoration, ivory armbands (*ngotho*) had a special place. From this flowed an "ivory aesthetic." This encompassed "an appreciation of its suppleness during carving, its ability to gleam when rubbed with oils or glow in a more understated fashion when brushed". That some ivory-carvers in other regions were veritable virtuosos is testified to by the well-known double, 14 cm. high armband, most likely from the hand of an Owo-Yoruba master, and now found in the P. and R. Tishman collection of African Art, Walt Disney Imagineering. Drewal (1992:202) describes the armband as follows:

> The two thin cylinders of ivory were carved from the same tusk,
> the inner cylinder made with loops within which the outer one
> (with almost three-dimensional figures) moves. Such movement
> facilitates the sounding of the ivory crotals suspended from the
> ivory links.

Much simpler are the small bowed pendants in the form of a legless human figure which the Luba carve from hippopotamus teeth (Cat. 34). They acquire a deep yellow to orange-red color after being rubbed with palm oil, and also due to continual contact with the body fat of the wearer. The Pende also sometimes make use of the same material for carving their famous miniature masks in the form of pendants called *ikhoko*. Most, however, seem to be made from elephant ivory, with others fashioned from bone or other materials[12]. Through wear, over the years the ivory examples have acquired the same patina as seen with the cited Luba pendants (Cat. 35-38).

Just as the case in other continents, Africa - and more particularly sub-Saharan Africa - too has yielded very many objects in ivory and related materials. Today most of these, and often the most beautiful examples, are found in museums and private collections. Unfortunately enough, we are only sporadically informed as to the details concerning the various aspects of their manufacture, the makers themselves, those who commissioned them and the public. Currently there are very few such objects still made in the so-called traditional style. The reasons are multiple. Since 1990 there has been an official ban on the use of elephant tusk and, together with the large-scale disappearance of the elephants themselves, also gone are those who in the past had commissioned such pieces, and with them the bulk of the cultural background from out of which the production of ivory art works had arisen[13].

STONE

In Africa, stone is less used for the making of sculpture than are wood and ivory. There are only a few regions where one comes across appreciable numbers of sculpted works in stone. In West Africa, areas of interest include Sierra Leone and Guinea where in past times respectively *nomoli* and *pomtan* (sing. *pomdo*) figures were made; other examples originate from the town of Esie in Nigeria, from Ife, Igbajo and the neighboring Eketi-land of the central Yoruba; and finally we mention the monoliths encountered in East Nigeria in the region of the so-called Ekoi or Ejaham. In central Africa, stone sculpture is largely limited to the Kongo group. Aside from these areas and peoples, such works are also very sparsely seen amongst various peoples in the Grasslands of Cameroon, with the Kurumba of Burkino Faso, as well as in the ancient culture of Great Zimbabwe, in southern Africa, in south Ethiopia and a few other regions still.

Quite little is known regarding the technical and ritual aspects of elaborating sculpture in stone, either because the sculptors themselves are long since dead, or that such activity is associated with secrecy - something even less conducive for the understanding of this specific subject. The little that is known is enumerated here.

CAT. 40

Figure
Loma (Toma) peoples, Liberia
Stone. H. 36 cm.
Private Collection

Outside Sierra Leone and Guinea, stone sculptures are rare in this part of West Africa. The Loma are mainly known for the making of large masks and some rare sculpture in wood. (F.H.)

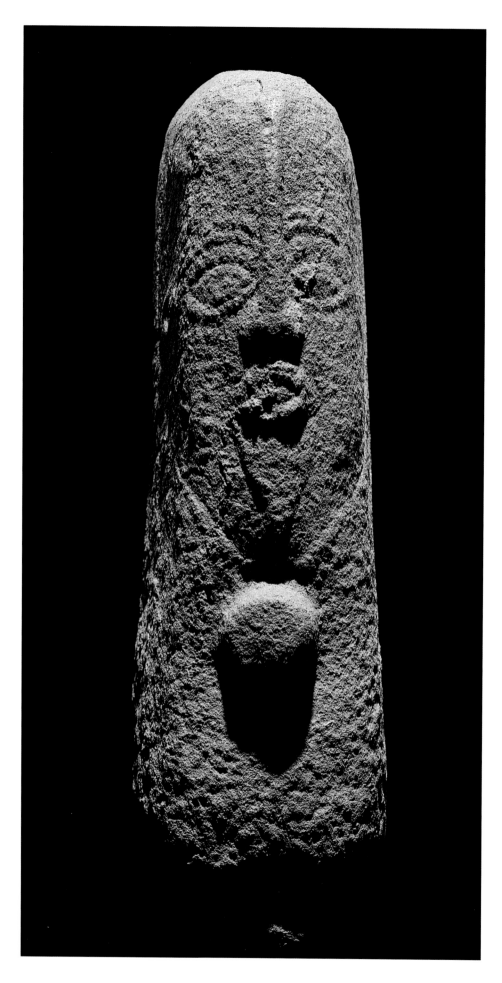

CAT. 41

Sculpture
Ikom, Cross River, Nigeria
Stone. H. 48.3 cm.
Toby and Barry Hecht

First are the monoliths found on the right-bank of the Cross River (Cat. 41). Thanks to the 1968 published results of Allison's limited investigations, some data are available. In East Nigeria's Ogoja province, he came across 295 stone images spread over 39 sites encompassing the territory of 11 different groups, all components of the "Ekoi." Among the Nta group, they seem to have been made over a period running from the early sixteenth to the early twentieth century. The sculpted figures, here and elsewhere, are primarily elaborated from basalt rock (probably dolerite), around fifty are in limestone and a few in sandstone. In every case it is local rock that is used. Basalt is known for its hardness, and it is difficult to work with primitive tools. Limestone is, as Allison (1968:24) rightly points out, "an unsuitable medium for carving and weathers badly." This material was nevertheless sometimes chosen, probably owing to the fact that it requires less effort to sculpt.

Along the riverbeds of the Cross River a good many rounded basalt boulders are found whose form is well suited for transformation into *akwanshi*, as these stone statues are locally known.

> *The carvers apparently selected boulders of a naturally suitable shape, these were smoothed and shaped to a certain extent before the carving of features and decorations began. The surface of most of the stone is carved with small indentations made, in the process of smoothing the stone, by pecking at it with another stone or possibly a metal tool. In some cases stones have been erected at this stage with no further carving or decoration. (Allison 1968:24)*

The monoliths' dimensions vary from around 30 cm. to 183 cm. They for the most part stand in groups (of up to thirty pieces) and ten of them are erected in the form of a circle. The stone sculptures are usually depicted with a large navel, some have a purely phallic elaboration without any other further decoration. The vast majority of the *akwanshi* have human traits, being provided with eyes, nose, mouth ears and a beard. Some also have arms with hands and circles to indicate breasts. Decoration ceases below the navel, and there is also no emphatic indication of genitalia. But given that the statues have beards one may suppose that they represent men. Their upper-body ornamentation, Allison tells us, probably represents scarifications signs or even body-painting. This same investigator indicates that in the vast majority of cases sculptors "produced a decorated boulder rather than a stone sculpture" (p. 28).

Six *akwanshi*, on the other hand, do indeed have a good deal of sculptural modeling, but only a few attempt to portray a full figure. Sculpting of the two large and smoothy carved phallic monoliths must have required a great deal of patience and skill. These are, for that matter, the only ones of true cylindrical form. The other *akwanshi* are closer to deep slabs. A half-finished abandoned figure gives an idea of the method used to arrive at its form. Allison (1969:28) provides the following details:

> *The stone was a large slab, over six feet long and wedge shaped in section. On the narrow edge, seven expressions had been notched into the stone, apparently with the intention of cutting it away so as to leave the navel and other prominent features standing away from the general level of the surface without involving too much labour. Even so the work must have been considerable and was probably undertaken by a number of assistants working under the direction of an expert. The presence of a number of notches on the working edge suggest*

that the preliminary work was carried out by several operators
working at the same time. The cutting is said to have been done
with metal as well as stone tools.

The stone tools employed for sculpting appear to be of basalt. Only a hard stone such as this is able to work an identical similar material. A sculptor who had learned his craft from his father, told Allison that in addition to a basalt stone he needed a "ground-down machete" to give the *akwanshi* its rudimentary form. The man refused, however, to let the investigator watch him at work or even get a look at his tools. Allison (1968:29) adds in this regard:

It is not surprising that the adepts of such an unusual art as stone
carving should wish to keep their methods secret, or that the
votaries of a cult should be reluctant even to admit that the cult
objects are of human origin.

A certain chief of the Nnam group confided that one of the old "age-grade companies was called 'Anepetal,' meaning the 'stone-makers' and he assumed that this particular company was responsible for carving the stones." It is not known if this also held for the other "Ekoi" groups.

The greatest concentration of sculpted stone objects in sub-Saharan Africa is found in the town of Esie where both Igbomina and Yoruba live. Esie lies in the Ilorin province of Nigeria, almost on the dividing line between savanna and forest areas. A great many stone sculptures were discovered in the immediate vicinity of the town several decades ago. Eight-hundred to one thousand anthropomorphic representations, in addition to some animal figures, between 14 cm. to over one meter tall - made from a robust variety of steatite - are today housed and on view in a local museum. The statues were originally located in a sort of necropolis located a few kilometers to the southwest of Esie. They were partially overgrown with grass, shrubs and trees, or covered with a thin layer of earth. Despite the chaotic sight, they nonetheless appear to have been erected according to a particular plan. Due to the fact that many of them are broken, their exact number is difficult to determine[14].

In the main these figures portray sitting men and women. Some are shown playing musical instruments or, more frequently, carrying some sort of weapon - including, unusually, the women as well. The men oftentimes have a bow and arrow and daggers, a great number of women hold up a sort of "cutlass." In reality this is most likely a machete used in agricultural activities.

The inhabitants of Esie maintain that their people came across these statues at the end of the eighteenth century, when they had made their way to their current home. A local legend relates that these figures are the petrified remains of visitors from a distant land. It is clear that the present local population has in fact no idea of how these statues got there, or where they came from, much less who made them or when. Western researchers, too, have for many years sought to come up with an acceptable answer, but certainty on this subject remains ever elusive.

Many figures are, as mentioned above, either broken or in one way or another damaged - apparently by intention - but others have remained relatively intact. One striking fact is that the appearance of these figures shows little or no connection with other Yoruba sculpture (which, for that matter, is predominantly in wood). Moreover, it bears practically no resemblance to any other form of Nigerian sculpture, and even less to the remainder of sub-Saharan African art. The full figures which are preserved have a short loincloth. Many of these are appointed with an intricate coiffure or headpiece, and are shown wearing necklaces and armbands. Globally the portrayal is - proportions notwithstanding - what may be termed realistic, though with a healthy dose of stylization and even pure convention. Many of the personages are indigenous in appearance, others show characteristics referring to peoples based more northwardly. A few exhibit full facial scarification, somewhat similar to that seen in some bronze works of Igbo-Ukwe and likewise on the bronze figures of Jebba, though there are no other parallels. The most commonly seen marking consists of three notched strips on the cheeks, a scarification not seen elsewhere. Some details are vaguely reminiscent of the Nok sculpture, others of the Nupe or present Yoruba examples. Nevertheless, taken a whole these works have an original style that stands totally apart from any other known sculptural design.

Ever since the discovery of the Esie statues, researchers have tried to find a reasonable answer to the problematic issues that continue to surround these unusual works. Over the last decades various hypotheses have been advanced. After years of investigation of the available data, including consideration of the most plausible of the proffered suppositions, Stevens comes to the conclusion in his 1978 study that there is a good chance that these sculpted images originate from Old-Oyo, the former capital of the kingdom of the same name. The city which in the fourteenth century was populated by a Yoruba group, and had possibly been founded some several centuries earlier, quickly became a flourishing commercial center with a distinct cosmopolitan character. This development occurred to the apparent detriment of the city of Ife, which nonetheless remained the most important religious and cultural center. The contacts which the Oyo had with, among others, the Hausa, the Nupe and Borgu (and via them with the Arab and Berber worlds) led to the absorption of all manner of influences which are reflected in Esie sculpture.

In the fifteenth century the prosperous city was overrun by Nupe warriors. The *alafin* (ruler) of Old-Oyo and his court sought and found refuge in the north of the Borgu region which lies to the north of their city. Stevens reasonably suggests that at the time of this event the sculptures which later came to stand at Esie had already been made, and that they were of great importance to the inhabitants of the then Oyo kingdom. The figures might perhaps represent a royal household with servants and messengers, and with women who with their raised machetes could be the symbolic embodiment of the concept "woman-farming-earth." The whole would be a representation of the "essence" of the Oyo kingdom, and thus considered as precious patrimony. For these reasons another part of the populace - who were charged with the preservation of the statues - would likewise have fled under pressure from the Nupe, this time towards the southeast. This group would have succeeded in - and not without considerable effort - moving the hundreds of sculptures to a safe unpopulated region that could serve as provisional refuge, at some 185 km. from Old-Oyo. After having been there a certain time, the Oyo refugees would have been attacked once again by the Nupe. Some became dispersed without having the opportunity to regroup, some were decimated and others taken into slavery. The abandoned figures were vandalized because they were not simply representations, but rather objects of undoubtedly great symbolic value. This explains the numerous broken-off heads and the intentional disfiguration that so many of these pieces were subject to. In the eighteenth century Igbomina immigrants - the current inhabitants of Esie - would have come across the necropolis and incorporated the many figures into their own cult.

This is the broad outline of the hypothesis that Stevens puts forward and reasonably argues. Although this remains a matter of supposition and not proven fact, in light of current knowledge it nonetheless offers a plausible explanation for one of Africa's most intriguing mysteries. The author, however, was not able to ascertain how many sculptors were responsible for these works - there are several recognizable sub-styles present - nor how long the production process lasted, nor under what circumstances they came into being. Also found at Esie were terracotta fragments which have been dated by thermolu-minescence to the twelfth century. It has likewise not been proven that all the sculptures originate from the same time-frame. Based on historical and other indications, Stevens believes that the fabrication of these pieces must pre-date the Nupe invasion in the fifteenth century. This same investigator points out that analysis of a number of the images shows that the soapstone (steatite) used originated from various sources. He does not offer other technical details. Seeing that steatite (a massive variety of talc) in the fresh state could easily be worked with then-current tools of the wood-sculptor, one may suppose that the stone-carvers also made use of adzes and knives. The less supple elaboration of the figures seems attributable to the use of steatite which once exposed to the air has the tendency to harden quite rapidly, something that subsequently invests the works with a greater degree of durability.

Esie is not the only place in Yoruba territory where stone sculptures were encountered, although to present only a quite limited number of examples have come to light. Here one may draw a distinction between monoliths, anthropo- and zoomorphic figures and, finally, stools. The best known in the first-named category is undoubtedly the so-called staff (*opa*) of Oronmiyon, named after the walking-staff - or the war-club - of the eponymous mythical hero who is the son of Ogun, the Yoruba's divinity of iron. This object is a monolith of granite-gneiss erected in the city of Ife and measuring ca. 5.75 meters in height. It is adorned with iron nails with spiral heads, such as is also seen on other stone figures in Ife, most likely for purely decorative reasons (Willet 1967:79). The "staff" has a beautiful, smooth finish, something that given the material's hardness must have entailed great effort on the part of its sculptor(s).

Among the figures in stone, deserving first mention are the two specimens originally erected in Ife's Ore Grove. The largest is sometimes referred to as Idena, which signifies

CAT. 42

Head
Guinea
Stone. H. 17 cm.
Private Collection, Milano, Italy

54

CAT. 43

Figure
Sierra Leone or Liberia
Stone. H. 24 cm.
Private Collection, Milano, Italy

"gatekeeper." The figure is male and measures some 101.25 cm. in height. He wears a large beaded necklace and a loin-garment with an striking knot. The realistic features of the face are topped by a head-dress fashioned from wrought iron nails driven into prepared cavities. The style of the figure is less fluent than with the "classic" terracotta and bronze heads and sculptures from Ife, perhaps due to the hard variety of stone employed (again local granite-gneiss) for the figures' carving, or else a logical consequence of the fact that here other craftsmen were involved. The smaller figure from the same Ore Grove measures around 80 cm. It is of broader design and more roughly executed than the Idena figure.

Other anthropomorphic stone figures originate from Eshure in the Ekiti country. In this location situated around 150 km. to the northeast of Ife, some sculptures in a variety of granite were found in the Orodi Grove (Igbo Orodi site). The largest measures 125 cm. and is strongly similar to the Idena figure in both its posture and clothing, though the design is less true-to-nature. A second figure is much more schematic. It has a round head and long arms alongside the body. Striking are the hundreds of iron nails randomly applied to the torso.

Under the category of anthropomorphic representations a few other more recent figures in steatite deserve mention. These are found in various shrines at Ife, like the one of Orishania. This sort of sculpture, made from a local variety of soapstone, is fairly schematically elaborated, in every way less fluent than the wooden Yoruba figures. One interesting stone figure is a 60 cm. tall representation of the divinity Eshu, found around 80 km. from Ife in the city of Igbajo. Originally there would have been three such stone figures located there. Given this Eshu figure's style, Allison (1968:21) suggests that it could be the work of a wood sculptor "...who, perhaps in relatively recent times, had tried his skill in a new medium and achieved considerable success." The variety of stone used here is not known.

Zoomorphic representations are extremely scarce. In 1957 in Ife's Ore Grove, Willet (1967:80) came across a stone image in the form of a snake or a fish, with iron nails for the eyes and mouth. More well-known is the granite "mudfish" found in the Ogun Ladin

CAT. 44

Half figure
Sierra Leone
Stone. H. 12 cm.
Private Collection, Milano, Italy

Figure
Guinea
Stone. H. 32 cm.
Private Collection, Milano, Italy

shrine of the Ife palace. This shrine is devoted to Ogun, the divinity of iron and war. The most striking stone objects from the corpus of Ife sculpture are undoubtedly the three complexly constructed stools (*apere*) of which the only intact specimen comes from the shrine of the divinity Oluorugbo, and now is housed in The British Museum. The stool - which also has counterparts in bronze - is 67.5 cm. broad and 52.5 cm. high, and made from local quartzite. This material is indeed quite difficult to carve, given that quartz - as Willet (1967:83) puts it - "... has a very coarse crystalline structure which does not break in easily predictable form. It would be necessary to grind the stone away, using a paste of coarse sand and water applied with strips of soft wood," entailing much labor, coupled with an extraordinary degree of technical knowledge. The result is a very smooth realization without any telltale traces of having been worked.

Down through the years several hundreds of small figurines have been found in Guinea and Sierra Leone, mainly carved from steatite. In Guinea they are called *pomtan* (sing. *pomdo*); in Sierra Leone the designation used is *nomoli*. They come from the territory of peoples including the Kissi, the Sherbro, the Koranko, the Mende and the Kono, but they are apparently not made by each of these groups themselves. These small images are predominantly anthropomorphic and measure between 10 and 20 cm., while some are as small as 4 cm. and a few as large as 90 cm. They were accidentally found in the ground and taken by those living there. Most of these examples are encountered among the Kissi and the Mende.

CAT. 46

Figure: Mintadi
Kongo peoples, Dem. Rep. of the Congo
Stone. H. 41 cm.
Private Collection, Milano, Italy

The Kissi mainly live in south Guinea, the Mende in central and east Sierra Leone (Cat. 42-45). Both peoples respectively ascribe the *pomtan* and the *nomoli* with characteristics pertaining to the religious-magical realm. The Kissi see them in connection with their ancestors, and preserve these small figures - often packed in cotton wrapping - in the shrine of the descendant. The Mende, too, place the *nomoli* in simple shrines and also mobilize them in cults for obtaining a good rice harvest. Some examples are several centuries old and are attributed by some investigators to peoples belonging to the Manes confederation (probably Mande conquerors who came from the region of present-day Loma). Others are more recent and in certain cases carved by the Kissi. In any case, taken as a whole the *nomoli* and the *pomtan* present an ensemble of various styles from different periods of elaboration. Jérémine (1945) carried out mineralogical and petrological examination of over 300 such pieces. He came to the conclusion that around 200 were carved in talc or steatite (mainly brown in color with various silicate minerals) and a minority in varieties of rock such as chlorite schist and amphibolite. A few were hewn from harder materials such as granite, dolerite and also in sandstone. This in itself can explain the difference in style, at least in certain cases. Steatite can indeed be carved with much greater ease.

In past times, a great many specimens in steatite were likewise seen amongst the Mboma, Solongo and Bakongo Ba Boma peoples (resp. Northwest Angola and Lower Congo). Locally such objects are known as *mintadi*, or "guardian spirits". Most were collected and described by Verly (1955). Cornet (1978), who calls them *bitumba*, also devoted attention to this subject. Nearly all the figures are human representations, frequently representations of chiefs. They measure between 30 and 55 cm, and are elaborated in varying attitudes. Typical is the portrayal of a sitting man with head held at a slant and resting on one hand, with the other hand on his hip. The legs are usually in a cross-legged, "tailor's" position (Cat. 46). Other statues have their hands turned upwards or they are kneeling. There are also mother-and-child representations. These figures are said to be the abodes of an ancestor spirit which aids and protects its descendants in difficult circumstances. Many *mintadi* were encountered in abandoned cemeteries. As for the types of stone used, it was one or other locally-found variety of steatite. Allison (1968:43) informs us that "... the form most favoured by the carvers was a sericeous schist which was usually obtained from exposure in river beds. It was carved with small adzes and knives, the normal tools of the wood-carver, and is more easily worked when fresh and damp and hardens on drying." This carving tradition may date back a good many centuries.

In the ancient culture known by the place-name Great Zimbabwe and famous for its imposing stone buildings constructed between 1000 and 1500 by the ancestors of the Karanga and the Shona, some sculptures in steatite have likewise been found (Cat. 47). There are some avian representations on pillars (bird pillars) as well as a pair of anthropomorphic images, respectively a woman of 40 cm. and a man of 36.9 cm., which perhaps originate from the same Zimbabwe culture pool. The male figure, which is part of the P. and R. Tishman collection of African Art, Walt Disney Imagineering, was made from a greenish serpentine, while the female, in The British Museum, was carved from soapstone. Both figures are represented very schematically. Instead of terminating with legs, they end in a conical shape. A few bowls with decoration applied in low-relief are also hewn from steatite (Allison 1969:49). In 1905 at the Umtali site, some 240 km. northeast of Zimbabwe, around 50 rudimentary sculpted soapstone figurines were found, the majority female images, along with other diverse representations made in the same material. Perhaps they constituted votive offerings. The exact period of their production is not known, though they are most likely several centuries old (Allison 1968:53).

Much more true-to-nature are the two heads - one of 15 cm. and one of 11.25 cm. - which were excavated in around 1900 and 1946 respectively in Kimberly (South Africa). The features of the first head show a similarity with those of a Bushman, and is more realistic than the second. According to Allison (1968:54), "... it is said to be carved from a 'material similar to kaolin." Equally exceptional is the head in volcanic tuff stone, found near the Uele River in Northeast Congo. It is 19.4 cm. tall and shows traces of black pigment. No further details are known.

For the sake of completeness, we now turn to the numerous stone monoliths of southern Ethiopia. The sculptures are mostly of phallic elaboration, like the examples from the region of Sidamo. A few, just like in Darassa, have an upper-part with rather schematically portrayed anthropomorphic traits. The monoliths are made from different kinds of hard stone. Most are in basalt, others are fashioned from granite and sandstone (Allison 1968:57-58).

Schweeger-Hefel (1981) found various stone figures during her fieldwork in the 1960s with the Kurumba of Burkino Faso, one at Ouré and another in Taga. Both are anthropomorphic figures in granite, flat and schematically hewn, with a strikingly small head. The most intact object measures 45-50 cm.; the second sculpture - broken-off and damaged - is 40 cm. tall, and seems more likely to be a torso which originally must have been larger than the object from Ouré. From a technical viewpoint both figures are "outstandingly elaborated" (1972:145). Schweeger-Hefel suspects that these statues were not made by the Kurumba themselves, but rather by an earlier people with a megalithic tradition.

Harter (1986:105-107), for his part, points out that sculpture in stone also occurs in the Grasslands of Cameroon. Here use is made of "white rock" (granite and sandstone) and "black rock" (basalt), while some works are carved from a grayish granite. The large mono-

Figure

Great Zimbabwe, Zimbabwe
Stone. H. 33.7 cm.
Paul and Ruth Tishman Collection of African Art,
Walt Disney Imagineering

liths encountered in the region are undecorated, but with one single exception. It concerns a cylindrical stone statue 1.25 meters high, with anthropo- and zoomorphic motifs carved in relief. Further information is lacking. In the Bamenda region, too, there have been rare finds of stone sculptures of medium-size. They apparently receive offerings of human blood in times of misfortune, when harvests are bad or when the ruler is ill (1986:106). The Bamileke are known to have small, very rare female figures, carved in steatite and originating from Batié. They had the same function as the wooden *mu po* figures[15]. And again according to Harter (p. 107), in Bayangam there was a sitting male figure with a fine glossy black patina.

There are a few other peoples where stone sculpture is or was sporadically made, but it is not possible to exhaustively deal with them here. What should be clear from the preceding discussion is that in sub-Saharan Africa the use of stone as basic material for sculpture is far less common than wood, or even ivory - and this for readily explainable reasons. We are also very less well informed when it comes to knowing details on just how these objects in fact came to be carved or hewn, and this state of affairs is regrettably all the more true when it comes to information on the sculptors themselves.

Conclusion

From the information presented above, it seems clear that for the making of sculpted works use is most often made of vegetal raw-materials, with wood by far the front runner. This is hardly surprising given that sub-Saharan Africa is sufficiently rich in vegetation. Many dozens of tree varieties - of high, medium and low density wood - are employed for the making of masks, statues and figuratively or otherwise elaborated utensils. Furthermore, wood is relatively easy to work with locally available tools. Hardwood varieties are indeed more difficult to manipulate, but they have the advantage of durability by virtue of their inherent resistance to insects and climatic conditions. Lighter woods, on the other hand, are better suited for the masks which dancers must often wear for hours at a time, as well as for other objects which are not intended for extended use.

Most figures and masks sculpted in wood function within the framework of local religious practices, including those which are - not entirely correctly - termed "magical." Others have a role pertaining rather to the social-political sphere, and such certainly includes the beautifully decorated everyday objects and utensils carved in wood.

Ivory - the bulk of which comes from elephants - is obviously much rarer, and thus much costlier than wood. In most cases ivory is in the possession of rulers and high dignitaries, and as a rule it is also they who commission the ivory-carvers. The carving of ivory is work for the specialist, but sometimes an adept wood-carver can also successfully turn his hand to ivory. Indeed, the tools used for working the two materials are much similar.

The fact that ivory is much more frequently used for decorative objects of prestige rather than for religious purposes, is due to its costliness. Peoples such as the Lega, who are experienced elephant hunters, do nonetheless make use of miniature ivory masks within the context of the Bwami association. In fact, these equally have a social function. This also holds for the richly elaborated ivory masks which the rulers of the ancient Benin kingdom wore on their belts, as well as for the ivory divination objects of the Yoruba. The majority of ivory objects consist of ornaments and leader's-attributes such as flywhisks, scepters, staffs, and large tusks decorated in relief. Spoons, combs and flutes, horns, finger-, arm- and leg-rings, hairpins, necklaces, pendants and other items might also be used or worn by people of lesser rank. The ivory pendants of the Pende (in the form of a "maskette") and of the Hungana, also have a protective function. The conventional Western distinction between the profane and the religious is, for that matter, considerably less clear in the African context. Many objects, in no matter what material, are indeed polyfunctional: they have more than one sole function and meaning.

Stone sculpture is very rarely encountered south of the Sahara. Only in around four regions do we find a few hundred specimens in this material. It is striking that the majority of statues are carved from soft varieties of stone, like steatite. This is the case for the *nomoli, pomtan* and *mintadi/bitumba* discussed above and also for the Esie images. Steatite or soapstone may be worked about as easily as wood, and thus the tools employed are also nearly the same. When hard stone varieties are chosen, the design is extremely simple; this is seen with the *akwanshi* of the Cross River region. The same is largely also true for the rare other cases where works have been produced from difficult-to-hew rock. Just as with wood sculpture, images made in stone likewise have a function and significance in religion as well as in social-political life. Such is probably the case for the statues from Esie.

If one surveys the whole of African sculpture, and in particular that made by subtractive methods, it is indeed remarkable that these sculptors have with such limited means often produced objects justly considered as true works of art in the West. Visitors to this exhibition are invited to ascertain this for themselves.

1. The section on the wood-carver in this contribution appeared in 1988 in Dutch and French in the exhibition-catalogue "Utotombo. Kunst uit zwart-Afrika in Belgisch privé-bezit (Brussel 25 maart-5 juni 1988) [French edition: "Utotombo. L'art d'Afrique Noire dans les collections privées belges) (see Burssens 1988). The original text has been and revised and enlarged for this volume. Although use is made of the "ethnographic present," it should be made clear that this does not imply that in every case the same situation still pertains as described.
2. Aside from the varieties mentioned, dozens of others more come under consideration for use. Dechamps, in the 1970s, published lists in *Africa-Tervuren* with the botanical origin of hundreds of figures and masks found among diverse Congo peoples. Here, a thorough knowledge is not only desirable from a scholarly point of view; it is also of practical use for tracing forgeries.
3. Bassani (2000) in his book *African Art and Artifacts in European Collections 1400-1800*, has published an entire series of art- and other objects which have made their way from Africa to the European continent over many centuries.
4. Martinez-Constantin (1999), who gives us these dates, has also provided much further early data concerning the Tellem, pre-Dogon, Dogon and stylistically related groups.
5. "... le sculpteur, face à sa pièce de bois - généralement un bloc cylindrique -, délimite les principales sections constitutives du personnage à réaliser : la tête, le corps et les membres inférieurs" (Lehuard 1989:89).
6. A distinction must be made between the different densities of various ivories. As general classification, ivory may be termed soft, medium soft, and hard. Ivory from the western half of the continent is usually harder than that from the east, and consequently more difficult to carve, not to mention more prone to crack. The original color of ivory varies according to the animal's diet, and runs from off-white to light green to light red and a brownish shade. One must also reckon with the aging process, as well as with any patina subsequently applied (of this, more below). Use is made both of elephant tusks from animals already long dead, as well as from the freshly killed. Tusks weighing between 25 and 30 kg. and measuring some two meters in length are considered ideal. The elephant's molar teeth can also be used for sculpting.
7. Ivory from the hippopotamus is much finer and harder than that from the elephant tusk. Given the limited measurements of such teeth, it is apparent that any small sculptures carved from this cannot exceed several centimeters in size. Jacob (1975:15) states that one finds fine specimens in Nigeria, in particular among the Nupe and the Junkun. More well-known are the examples made by the Luba from Congo.
8. Biebuyck (1986:40) tells us that for the sculpting of figurines in bone, mainly used are the thick parts of the rib or the joint bones that are flat in the articular areas. "These sculptures have porous surfaces that preserve the natural brown-gray colors of the dried bones. Their patinas are varied but duller than those of the ivories. The bone figurines may be so well polished and coated with oily and resinous mixtures that it is hard to distinguish between tham and ivory sculptures..."
9. "Hoewel de olifant vaak ook machtige en opstandige hoofdmannen symboliseert, staan hier vooral zijn eigenschappen als koninklijk dier op de voorgrond: aanvoerderskwaliteiten, wijsheid en hoge leeftijd, eigenschappen die ook aan de Oba werden toegeschreven. De ivoren slagtand, met zijn gecompliceerde symboliek, werd een koninklijk materiaal bij uitstek: hard en sterk, en duurzaam leende het zich als de ideale grondstof voor het registreren van historische gebeurtenissen voor de volgende generaties."
10. "De donkere verkleuring op de slagtanden ca. 60 tot 70 cm. van onderen naar boven zou afkomstig kunnen zijn van de inwerking van offerbloed dat men op de tanden smeerde, hoewel die nadien werden afgewassen. De verkleuring zou ook terug gaan op het met de handen vastnemen van sz tanden waneer deze werden opgetild, omdat vooral de meest verheven delen donker zijn, terwijl de diepere delen lichtere kleur vertonen."

11. "Selon la fréquence des enrobements, selon l'insistance avec laquelle les assistants du Maître imprimaient leur nappage huileux, selon la forme d'utilisation de la sculpture, la translucidité du pigment permet aujourd'hui d'admirer des tons allant au jaune clair au brun violacé, en passant par toute la gamme des oranges." (Lehuard 1989:100)

12. The so-called ivory palm yields large, hard white seeds. They have something of the appearance and consistency of ivory. The Pende - and other Central African peoples - have also possibly made use of this material.

13. Given the large existing stocks of tusks, and due to economic considerations, this prohibition was slackened in the beginning of 1999 in Botswana, Zimbabwe and Namibia.

14. Although Leo Frobenius, the German ethnologist who was central to the discovery of Ife sculpture, in 1920 in Offa (some 20 km. from Esie), had collected three heads in the same style (yet without publishing details regarding this), it was H.C. Ramsay, a British school inspector, who is attributed with the find of Esie stone sculpture. This is because he was, in 1933, the first European to visit the statue cemetery and to have seen the entirety of these pieces *in situ*. In 1955-56 Philip Stevens conducted a thorough investigation into the origin of the makers of the sculptures about which so little was known. His findings appeared in 1978 in book-form under the title *The Stone Images of Esie.*.

15. *Mu po* are small, "active" figurines which are worn (unseen) by members of the Bamileke's *ku n'gan* association.

Material
Differences
Art and Identity
in Africa

Transforming Through Fire

CAT. 48

Animal figure
Karagwe peoples, Tanzania
Iron. L. 30 cm.
Private Collection

Iron Sculpting in Africa

WILLIAM J. DEWEY

The intractability of iron seems totally at odds with the incredible variety of forms it takes throughout Africa. Iron is the toughest of all the materials that are regularly worked in Africa, but at times can also seem the most pliant and fluid (see, for example, (Cat. 49). Some pieces made of iron are weighty and massive, while others are pointed, sharp, and threatening (Cat. 55, 65). Others display almost impossibly thin spirals and extensions (Cat. 50), seemingly suspended in midair. This is because iron, though hard when it cools, is malleable when red-hot.

The context of iron in African cultures is central to understanding this seemingly contradictory sculptural material. Over the centuries, iron has been the substance and agent of transformation that has allowed Africans to forage and hunt, and to till the soil; and they have used objects made of iron to assure their own protection and prosperity. Thus, iron has been essential for their continued existence and has even saved people's lives, but it can take lives too. Iron working has been the preeminent transformative process, a technology greedily sought and jealously guarded, for it could turn rocks into metal, and unshaped iron into tools, weapons, and art. It is not surprising that the use of iron has gone beyond the strictly utilitarian and is also employed for a variety of ritual and symbolic uses. In some areas of Africa, blacksmiths are respected for their skill but are usually not accorded special status or privileges. In other parts of Africa, the transformative powers of iron-workers are deemed so great that blacksmiths are considered dangerous and are avoided by ordinary people. The iron-working and -making technologies are so important that African culture heroes and kings are often linked actually or metaphorically to the knowledge and skill of blacksmiths.

Many Westerners might be familiar with the way iron ore is smelted in a blast furnace and then cast into ingots to produce pig iron, but most are unfamiliar with African techniques of making iron. In the direct (or bloomery) method, which is the traditional way of making iron in sub-Saharan Africa, the iron does not become molten, instead congealing into a mass known as a bloom that must be extracted from the furnace. After some forging, the metal is immediately ready for fashioning into a wide variety of items (Kense 1983:35).

African furnaces have traditionally been constructed in three basic types: the bowl furnace, the low-shaft furnace, and the high-shaft furnace. The first two require air to be forced into the furnace area by using bellows, while the third one uses a naturally induced air draft. A sufficiently powerful draft can only be achieved in this latter case by keeping the air-intake holes low on a tall furnace. Historically, these three different furnace types were scattered across Africa, with areas of concentration that probably reflected historical migrations, trade, and other modes of technology transfer (Cline 1937; Childs 1991; Kense 1983). Varying greatly in size and shape (Herbert 1993:9), their sculptural form was as rich and diverse as other African art forms in clay such as pottery and architecture, but the furnaces are not well known beyond those who investigate African ironworking.

Sexual and reproduction metaphors in conjunction with iron smelting are common in

CAT. 49

Stand
Banyambo peoples, Tanzania
Iron. L. 72.4 cm.
Marc and Denyse Ginzberg

many areas of Africa (Herbert 1993). The smelting furnaces were usually located away from the villages. Women, except those past menopause, were not allowed near the furnaces. Wooden bellows feeding air into the furnace were carved in phallic forms, and fertility magic was placed inside the furnace to encourage and protect its "fecundity." Master smelters controlled this magic, organized the long months of labor necessary to bring smelting to fruition, and imposed on their workers certain prohibitions from ordinary activities such as sexual contact. They also led dances, songs, praises, and other activities necessary to make the entire performance of smelting a success. Observing the Shona in the late 1800s, Bent noted that a furnace

> *is made of clay, and is another instance of the design being taken from the human form, for it is made to represent a seated woman; the head is the chimney, decorated in some cases with eyes, nose and mouth, resting on shoulders; the legs are stretched out and form the sides of the furnace, and to complete the picture they decorate the front with breasts and the tattoo decorations usually found on female stomachs (1892:46).*

The metaphors of Shona smelting are also linked to kinship and the perpetuation of society. Married iron workers could not sleep with their wives during smelting, because this "adultery" against the furnace as their "true wife" would cause the death of the expected child/iron. Many gynecomorphic furnaces across Africa include breasts and scarification marks (Herbert 1993:32-51), and I found that some Shona furnaces were also built with a representation of a woman's waist belt known as a *mutimwi* (Dewey 1990). These belts not only have an erotic connotation—they are manipulated during lovemaking—but are also used, symbolically, to mark important stages in a Shona woman's life, such as first menstruation, marriage, and childbirth. The belt's most important function, it is believed, is "to strengthen [a woman's] sexual power and to safeguard her fertility" (Aquina 1968). When a husband pays bridewealth, some of which is often used to buy beads for a new waist belt, he temporarily acquires the use of his bride's fertility to produce children. The smelters were symbolically doing the same, acquiring the fertility of the furnace to produce iron offspring.

Bellow types also adhere to a limited number of designs. One type, known as a bag bellows, is usually constructed of an animal skin. Another type, known as a bowl bellows, is usually carved of wood, although some are also made of clay or hollowed out of the ground. Bowl bellows are made with either two or four bowl chambers that are linked to the tube inserted into the ceramic pipe *(tuyere)* entering the furnace. These bowls are covered with a membrane to which sticks are attached. By repeated alternate pumping, the operator (or operators) of the bellows can produce a steady draft of air (Cline 1937, Kense 1983). Many carved-wood bowl bellows are simple in appearance, but some also have anthropomorphic heads or full figures incorporated into the design. Figurative bellows, such as the four-chambered example from the Songye people shown here (Cat. 51), were usually the prerogative only of chiefs and kings emphasizing the symbolic connections between metalworking arts and sacred kingship.

Most Westerners are even less familiar with African smithing techniques than with African iron smelting. Some forges are elaborate clay constructions, but those that many Africans use are no

CAT. 50

Staff with birds
Yoruba peoples, Nigeria
Iron. H. 94 cm.
Private Collection

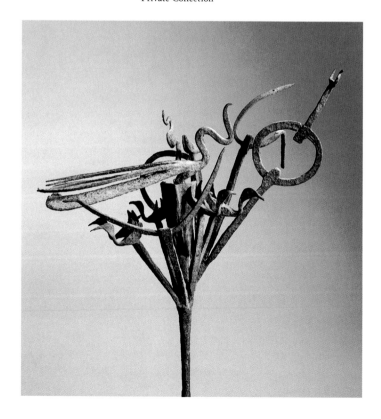

CAT. 51

Bellows

Songye peoples, Dem. Rep. of the Congo
Wood, fiber. H. 70 cm.
Stewart J. Warkow

more than a pile of charcoal. In central Africa, hammers are generally conically shaped and can serve a dual purpose as anvil or hammer. Tongs are often made by simply bending a stick of green wood or a piece of bark to act as a pair of pincers. Hinged metal tongs and another type with a bent strip of metal, controlled with a sliding iron, are seen in many parts of Africa. The simplicity of the tools used at the forge makes the beauty of the objects all the more astonishing. African smiths are highly skilled; they understand the properties of the various types of iron they produce (which range from malleable wrought iron to carbon steel) and know how to use and adapt them for particular functions. Blacksmiths are adept at folding, hammering, stretching, and annealing (heating the iron and allowing it to cool slowly in order to toughen it). Pressure welding (hammering together different pieces of metal at high temperatures) is used in the production of many objects.

The role of blacksmiths in African societies varies tremendously: Some have high status and are greatly respected, while others have the same status as ordinary citizens. Central and Southern African smiths are neither despised nor feared, as they are in some East and West African societies, nor are they segmented into endogamous "castes." For example, in Zimbabwe, Shona blacksmiths do not have a special status. There are no guilds or workshops of artists (other than occasional family groups where several members work together), and the predominant pattern is of individual artists working on their own. Training is very informal and skill is often considered either inborn or acquired through supernatural intervention. Nevertheless, many blacksmiths gain reputations as accomplished artists and attract clients from villages at some distance away (Dewey 1986).

Around the turn of the century, European colonizers prohibited local African industries such as iron smelting in order to decrease African self-sufficiency. Africa was flooded with iron objects produced in Europe that were often inferior in quality to the local products they replaced. Smelting became obsolete in most parts of Africa, although there are reports that it is still occasionally done in very remote areas. Scrap iron provided new sources for African blacksmiths (Roberts 1996), who transform discarded iron into all sorts of useful things, from plowshares to keys for thumb pianos.

CAT. 52

Rattle

Bamana peoples, Mali
Iron. H. 30.5 cm.
Richard H. Scheller

Double gong
Igbo peoples, Nigeria
Iron. H. 57 cm.
Private Collection

Gong
Igbo peoples, Nigeria
Iron. H. 93 cm.
Private Collection

CAT. 55

Knife
Ingessana peoples, Sudan
Iron, leather. L. 97.2 cm.
Marc and Denyse Ginzberg

CAT. 56

Knife
Njem peoples, Cameroon
Iron, leather, fiber. L. 48.3 cm.
Marc and Denyse Ginzberg

Africans use iron to make a wide assortment of musical instruments (DjeDje 1999). Many are percussive, such as the Igbo gongs (Cat. 53-54). Among the Igbo, such bells are the prerogative of individuals with high status, such as Ozo titleholders (Cole and Aniokor 1984:52). Double gongs are a symbol of leadership throughout much of central Africa (Vansina 1969). Among Bamana and related Mande peoples of Mali, iron rasps or scrappers are a common musical instrument; but perhaps such an embellished example as (Cat. 52), with its antelope head, was made for a special purpose. Wooden rasps are used by musical troupes known as Nkenye undergoing initiation into the Jo society (Brincard 1989:120–21, citing Ezra 1986); and Bamana flutes made of iron are known to have been used by the Komo society (McNaughton 1988).

Although iron tools and weapons serve primarily functional purposes, a blacksmith will often demonstrate his aesthetic sense even as he skillfully executes his craft. The Ingessana and Njem throwing knives of Sudan and Cameroon (Cat. 55-56) suggest that form can be both functional and of great beauty. While such blades are most frequently used as hunting or agricultural tools, they can be quickly drawn from over one's shoulder to swing at—or throw at—an attacker (Elsen 1996, 2000; Felix 1991; Spring 1993:68–93). The Mbum throwing knife from Cameroon (Cat. 58) represents an interesting variation. If it had been used as a weapon, it would have been skipped along the ground, rather than thrown end-over-end like the two previous knives; but its stylistic refinement indicates that this particular knife served as a currency token.

Pre-colonial African currency tokens occur in a fascinating array of shapes and sizes (Puccinelli 2000). Although they could be used as practical tools or weapons; their foremost purpose was symbolic rather than utilitarian, for they represented value itself. Value is essentially an arbitrary social construction that is constantly being negotiated. It depends on the trust of both sides of a transaction concerning the "worth" of something. Currencies, such as the elegant sculptural shapes from the Idoma, Lobi, and Mbum peoples shown here (Cat. 57-59), did not function the way coins do in our own society. They are what is called a special-purpose (as opposed to our general-purpose) currency and were often used exclusively for such things as ransoming prisoners of war or negotiating marriage agreements. The shape is derived from iron tools such as throwing knives and hoes, but the tokens are too thin and fragile to be utilitarian and instead represent the value of work that could be done with such tools.

> [S]uch a blade may stand for the totality of the work performed and the harvest gained, of the cooperation to accomplish the task and the sharing of food thereafter, and of land rights and work responsibilities. The value of the iron hoe blade, then, is this totality, that, in many ways constitutes the lifeblood of society itself.
> Iron hoe blades were often used as currency tokens in the context of bridewealth, when a groom and his family exchanged wealth for the hand of the bride. Bridewealth was by no means a "purchase," however. Rather, hoe blades given as bridewealth represented an exchange of responsibilities and expectations between the families of the bride and groom. To raise required bridewealth, the groom had to borrow from his kin; in accepting bridewealth, the bride's family redistributed wealth to those from whom they had borrowed in the past. In this way, a woman's bridewealth allowed her brothers to marry, thus furthering their lineage. The exchange of bridewealth cemented these bonds, and was the "glue" of social continuity (Dewey and Roberts 1993:11).

Staffs for the Yoruba deity of the farm, Orisha Oko (Cat. 65) are masterpieces of ironworking. Pemberton (1989:167) recounts that Orisha Oko was once a hunter and friend of

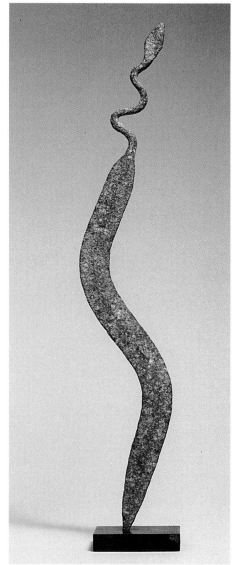

CAT. 57

Currency(?)
Lobi (?)peoples, Burkina Faso
Iron. H. 40.6 cm.
Mr. and Mrs. Carrie-Vacher

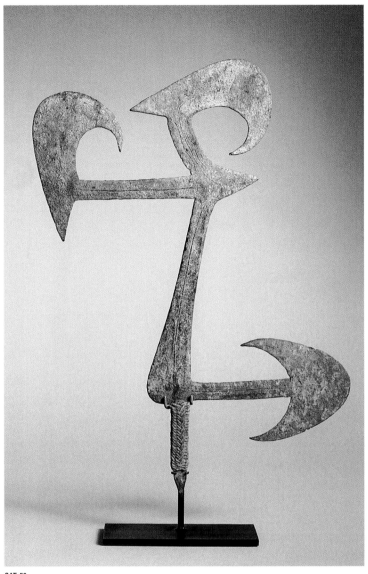

CAT. 58

Currency
Mbum peoples, Cameroon
Iron. H. 49.5 cm.
Michael Oliver

CAT. 59

Currency
Chamba peoples, Nigeria
Iron. L. 45.1 cm.
Mr. and Mrs. Carrie-Vacher

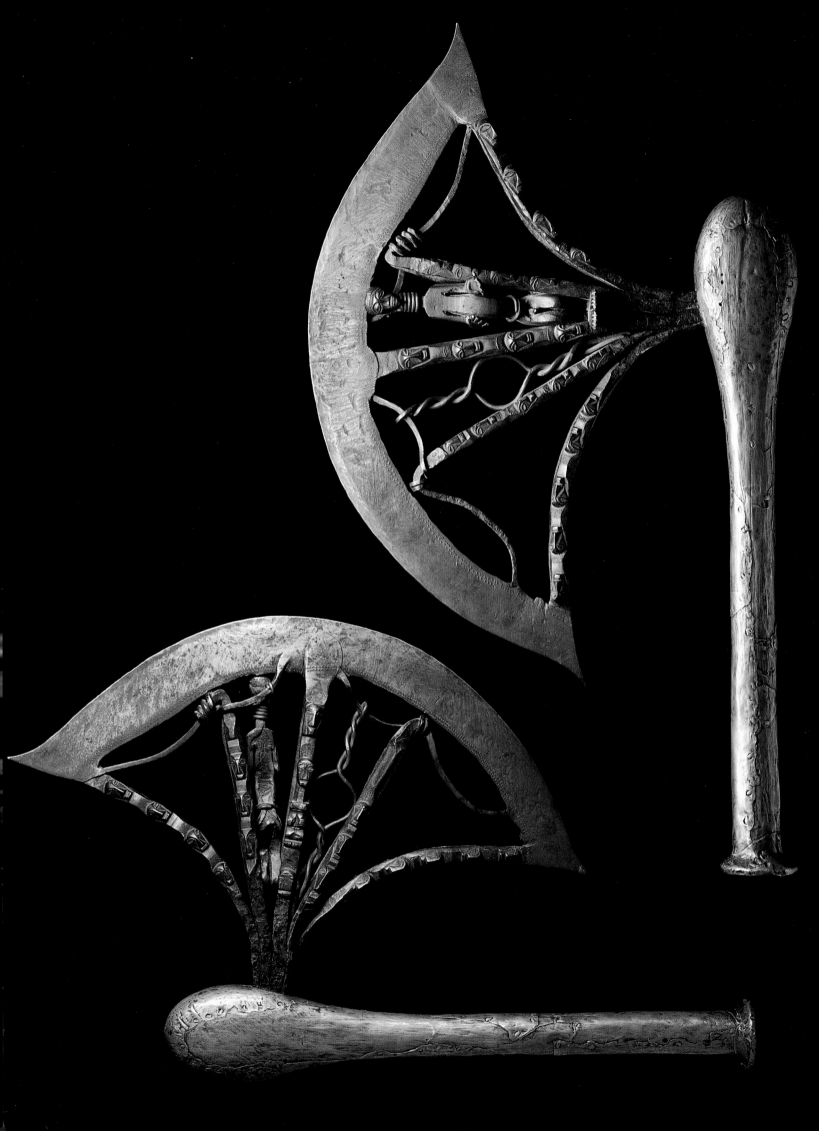

Axe

Nsapo peoples, Dem. Rep. of the Congo
Wood, iron, copper. L. 31.75 cm. (blade)
James Willis Tribal Arts

CAT. 61

Assemblage

Dogon peoples, Mali
Iron. H. 59.7 cm.
Private Collection

CAT. 62

Miniature tools

Dogon or Senufo peoples, Mali or Ivory Coast
Iron. L. 15.2 cm (box)
John Crawford.

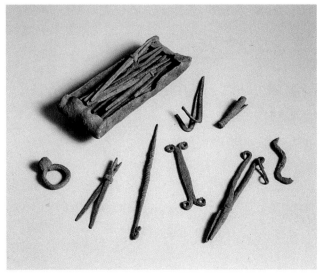

CAT. 63

Statuette
Kuba peoples, Zaire
Iron. H. 19.5 cm.
Etnografisch Museum, Antwerpen

Ogun, the Yoruba deity of war, hunting, and iron, but gave up hunting to become a farmer. Orisha Oko is described as a woman who acquired great wealth through the power of her staff, or as a barren woman. These staffs are now said to protect their owners and farms, and to have the ability to grant children to barren women (Thompson 1971:chap. 10). Although the cult of Orisha Oko is found in many Yoruba towns, its historic center is the northeastern Oyo town of Irawo, where the staffs are manufactured. There, devotees bring hoe blades to the master blacksmith who re-forges them into the components that are assembled into the distinctive Orisha Oko staff form. Female devotees of the cult commission these staffs in various sizes according to their wealth (Cornelius Adepegba 1993, personal communication) and must never allow them to touch the ground.

One of the most renowned groups of Congo blacksmiths, the Nsapo, made and sold elaborate luxury display axes (Cat. 60) at the end of the nineteenth century. Many of their neighbors (and also foreign officials and missionaries) acquired them as symbols of wealth and power for men of high status. The ornate ironwork blade is constructed with iron currency bars used as the spokes of the openwork construction, and the wooden handle is sheathed in copper, another symbol of wealth (Kriger 1999:146–49).

Blacksmiths hold a prominent place in Dogon mythology. The first smith was one of the primordial beings who first populated the world, known as the Nommo. While descending in the celestial ark to earth, this blacksmith noticed that there was no fire among the items assembled to begin the world, and so stole a piece of the sun (Roberts 1988). Dogon blacksmiths are still "hot" because of their transformative powers, and must not walk in people's fields, lest they cause the crops to wither. Instead, they use their extraordinary powers to heal, divine, and create. Smiths and Nommo are regarded as twins and are believed to have certain powers in common, such as the ability to bring rain. Objects made of iron are prominent in shrines dedicated to totemic ancestors *(binu)*, in houses of religious and political leaders of Dogon communities *(hogon)*, and in altars to Nommo. Miniature iron sculptures such as hunters' bows, sandals, and sets of blacksmiths tools (Cat. 62) are placed in *binu* shrines (Ezra 1988:7–83).

The Dogon assemblage of iron objects seen in (Cat. 61) probably once ornamented one of these previously mentioned contexts or a rain-making shrine. The disk may represent a warrior shield with a minimalistic figure above it surrounded by the accumulation of hooks, dangles, and other iron forms that focus and attract spiritual forces to Dogon shrines. The leaflike projections, common on rain-making staffs made of iron, are "suggestive of growing plants, which for the Dogon people thrive on the moisture provided by Nommo, the primordial being who brought order, purity and fertility to the universe and who is manifested in life-giving water" (Ezra 1988:81).

Iron objects are made to honor the god Ogun (or Gu) among the Yoruba, Fon, and other coastal West African peoples. This deity of blacksmiths and warriors is, as Robert Farris Thompson has noted, "Lord of the Cutting Edge" (1976:chap. 7, p. 1) In one Fon version (Cat. 64), he carries a rifle and a ceremonial sword called a *gu-bassa*. Ogun has come to the New World, too, and is important to many syncretic religions such as Santeria in Brazil or Vodun in Haiti (Barnes 1980; Barnes and Ben Amos 1989; Cosentino 1995). It is no surprise, then, that Ogun is among the most popular and important deities in contemporary west Africa and throughout the diaspora of African America, for Ogun still personifies the creative transformation and ironies of iron.

In many parts of Africa, there was and still is a close relationship between iron working and leadership. This may be because pre-colonial leaders controlled the sources of iron ore and the means of production and trade. Underlying such history, though, was a conceptual association between iron working and the culture heroes who introduced human civilization, such as among the Dogon and Bamana of Mali, or the Luba of the Democratic

CAT. 64

Figure representing Ogun or Gu
Fon peoples, Republic of Benin
Iron. H. 47 cm.
Private Collection, New York

Republic of the Congo. The relationship between iron and authority in African is especially well illustrated by a cluster of objects in the exhibition.

The symbolic associations among iron, social status, and sacred authority may be based on the leader himself as a master smelter or smith. An excellent example comes from the Karagwe people of northwestern Tanzania, where the early nineteenth-century King Ndagara is said to have fashioned at least 120 extremely intricate iron accoutrements, including staffs, spears, and standards (Cat. 49). The standards held sticks (known as *omusinga*) that shielded royal drums from view during new moon ceremonies. At least fifty *omusinga* were once in the treasury of the kingdom (Sassoon 1995:157). In a virtuoso display of skill, the iron rods descending below the multiple *omusinga* sockets are plaited together as if they were as supple as green vines. The masterpieces of these royal collections are the iron figures of oxen or cows (Cat. 48). These expressive objects symbolize the great importance of cattle to the pastoral peoples in the interlacustrine states (kingdoms between lakes Albert, Kivu, and Victoria) such as the Karagwe. The royal insignia of many of these kingdoms include royal anvils, several of which (including the Karagwe) feature odd, curving representations of horns sprouting from the top (Sassoon 1983). To make the cattle figures, the blacksmiths seem to have taken a different tack, welding several of the conical anvils together. These figures may have had magical powers to increase the royal herds through an association between the smelting of iron and the birth of cattle.

Among the Kuba, royalty were also said to be excellent blacksmiths. One eighteenth-century prince, Myeel, is by tradition credited with forging a full-size house, a boat, and several unusual human figures, two of which are now housed in Antwerp (Vansina 1978:182). The hairline and conical hat seen on (Cat. 63) confirm its Kuba attribution, but there is no independent way of confirming the eighteenth-century date attributed by oral tradition. The figure was once supported on an iron post (now broken at the genital area, but still attached on a second example); and the unusual treatment and gesture of the hands has been interpreted as meaning that the figure once held something (Claerhout 1976). Another possibility is that a symbolic gesture, akin to Kongo gestural cosmograms seen on objects such as Bembe *muzidi* and Bwende *niombo* figures (see Thompson and Cornet 1981), may have been intended.

Blacksmiths and items made of iron also figure prominently in Luba mythology. Kalala Ilunga, the founder of the Luba state, is one of the figures who is most intimately linked with the introduction of iron making and iron. In a ceremony enacted after the enthronement of each Luba king, an official would cry out

> *"Let us strike the anvils" and, raising his two fists in the air proceeded to beat the bared knees of the king. "May you be firmly fixed in the kingdom," he added, beating again, "and live and reign as long and as well as your illustrious ancestor Kalala Ilunga Mwine Munza," . . . "I do this to remind you that your forefather Kalala Ilunga introduced ironworking into this land. He was a wise man. Whether weapons of war or tools of peace, whether for arrows and spears or for axes and hoes, the anvil is the secret of power and progress." (Womersley 1984:71)*

Like the transformation of unformed iron into an object, so the once common man is symbolically transformed into the king (Dewey and Childs 1996).

A related type of object that deserves attention is the bowstand (Cat. 66). Bowstands seem to be unique to the regions of southeastern Democratic Republic of the Congo, northern Malawi, and Zambia (Neyt 1993:59–71); but, as Audrey Richards has noted in commenting on similar iron ones found in Zambia, their owners "declare emphatically that the arrowstands came from Lubaland" (Richards 1935:31). For the Luba people, they are one of the most important symbols of chiefly power.

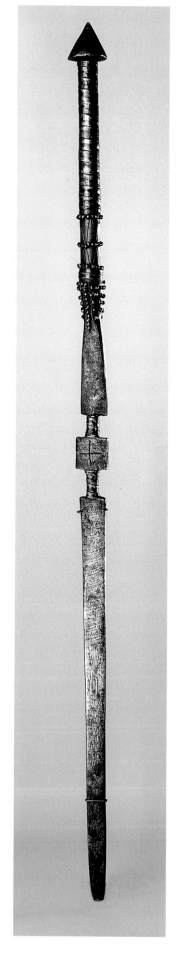

The great mythic culture hero of Luba kingship [Mbidi Kiluwe, father of Kalala Ilunga] was a renowned hunter whose cherished possession was his bow. Although bowstands serve literally to hold bows and arrows, they are primarily symbols of chiefly authority subject to elaborate ritual and taboo. Never displayed in public, they were guarded in a special house by a female dignitary whose role was to provide prayers and sacrifice (Nooter 1990:65).

The overall form of these tour-de-force sculptures (see Nooter Roberts and Roberts 1996:81) combines elements seen in the other ceremonial and utilitarian items, such as arrow-points, axes, and spears, along with hairpin-razor and conical anvil-shaped hairpin/nail forms. The master blacksmiths seem to have been deliberately combining much of their formal repertoire in these extraordinary objects. The special symbolic meanings of forged metal and their associations with political power and leadership coalesce in iron bowstands to make a powerful statement about iron and its importance in the Luba worldview. In this one object, many aspects of iron and the "forging" of Luba royalty are visually summed up.

CAT. 65

Staff for Orisha Oko
Yoruba peoples, Nigeria
Iron, wood. H. 150 cm.
Marc and Denyse Ginzberg

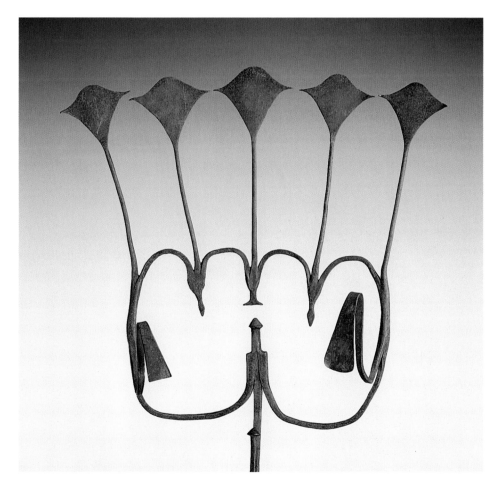

CAT. 66

Bow stand
Luba peoples, Dem. Rep. of the Congo
Iron. H. 62 cm.
Private Collection

African Ceramics

JEROME VOGEL

CAT. 67

Ancestral pot
Ga'anda peoples, Nigeria
Ceramic. H. 59.7 cm.
Simmons Collection

Pottery is produced just about everywhere in Africa. Archaeological excavations both north and south of the Sahara have found pottery that can be dated to between ten and fifteen thousand B.C., the time when nomadic hunter-gatherers began to settle in permanent communities and to use clay for making pots and as the basic material for architecture. Domestic pottery from predynastic Egypt is on view at New York's Metropolitan Museum of Art, as is figurative pottery from this period at the Brooklyn Museum. From earliest times, figurative and utilitarian pottery seem to have existed together. In South Africa the Lydenburg heads—dated to 500–700 A.D., and the oldest sculptures found in the region—were discovered with large amounts of "domestic" pottery. In many parts of Africa, perhaps because the climate prevented the survival of wooden objects, the earliest and most plentiful art to have survived is ceramic. For many cultures (Nok, in Nigeria, for example), ceramics provide us with our only sources of knowledge.

CAT. 68

Vessel
Hausa peoples, Nigeria
Ceramic. H. 63.5 cm.
Simmons Collection

Western art historians have tended to treat African ceramics (along with textiles and baskets) as of secondary importance. These objects are often referred to as "craft," or "decorative" art, in contrast to "high" art, which is wood or metal sculpture. This stance reflects attitudes toward European art: many museums show European painting and sculpture separately from European decorative arts, though this is not true of Asian arts. African figurative clay sculpture (often called "terra cotta" rather than pottery) has been included with wood and metal sculpture as "art," while clay containers are just "domestic pottery." In fact, however, this distinction between "art" and "craft" does not exist in Africa any more than it does in much of Asia. A wooden mask or statue is a utilitarian object in Africa, because it is used for communicating with spirits. Establishing a hierarchy of materials or genres in relation to African art does not help us in understanding or appreciating it. In this exhibition we will present both figurative and nonfigurative objects made of clay. They are together here as they seem to be throughout Africa.

Throughout Africa, pottery is made primarily by women. In many areas, indeed, it is literally in the hands of women from the first stage to the last—from the digging of the clay, to the modeling and firing, to the commercial stage of selling it in the market. The final product is also primarily used by women, as they are responsible for cooking and serving food, getting water, and brewing beer. Being a potter is a good business for a woman in contemporary Africa, and one over which she has complete control.

Men do make pots among a few groups, like the Hausa of Northern Nigeria, but this is an exception. There are also some groups in which women make domestic pots and men make figurative pots used for religious purposes, but this seems to be a rare division of labor. Some scholars, mostly men, have claimed that much archaeological clay sculpture, such as Nok, Jenne, or Bura, must have been made by men. As we know nothing about pottery-making in those times, this seems to be speculation based on the belief that only men are artists. Also, among the little we do know about these sites is that they contain huge quantities of shards of the kind of pottery that has been made by women for hundreds of years. There is simply no proof that men made the forms we most value. As in most realms of production in Africa, pottery-making is gender specific. It is women's work.

There have been many attempts to explain why women are the potters throughout Africa. As clay comes from the earth, and as many cultures throughout the world consider the earth to be female, it seems natural and appropriate that women should be potters. Iron ore, however, also comes from the earth, but iron workers in Africa are always men. While it seems "natural" that women should form pots out of mother earth, we can observe a given fact but not explain it. The classic ethnographic explanation applies here: "It is like this because it has always been like this." Suffice it to say that the earliest accounts we have indicate that pottery was made by women.

Except in urban North Africa and in modern art schools, African pottery is made without a wheel. Clay is dug, usually along the banks of a stream. It is dried, pounded to separate it from small impurities, then mixed with water until it is smooth and flexible. Sometimes the potter adds grog, a powder made of broken, already fired pottery. The mixture is kneaded with the hands or feet to make it pliable. The potter either punches out the bottom with her fist or begins the molding of the pot from the bottom of a broken one. The sides are raised by the use of winding coils. Inside and outside are smoothed with simple tools, often seed pods. The pot is allowed to harden and dry somewhat, then it is decorated with an incised or raised pattern and finally burnished with a smooth river stone. It may be given a pattern by pushing a piece of matting, a cob of corn or millet, or a carved wooden roller against the surface. Incised decorations may be carved with a sharp stick; raised decorations may be molded and attached. After a final drying, the pot is fired, usually on the ground in a fire of wood and straw. There is no kiln, and the firing is brief and at a relatively low temperature. The pot is often removed from the fire with a long pole, and then, while still red hot, brushed with water containing a resinous mixture of plant materials to make it shiny and somewhat waterproof. Sometimes it will be blackened by a second firing in sawdust or rice chaff with reduced oxygen, making a kind of raku.

Because of the low temperature of the firing, the resulting pottery has not vitrified. While it is somewhat fragile, this gives it definite advantages: it can expand and contract and thus resists thermal shock. It can be placed directly on a fire without shattering. Because it is somewhat porous, water stored in the pot passes through the wall and evaporates on the exterior. This keeps the water inside cool and pleasant for drinking, unlike water stored in a metal or plastic container. As cooking and water storage are primary uses for African pottery, these are among the many examples of the way traditional methods are well adapted to the African climate and life-style. Some African pottery is painted, and some has had simple slips applied, but most of it is made by the methods described. Although kaolin, the additive that turns pottery into porcelain, is readily available in Africa, it isn't used. Porcelain would not function as well as the low-fired pottery described.

While much African pottery is made for everyday use, rituals are still performed in the course of its production. Clay is usually dug from the bank of a stream, sometimes only by

Vessel
Lobi peoples, Burkina Faso
Ceramic. H. 47 cm.
Simmons Collection

Vessel
Senufo peoples, Ivory Coast
Ceramic. H. 84.4 cm.
Simmons Collection

Vessel
Sudan
Ceramic. H. 62.2 cm.
Simmons Collection

CAT. 72

Vessel
Grassland Region, Cameroon
Ceramic. H. 36.8 cm.
William Itter

CAT. 73

Basket
Grassland Region, Cameroon
Rattan. H. 35.6 cm.
William Itter

The closeness in size and shape between the two vessels
shows a similar provenance. The materials from which
they are made, however, are different. Both, basketry
and ceramic vessels are women's occupancies among
the peoples of the Grassland region of Cameroon.
(F.H.)

women, sometimes by men and women. A sacrifice is often made to propitiate the spirit of
the site. The digging of clay may be forbidden on a particular day of the week that is sacred
to the earth, as among the Baule. Senufo potters must make small double pots for the spirits of twins, and must include them in every firing, or else their pots will break. In many
areas, menstruating women are not allowed to dig clay or mold pots. Some special ritual
forms can only be made by elderly, postmenopausal women.

Pots often have ritual or medicinal uses. Special shapes have to be used for medicines
and protective shrines. (Across West Africa pots covered with points, like the Lobi pots in
this exhibition, seem to be associated with protective medicines.) Often a shrine or altar
will be covered with pots, figures, or both that contain medicines or are the abodes of spirits. Pottery seems to have widespread associations with death. Many figurative pots, as
among the Akan peoples of Ghana and Ivory Coast, are funerary figures for cemeteries,
which are called "the place of pots." Among many other people, a woman breaks a pot after
the death of her husband to signify their separation. Often a broken pot, or a pot that has had
a hole punched in it, is placed on a grave. This seems to be a very old tradition, dating back
at least to Bura burials in Niger in the first millennium. It is tempting to see symbolic connections among pots, the earth, death, and burial, but again this is an area that needs study.

This exhibition includes pottery objects made over a large expanse of time and space.
For both practical and moral reasons it has been impossible to include examples of the oldest known objects from the Sahara, the Sahel, and the Nile Valley: they are fragile and in
many cases have been illegally excavated and exported from their countries of origin. These
are figures that we assume had a religious function.

When we turn to the Nok culture of northern Nigeria, which has been dated to 500 B.C.,
we have thousands of heads and body fragments and a considerable number of almost life-
sized figures. In technical terms, making and firing these objects was an extraordinary
achievement. Like later clay figures (1100–1500 A.D.) found in the Niger Valley, they carefully show jewelry, coiffures, and body decoration and seem to represent people of importance. A tradition of clay figures stretches across a wide belt of West Africa from Mali to
Chad, and continued for about 1,500 years. As most of these figures were found in uncon-
trolled digging, we know little about their function in their own cultures. It is hard to com-

CAT. 75

Head
Krinjabo Agni peoples, Ivory Coast
Ceramic. H. 25.4 cm.
Museum for African Art, Gift of Mala Silson Estate

CAT. 74

Head
Akan peoples, Ghana
Ceramic. H. 30.5 cm.
Francoise Billion Richardson

pare their styles to wood or metal sculpture from the same period, as very little of it exists. Two general stylistic elements can perhaps be related to the technical qualities inherent in modeling clay. Compared to much African wood sculpture (of a more recent date), these figures have great freedom of pose. Their postures are very varied; they stand, sit, crouch, slouch, do acrobatic contortions, and hold their arms and legs in all kinds of positions. Some are so twisted that they have no principal view, in contrast to the essentially frontal pose of much wood sculpture. I would propose that this freedom is partly the result of the clay modeling process, where the artist is not restrained by the shape of a piece of wood, as a wood carver is. The similarly free poses of certain bronzes could well be the result of the fact that the wax model from which the bronzes were cast was also the result of modeling. The elaboration of coiffure and surface decoration may also be related to the ease of adding decoration while modeling, as compared to including it during the subtractive process of woodcarving. This is speculative, as we know nothing about the making of clay sculpture long ago, but these ideas are based on observation of contemporary artists. There must of course be aesthetic and functional reasons for free poses and abundant surface decoration; but the technique of working in clay makes them feasible.

Domestic pottery made in an area 4,500 miles wide and about as long, and by hundreds of different groups, presents an enormous variety of styles. Nevertheless, certain general points can be proposed. Pots throughout Africa tend to have similar uses; they are used for carrying and storing water, for cooking and serving food, for brewing and serving beer in dry areas, and for fermenting and serving palm wine in forest regions. Pots are also used as containers for protective medicines, on shrines and altars, sometimes even as containers for the dead. In most areas the techniques for making these pots are similar: the walls are built up of coils and the firing is done at low temperatures. Leaving aside details of surface decoration, African pots show great similarities of size and shape. They tend to be round, because the method of their construction leads to a round shape. Water pots tend to be similar in size, perhaps because the women who carry them are similar in strength. Cooking pots are related to the quantities to be prepared (and so to family size) and to the amounts a woman can carry and maneuver. Large beer pots relate to the quantities of beer prepared or sold. Serving dishes and prestige drinking-vessels tend to be relatively small because of their function. Since pottery is made by a similar process and used for similar functions, a pot from Burkina Faso often basically resembles a pot from South Africa. Their decorations vary and there are differences in form—a wide neck, a narrow neck, no neck, a tall neck. Many of these differences are related to function; a high neck, for example, makes sense in a pot used to transport water or beer, while a low neck makes sense if liquid will be served with a ladle. Aesthetic preferences are important, but practical considerations should be not ignored as influences on form.

We have a considerable corpus of African pottery from the distant past. One of the most striking features of many archaeological sites is the incredible quantity of shards of everyday pottery. Most of the everyday pots we know, however, are of recent date—many of them from the last fifty years. Only recently have museums and private collectors become interested in pots. There have been few exhibitions and the literature is meager. Pottery is fragile, hard to ship, and does not command high prices, so that it is relatively unimportant in the African art market. Collecting and shipping it was of course even harder in the colonial period. As wood and metal sculpture becomes harder to find, however, dealers are starting to look for old pots, and a few pottery collectors have appeared. While some scholarly attention is being paid to pottery—particularly by women scholars, since it is the prime example of women's art—it remains inadequately studied and poorly documented.

CAT. 76

Pipe bowl
Grassland Region, Cameroon
Ceramic. H. 10.8 cm.
Charles and Kent Davis

Pipe bowls are made by men. The clay is carved with knives and spatulas, similar to the subtractive technique used on wood. (F.H.)
(Harter 1973: 22)

Half figure
Longuda, Cham or Mwana peoples, Nigeria
Ceramic. H. 22.9 cm.
Drs. Jean and Noble Endicott

Among the Longuda, each disease or class of disease is
personified. During consultation with a healer, the sick
body is touched with some of the clay that will be
used to make the figure. It is believed that the disease-
producing spirit enters the clay. When the shaping of
the figure is almost complete, the male or female healer circles the pot around the patient's head, while con-
tinuing to mold it over him. The patient then fires the
finished pot and deposits it on a shrine. (F.H.)
(Barley 1994: 91; and Berns 1993: 137)

CAT. 77

Ancestral vessel
Ga'anda peoples, Nigeria
Ceramic. H. 30.5 cm.
Private Collection

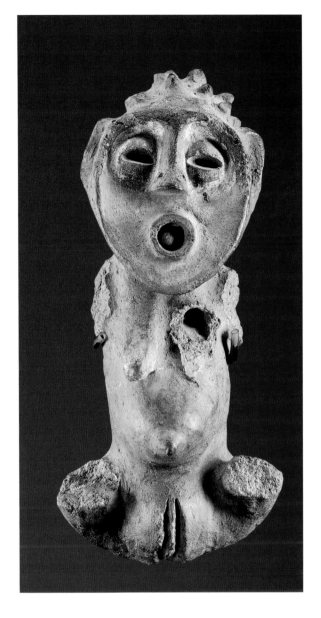

CAT. 79

Figure
Mambila peoples, Cameroon
Ceramic. H. 32 cm.
Private Collection, Milano, Italy

CAT. 80

Figure
Mambila peoples, Cameroon
Ceramic, polychrome. H. 26.7 cm.
James Willis Tribal Arts

The male and female figures show a great resemblance
in the modeling of the head and facial features.
Presumably, they were made by the same artist and
may have been used as a pair. (F.H.)

Figure of an Ogboni or Oshugbo Chief

Ijebu Yoruba peoples, Nigeria
Ceramic. H. 76.2 cm.
Paul and Ruth Tishman Collection of African Art,
Walt Disney Imagineering

Contemporary Potters and Pottery

We have made a point of including the work of three contemporary potters in the exhibition, both because of the high quality of their work and because detailed studies of their technique are available. Their pots show that beautiful and original work is still being produced in the African tradition. These potters come from different parts of Africa—west, east, and south—and have quite different relationships to their own traditions, to Western influences, and to the foreign market. Foreign researchers have given us insight into the means by which they create new forms as well as into how they work.

Kouame Kakaha is a potter working in a pottery cooperative in the small Baule village of Tanoh Sakassou, Ivory Coast. The Baule have a long tradition of making pottery for domestic use. From what we know, most villages used to have a potter or potters, just as they had weavers and sculptors. Potting was not a profession in the sense that women earned a living at it. Potters, like most artists, potted part-time and worked in the fields during the growing season. This is still the case for many of the Tanoh Sakassou potters. We have very, very little old Baule pottery, largely because their long war against the French in the early twentieth century resulted in the destruction of many villages. While the Baule speak an Akan language, there are no signs that they ever made figurative clay funerary heads, as did most of their Akan neighbors. Their pottery resembles their other art in that it places great emphasis on elegance, rounded forms, fine surface decoration, and smooth, highly polished black surface. They have made water pots, cooking pots, and a number of prestige vessels such as palm wine containers and small serving pots. As in other realms, pottery is appreciated for its aesthetic qualities. Potters enjoy animated discussion of the relative quality of pots, and have well-formulated criteria for evaluating them.

The Tanoh Sakassou pottery cooperative was founded in 1972. At the time, the traditional buyers of pottery, Baule women, were turning to plastic and metal containers, but a new market of urban Africans and foreigners was becoming important. The cooperative's potters no longer bother to try to sell their pots in local markets (not even in the nearby large city market in Bouake). They sell from their attractive showroom, built for them by a foreign embassy, and in craft fairs in Abidjan, and they supply European and American wholesalers who place orders and sell overseas. They make "traditional" forms like cooking and serving vessels, but they also create new forms, for their urban and foreign clients demand novelty. When making classic Baule vessels they feel that they must conform to traditions of shape, size, and decorative motif. As they explain it, if you changed these the pot could no longer be called by its name. It would become something else. If their clients ask them to, however, the potters are willing to produce new pots that relate to a Western life-style, if requested by their clients, such as votive lights ordered by local Baptist missionaries, or enormous planters for a hotel in Abidjan. They also invent new forms, often inspired by things seen in village life like chickens, goat, and women carrying water. Since there is no tradition of figurative pottery to build on, these forms are a new kind of art. They are the property of the individuals who create them; while everybody who has the ability can make the old forms, the creator of a new one has a copyright on it. When asked how they create new forms, the potters speak of observing village life. They may also say, though, that ideas appear to them in dreams. Interestingly, this is the same explanation that wood sculptors give for the origin of their masks. While the subject matter of the new forms is original, the pottery itself is still black, shiny, highly

CAT. 82

Vessel

By Kouame Kakaha, 2002. Baule, Tanoh Sakassou pottery cooperative, Ivory Coast.
Ceramic with organic glaze. H. 55.9 cm.
Jerome Vogel

decorated, elegant, and refined. It is still high-quality Baule pottery.

Kouame Kakaha works in this context, though her pottery is somewhat idiosyncratic. She has always worked in the village, has raised her children there, and lives the life of a village woman. I have seen her participating in village ceremonies and have sometimes been told that she is away in her field. She first came to my attention years ago when I saw a pot (Cat. 82) that was totally outside the usual repertory of forms. I assumed that it was inspired by the shape of a woman, as it strongly resembled an ancient Anatolian goddess. It took repeated questioning to overcome the potter's reluctance to explain that it was actually inspired by the testicles of a ram. (Goats, in large numbers, wander through this part of the village.) The abstract form, the result of dreams and internal meditation, then underwent a long process of trial and error to develop it into a form that was aesthetically pleasing and able to survive the firing process. The first version, now unfortunately broken, required a support between the two parts of the base. It was also markedly asymmetrical and somewhat rough in surface. While these qualities were pleasing to my Western eye, they did not please a Baule eye. Subsequent versions have dropped the supporting strut and are symmetrical, smooth, and shiny. Improvements in their construction have made them more resistant to the stresses of firing. A form that was outside the Baule canon has become "Baule-ized."

Kouame Kakaha has continued to make forms that are markedly different from those made by the other potters. She has created a number of vessels ranging from containers to ashtrays with ram decorations, although the other potters prefer birds, chickens, and fish. This makes me suspect that the ram motif has a personal significance for her. She also invents pots with wavy, irregular decoration on highly irregular shapes. She rarely uses the fine, overall incised decoration that characterizes most of the Tanoh Sakassou pottery. She is, in short, an original artist. She has commercial success with Western clients who respond to her original and sculptural style. In the past couple of years her son has started making pots (he is the second of his mother's sons to have followed in her footsteps), and he, too, makes odd, irregular vessels that depart markedly from the norm. Although his pottery is not technically perfect, it too sells well because of its originality. Both of these potters use traditional methods to express a personal vision. The new foreign market has encouraged innovation, and has made it possible for men to make pots, but Tanoh Sakassou potters are still in touch with their social and artistic traditions. They enjoy the freedom of inventing new styles and say that it is actually harder to make traditional pots because of all the rules that must be followed.

The second contemporary potter we are presenting is Nesta Nala, a Zulu potter from South Africa.[i] She works according to very traditional methods in a small Zulu village, but she has become well-known in South Africa and abroad. She learned potting from her mother and has passed on the profession to her daughters. There is an old Zulu potting tradition, much of it associated with making beer pots used in the ceremonies of hospitality. Although Zululand has conserved more traditions than many parts of South Africa, pottery was almost a dying art by the 1970s. According to Rhoda Levinsohn, Nala was one of a very few potters determined to conserve not only the tradition but the high standards of craftsmanship that were disappearing as South Africa underwent profound social changes. Nala worked, and works, very much as do the Baule potters, building up her pots with coils and doing simple firing, though she produces her shiny black surfaces with animal fat (Cat. 83).

Nala's forms are very similar to old Zulu beer pots, but are more elegant than anyone else's (including those of her daughters). You can identify her pots by weight; they are much lighter than those of other potters because of the extreme fineness of the walls. The surfaces are smooth and perfect, the decoration rather sober and restrained and very much in the style of old pots. If they have a defect, one might say that they are almost *too* per-

90

CAT. 83

Beer pot
by Nesta Nala, 2002. Zulu peoples, South Africa
Ceramic with organic glaze. H. 24.1 cm.
Dr. Gary van Wyk and Lisa Brittan/ Axis
Gallery, New York

CAT. 84

Vessel
Zulu peoples, South Africa
Ceramic. H. 39.4 cm.
Simmons Collection

fect—that they lack individual character and invention. Indeed, Nala makes the same sizes and shapes of pots many times, although there are of course small variations. She does create new and nontraditional forms of decoration; she has, for example, experimented with foliage decoration (leaves incised on the walls of pots). By and large, her pots give the impression that she wants to stay close to Zulu forms, and that her innovations are mostly in decorative motifs.

There has been something of a resurgence of Zulu pottery-making at the moment, encouraged by interest in South African traditional arts on the part of foreigners and urban South Africans. An active market is developing for Zulu baskets, beadwork, and pottery, and for the new baskets made of colored telephone wire. The contemporary Zulu artists are not anonymous; galleries are careful to provide names and biographical details on individual artists. Some have become very well known, and their works command premium prices. Although she continues to live and work where she always has, Nala has become a cultural celebrity. She has won awards in national ceramic contests, which until recently were dominated by white, studio potters. Dealers vie for her rather limited production, and emphasize the prestige of having a Nala pot. Her pots are now much too expensive for a rural Zulu clientele. They are works of art, proudly shown in large cities throughout the world. Nobody would think of serving beer in them; they are works of art, not utilitarian objects.

It is hard to write about this without a certain irony. African friends have often laughed at me for displaying everyday objects as art—objects they used as children. It is however true that many traditional African arts or crafts have been preserved by the emergence of a foreign market or of a sophisticated urban market. The Tanoh Sakassou potters sell mostly to foreigners, and they have profited from the higher prices tourists can pay. Tuareg silver-workers now work primarily for foreigners, as do Baule bronze-casters. Craft traditions are being preserved that were disappearing, but the function of the objects has changed. Whether good or bad, this seems to be inevitable.

Our third contemporary potter, Magdalene Odundo, came to making pottery from an entirely different direction.[ii] She is African, but it was as a student of graphic arts in England that she became interested in African art and began experimenting with making pots. Eventually she went to study in Nigeria at the center started by Michael Cardew, and it was here that she learned the technique of hand-building pots. She later did research on women potters in Kenya, her home. Odundo's technique is basically African. Although she fires her pots in a kiln, she blackens them in a way very similar to that of the Baule potters. She says, however, that all of world art is part of her inspiration, and she sees no reason to limit herself. While her ceramics are pots—she keeps the container form—they function as Western-style ceramic sculptures. Their perfection and their overwhelming presence dominate. It is instructive that one of her pots was exhibited at New York's Metropolitan Museum of Art with works of twentieth-century European decorative arts. It looked perfectly at home, perhaps because Odundo is consciously making works of art. She has moved African pottery into a Western (or Asian) context. African technique is in the service of a modern sensibility (Cat. 85).

It is impossible to tell whether Odundo represents a direction that African pottery may increasingly take. Students in many African art schools are taught to make pottery on a wheel, but there is also increasing interest in trying to work in the old ways. At the moment, pottery continues to be made in a number of different kinds of world in Africa. It does not seem in danger of disappearing, even though much of it is made for different uses by different clients.

1. As Nesta Nala's working methods have been carefully studied by Rhoda Levinsohn and were published in *Art and Craft in South Africa* in 1984, I have not gone into as much detail here as with the Baule potters.
2. Magdalene Odundo's pottery has been studied by Marla Berns, to whom this section is heavily indebted.

CAT. 85

Ceramic in the shape of a vessel
by Madeleine Odundo, 2001
Oxidized terracotta. H. 80 cm.
Courtesy Anthony Slayter-Ralph

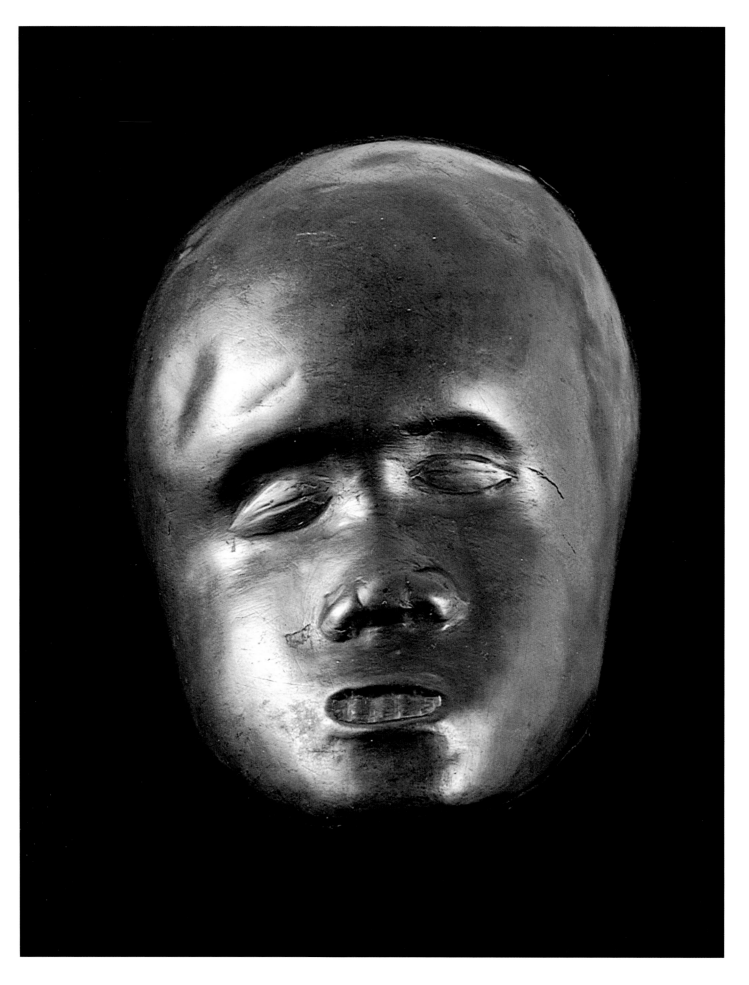

Sculpting in Copper Alloys

FRANK HERREMAN

*I*n many African cultures, brass and bronze alloys are reserved for prestige objects and royal art forms. Metallic alloys are cast in highly detailed, small-scale pendants and weights; realistic heads made for altars; and used as an additive element to numerous types of regalia and ritual objects. This section introduces contexts where copper alloy sculptures are used, and can still be found today. Paula Girschick's essay "Brass Never Rusts; Lead Never Rots"; Brass and Brasscasting in the Edo Kingdom Of Benin", explores royal prerogatives that reserve the use of brass, the social position of the artists, and other historical and economic factors involved in obtaining the metals used in these artworks.

Brass sculptures made from copper and tin alloys from the Nigerian cities of Ife and Benin are considered to be among the major masterpieces in the cannon of African art. The first Ife sculptures were created between the twelfth and fifteenth centuries, while the sculptures from Benin were made between the sixteenth and nineteenth centuries. These pieces were preceded by a series of ninth century sculptural objects in bronze such as vessels, staffs and pendants, found in 1938, in the village of Igbo-Ukwu, near Awka in eastern Nigeria. In 1959-1960 and again in the mid sixties systematic excavations were conducted in the same location by Thurstan Shaw (Shaw 1978: 100). Ekpo Eyo states that it is believed that the copper used to make the Igbo-Ukwu sculptures was traded across the desert from North Africa, and the tin might have come from the Jos Plateau. Or, he suggests, the copper, tin, and lead might already have been mixed and traded across the Sahara as bronze (in Eyo and Willet 1980: 9). The latter would suggest that the metal trade across the Sahara desert started more than one thousand years earlier. This would change from the last quarter of the fifteenth century when most of the metal would be transported by European merchants by sea, as they established contacts with different coastal peoples from the Niger Delta. Bronze or brass cast manilas were exchanged for slaves, pepper, ivory, and other precious goods[i]. In the fifteenth and sixteenth centuries, the powerful Kindgom of Benin expanded its boundaries and used art and ritual to reinforce the power and mystique of a divine king (Ezra 1992: 11). In 1486, The Portuguese sailed up to the waterways into the area then known as the "slave rivers" and made contact with the Kingdom of Benin.[2]

However, the importation of copper and copper alloys by sea would not remain limited to the Kingdom of Benin. During several centuries, other Nigerian peoples, including the Yoruba and those who live in the Niger Delta, would also create important works of art by the method of lost-wax casting. Nigel Barley describes the method as follows:

> "...An object is modeled in wax, usually over a clay core and covered with further layers of clay. Baking hardens the clay, melts the wax and allows it to be poured off so that a hollow mould is left, ready to receive molten metal. Each object is thus unique as the mould must be broken to extract the casting"(in Mack 2000: 98).

CAT. 86

Head
Abomey, Republic of Benin
Brass. H. 21.6 cm.
Buffalo Museum of Science

The exact function of this head is uncertain. Because of the four holes at the base, it may have been attached to a full figure that represented a former ruler or deity that was made of separate metal plates riveted together. The same artist who made this head also created the famous nude figure that carries a sword in the collection of the Dapper Museum, Paris. (F.H.)

Face bell: Omo
Ijebu-Yoruba peoples, Nigeria
Brass. H. 25 cm.
W. and U. Horstmann Collection

Pair of Ogboni figures
Yoruba peoples, Nigeria
Bronze. H. 29.2 cm.
Private Collection

Among the different types of metal sculptures of the Yoruba peoples, the casting of copper alloy figures would be specially practiced in connection with the *Ogboni* society, dedicated to Onile, "the owner of the earth" in forms such as *edan* figure pairs. The *edan* figural pair of a man and woman linked by a chain is the principal emblem of this society (Cat. 87) (Fagg, Pemberton and Holcombe: 195). Some of these sculptures were already known before the Biafran war, in the late sixties. However, most of the *edan*-related sculptures would appear on the art market after this war. Because of the lack of documented information, it is difficult to date these objects. Yet, it may be assumed that, already in the sixteenth and seventeenth centuries, the Yoruba created sculptures for the *Ogboni* society (Dobbelman 1976: 6).

The lack of conclusive information about age, use, and exact provenance also characterizes a large number of important lost-wax objects created in different copper alloys and

CAT. 89

Bell
Lower Niger, Nigeria
Copper alloy. H. 10.2 cm.
Toby and Barry Hecht

CAT. 90

Helmet
Koma-Builsa peoples, Ghana
Copper alloy. H. 23 cm.
W. and U. Horstmann Collection

known as "Lower Niger Bronzes", a designation was given by William Fagg (Fagg 1960: no. 15). As with the *ogboni bronzes*, many Lower Niger objects were offered after 1968 by dealers. Philip Peek describes the Lower Niger Bronzes as:

> *"...a grouping primarily because they do not fit within more defined traditions. The thinking is that if bronze objects are not from the court of the Benin Kingdom or do not belong among those found at Igbo-Ukwu or are not part of the Yoruba Ogboni bronze traditions, then they must be Lower Niger Bronzes"*
> *(in Anderson and Peek 2002: 39).*

These metal sculptures include figural and abstract prestige objects like fly-whisks, staffs or adzes and axes, and adornments such as bracelets and pendants; or ritual objects such as free standing figures, vessels, figural gongs and bells or divination tools (Cats. 89). Philip Peek also notes that for the Lower Niger Bronzes:

> *"The variety of forms, styles, alloys, and contexts incorporated within this category should, however, be ample warning that they cannot possibly be products of a single tradition" (Anderson and Peek 2002:39).*

Peek believes that it is far more likely that there was a basic knowledge of bronze casting in many locations throughout Southern Nigeria. Therefore it is possible that these objects were made by local casters or itinerant artists and that these objects may also have been used far away from their place of creation. These sculptures in copper alloy are figural or abstract.

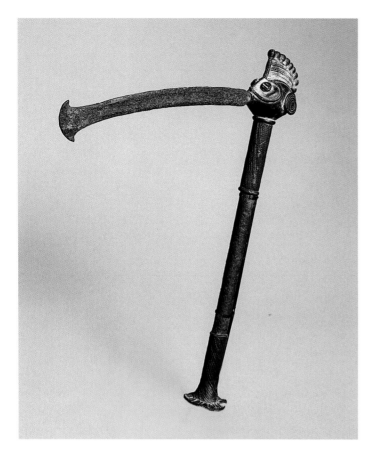

CAT. 91

Axe
Tiv peoples, Nigeria
Wood, iron, pigment. L. 42 cm.
Mr. and Mrs. Carrie-Vacher

CAT. 92

Dance hoe
Verre peoples, Nigeria
Copper alloy. H. 28 cm.
Toby and Barry Hecht

The creation of lost-wax sculptures is certainly not confined within the borders of contemporary Nigeria. Archeological findings from Djenne in Mali show that there is a long-standing tradition of metal casting that may go back to the thirteenth century. Other peoples, including the Dogon in Mali; different peoples from Burkina Faso; the Senufo in Ivory Coast; Akan peoples in Ghana and Ivory Coast; and the Fon peoples, Republic of Benin, are among those with an important metal working tradition (Cat. 86, 90). Artists from the Kingdoms of the Grassland region in Cameroon created objects that emphasize the prestige of local kings and their dignitaries. In Central Africa, casting of copper alloys is much more limited. It consists of currency, adornments like the bracelets of the Kongo and Teke peoples and anthropomorphic pendants by the Pende peoples. Most remarkable by their theme are the crucifixes, made by artists from the Kongo peoples (Cat. 93). This Christian motif was introduced to them at the end of the 15th century, when Portuguese missionaries were sent to convert the King, his court and subjects to Catholicism. Over the years, the function of crucifixes, as a major symbol of the Catholic religion, would shift in meaning and they become vehicles for the transmission of original local concepts and beliefs. When comparing a number of Congolese crucifix figures on the crosses, one can sometimes recognize different European style traditions, including Gothic, Renaissance or Baroque.

It may be concluded with certainty that the creation of objects made of copper alloys, is most closely linked to leadership and economic prosperity (Cat. 91,92). In many cases, the use of this precious material is a prerogative of kings or chiefs who often controlled the trade with the importers of the metal.[3] Copper alloys are mainly used to create symbols of authority, sculptures that represent ancestors, or ritual objects like gongs and vessels that are used by religious dignitaries or placed on shrines. The association of leadership and the use of metal sculptures can also include specific iconographical motifs. This can be illustrated through a small series of equestrian figures, images of power and leadership par excellence, from different West African peoples (Cat. 94-98).

CAT. 93

Cross
Kongo peoples, Dem. Rep. of the Congo
Bronze figure on wooden cross. H. 38.7 cm.
Pace Primitive Gallery, New York

In contrast with wooden objects that are susceptible to erosion or decay, copper alloys are reasonably durable. Therefore, a vast number of these sculptures have survived. However, recasting alloys to create new objects or to replace ones that were damaged is a common practice among many African peoples. Nevertheless, the research in Igbo Ukwu, Ife, and Benin provides us with information with a depth in time, nowhere else found in sub-Saharan Africa.

1   Hodgkin (1975:121) mentions that the expanding Kingdom of Benin sold the captives they took from enemies for twelve or fifteen brass bracelets each, or for copper bracelets which they price more.
2   The Portuguese Were succeeded by the Dutch in the 17th century. Eventually the British replaced the Dutch in the Nineteenth century. In 1897, British troops sacked the City of Benin during a punitive expedition.
3   It is significant that, when the Benin vassal city of Udo made a bid for power in the sixteenth century, it apparently seized Benin Brass casters and set them to work making its own casting as a sign of independence (Barley in Mack 2000: 98). The Bronze head Cat. 102, created in Udo, used a similar purpose as the ones used by the Oba in Benin.

CAT. 94

Equestrian group

Yoruba peoples, Nigeria
Copper alloy. H. 30 cm.
Private Collection, Belgium

The casting of equestrian groups in copper alloy is
common in the art of different West African peoples.
The material, reserved for the making of precious
objects, is perfectly suited for the representation of
ancestors, kings, and chiefs. (FH)

CAT. 95

Janus figure riding an animal, staff

Yoruba peoples, Nigeria
Copper alloy. H. 26.7 cm. (figure); 104.8 cm. (staff)
Myrna and Ira Brind

CAT. 96

Equestrian group, amulet
Kotoko(?) peoples, Chad
Copper alloy. H. 7 cm.
Charles and Kent Davis

CAT. 97

Equestrian group
Senufo peoples, Ivory Coast
Copper alloy. H. 10.8 cm.
Mr. and Mrs. J. Thomas Lewis

CAT. 98

Equestrian group
Yoruba peoples, Nigeria
Copper alloy. H. 19 cm.
Private Collection

"Brass Never Rusts, Lead Never Rots": Brass and Brasscasting in the Edo Kingdom of Benin

PAULA BEN-AMOS GIRSHICK

In memory of Roy Sieber

In February 1897 the Benin Punitive Expedition, a British colonial force, captured Benin City, capital of the Edo Kingdom of Benin. As Expedition members moved through the compounds of the royal palace, they discovered thousands of pieces of metal sculpture, including "very antique" brass heads, figures of horseback riders in "chain mail," and an immense brass snake crawling down the roof (Roth 1968 [1903]:173–75). The chief medical officer, Dr. R. Allman, who happened upon the workplace of the royal brass-casters, provides us with the earliest European description of the lost-wax process in Benin:

> The manufacture of bronzes was evidently carried on under the direct supervision of the kings, as the smelting pots and the clay and beeswax for moulding, etc., were all arranged in a compound adjacent to the palace. Several moulds in various stages of completion were found here; those ready for casting represented when broken the following appearance. A mould of special clay formed the base, over this a likeness of what was required was beautifully modelled in beeswax, and outside this a covering of "potters clay," the whole being enwrapped in ordinary mud or mortar. I can only conjecture the final process to complete the operation—i.e., the mould, after being sufficiently sun-dried, is transferred to the smelting pot and completely submerged in the molten metal, which takes the place of the wax, and the object is accomplished (Allman 1897:44).1

Members of the Expedition carried off thousands of objects as war booty, many of which they put on auction upon their return. The arrival and dispersal of Benin art in Europe captured public interest and stimulated scholarly debate about how and when the Edo had learned the lost-wax technique and where they had obtained the metals.[2] The earliest speculations on the origins of their casting techniques pointed to Portugal (Buchner 1908), India (Crahmer 1909), or ancient Egypt via migrations across the Sudan (Murray 1941, Jeffries 1951). While the ultimate knowledge of casting is likely to have diffused into what is today Southern Nigeria from elsewhere, archaeological research at the sites of Igbo Ukwu and Ife provide clear evidence for an internal development that predates European contact by several centuries (Shaw 1970, Willett 1967). As a result of these discoveries, scholars turned their attention to the relationships among sites in Nigeria. The artist Leon Underwood (1949) was the first to suggest a linkage between Benin and the nearby Yoruba kingdom of Ife. His analysis was based on stylistic and technological similarities. William Fagg, a curator at the British Museum, picked up on Underwood's suggestion and bolstered it with evidence from oral history.

In 1934 a local Benin historian, Jacob U. Egharevba, had published an oral tradition that brasswork was introduced to Benin from Ife during the reign of Oba Oguola, the sixth in the present dynasty. According to Egharevba, "Oba Oguola wished to introduce brass-casting into Benin so as to produce works of art similar to those sent him from Ife. He therefore sent to the Oni of Ife for a brass-smith and Iguegha was sent to him. . . . The practice of making brass castings for the preservation of the records of events was originated

CAT. 99

Plaque
Benin, Nigeria, 16th-17th century
Bronze. H. 47.5 cm.
Laura and James J. Ross

Rectangular brass plaques often portray persons and events associated with the court. This plaque represents the *Oba* or a chief. (F.H.)

during the reign of Oguola" (1968 [1934]:11). Fagg (1960) used this tradition as the basis for a chronology of Benin brasswork based on its degree of adherence to Ife naturalism. His hypothesis, which has been widely accepted in academic and commercial circles,[3] depends to a large extent on the dating of the reign of Oba Oguola, about which there is disagreement: Egharevba places it around the end of the thirteenth century (1968:11) while the anthropologist R. E. Bradbury suggests the end of the fourteenth century (1973:42). At this stage of our knowledge, unfortunately, neither date can be supported by corroborative data.

Evidence that has been mounting since the 1960s makes the picture more complicated and ultimately challenges the notion of a simple linear progression. In the first place, Graham Connah's excavations in Benin City have provided evidence that casting was already practiced in Benin by the thirteenth century A.D.,[4] although probably on a small scale. At the Clerks' Quarters site (Feature 21, Early Phase) Connah found a fragment of a crucible used for nonferrous casting (1975:64). In a mass burial (Cutting II, Early Phase) he also discovered some droplets of copper alloys (ibid.:146), five heavy penannular objects forty-eight bracelets, and three rings (ibid.:142), (fig. 2). The penannular objects were decorated with chasing and punchwork, which led Connah to assume they had been smithed rather than cast. Timothy F. Garrard, however, has argued that incised and punched decoration is actually easier to produce by casting from a wax model than it is by smithing (1983:18). He suggests that had Connah looked elsewhere in West Africa, particularly among the Akan, he would have found similar designs on early lost-wax castings. Consequently there is no reason to assume a priori that these early Benin pieces were smithed rather than cast. If Garrard is correct, this could put the knowledge of casting in Benin contemporaneous with—or even earlier than—the earliest thermoluminescent dating for the Ita Yemoo pieces at Ife: A.D. 1365+/-70 and A.D. 1420+/-45 (Willett and Fleming 1976:138). Further, the dates obtained by Willett and Fleming from a series of Ife and Benin copper castings fall into roughly the same time period in the fifteenth and sixteenth centuries,[5] indicating that claims to a clear-cut Ife origin are difficult to sustain.

Connah's bracelets, rings, and penannular objects constitute the earliest forms of Benin metal art known so far. They were made of tin bronze. There are sources for tin on the Jos Plateau and for copper, lead, and zinc in the Benue Rift in Nigeria, but no clear evidence of copper mining (Chikwendu and Umeji 1983). The closest sources are probably in Agades and Azelik, in Niger, but Akjouit, in Mauretania, is also a possibility (see Herbert 1984:15–19).

Much more is known about metal imports from the fifteenth century on, that is, after Benin came into contact with the European world. In 1486 the Portuguese prince John II sent an exploratory expedition to the West Coast of Africa with the aim of consolidating his trade monopoly. In 1487 he established a trading post at the Benin port of Ughoton, which continued until 1507. The Portuguese paid the Edo in manillas, an "open bracelet in the form of a horseshoe with lozenge-shaped ends" (Herbert 1984:201). There is no indication in the literature of whether the Portuguese introduced this form of currency or found it already in use, although Connah feels that the penannular objects may have been precursors (1975:57). The Portuguese used manillas as a general currency, using them to pay for slaves, Benin pepper (*Piper guineacene*) (Ryder 1969:31), rental for a house for the pilot, porters, provisions, and blacksmiths to make slave manacles (fig. 3). As the price of slaves went up, more and more manillas were imported; 13,000 of them, for example, were imported in a single

CAT. 100

Plaque
Benin , Nigeria, 16th -17th century
Bronze. H. 47 cm.
Buffalo Museum of Science

The plaque represents two fully attired dignitaries.
(F.H.)

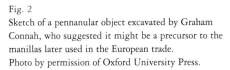

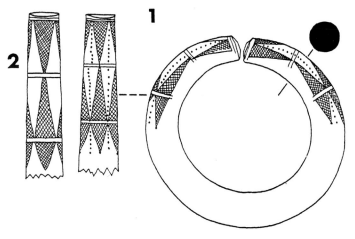

Fig. 2
Sketch of a pennanular object excavated by Graham Connah, who suggested it might be a precursor to the manillas later used in the European trade.
Photo by permission of Oxford University Press.

voyage in 1517 (Ryder 1969:53). Trade records show that the manillas were initially made of copper, but by 1517 the emphasis had shifted to brass, although not to the total exclusion of the copper versions (ibid.:40). This preference for brass can clearly be seen in the 1603–4 report by a German traveler that in Benin "they do not care for gold, nor for silver. Brass, however, they value highly, and also everything red"—a preference that was to continue until the present time, as we shall see (Ulsheimer in Jones 1983:41).

By the end of the sixteenth century the Portuguese were superseded by the Dutch, who continued to use manillas as a staple currency. Manillas generally lost their place as the medium of exchange around 1715 (Ryder 1969:144), and seem not to have featured at all when the Frenchman Landolphe was there in 1769 (ibid.:199); but this did not signal the end of metal imports, for Dutch, English, and French ships' records show a thriving trade in brass stew-pans, copper buckets, pewter ware, lead, knives in the thousands, and brass bowls. These bowls, called neptunes, ranged in size from a diameter of one foot or less to dishes weighing eight pounds. They were imported by the thousands of pounds. This emphasis on brass basins and other practical copper-alloy objects continued until the British takeover (ibid.).

The Edo certainly put these manillas and basins to use as adornment and as ritual vessels. In 1652, for example, Spanish Capuchins noted that at marriage ceremonies the woman is "fully adorned with coral, brass manillas, glass beads, ivories and cowries" (Ryder 1969:314), while the French trader Landolphe's feet were ritually bathed in a nine-foot brass bowl in preparation for his visit with a powerful Benin chief (ibid.:202). Both Fagg (1963:35) and Dark (1973:2) contend that art production in Benin was stimulated in the 15th and 16th centuries by the sudden appearance of larger quantities of imported metal, particularly the manillas, which were probably melted down. They note the coincidence of these imports with oral traditions of expansion in the arts associated with King Esigie, who is traditionally assumed to have been on the throne during the Portuguese period. However, as Craddock and Picton point out, "The trouble is that, although it seems obvious enough to suppose that the expansion of the Benin brass-casting industry [at the time of Esigie] was made possible by this new and readily available supply of metal . . . we have no evidence that these manillas really did find their way into the Edo caster's crucibles, nor do we know what they were actually made of" (1986:9). Assumptions that manillas were standardized have not held up under (albeit limited) testing, so that any attempts to correlate African alloys with European and Muslim ones are "dogged by the lack of precise information about the metallic content at any one time of the principal forms of copper exported to Africa, namely manillas, rods, and basins of various kinds" (Herbert 1984:99).

When Benin metal sculptures reached England at the end of the nineteenth century, preliminary metal analysis revealed that they were mainly brass.[6] Much more extensive analyses were carried out in the 1970s in Berlin by O. Werner (1970; see also Werner and Willett 1975), whose results show that his sample of several hundred pieces are mainly zinc-brass, although a number of rectangular plaques are tin-bronze and others are a mixture of zinc-brass and tin-bronze (Willett 1981:38).[7]

Brasscasting in Benin

The casting of copper alloys is in Benin a specialized skill that rests in the hands of a guild, Igun Eronmwon (literally, "brass-smiths").[8] The guild holds a series of ranked titles that belong within families, being inherited by the senior son. Each family has its own tradition of origin stating which Oba gave them their title: the Ine from Oba Oguola (late fourteenth century), the Ihama from Oba Ewuare (early fifteenth century), the Olague from Oba

Fig. 3
Fifteenth or sixteenth century Benin brass plaque depicting two Portuguese, each holding a strand of manillas. H. 45.7 cm. (18 in.). The Metropolitan Museum of Art, Gift of Mr. and Mrs. Klaus G. Perls, 1991. (1991.17.13).

CAT. 101

Head
Benin, Nigeria
Bronze. H. 20.3 cm.
Drs. Daniel and Marian Malcolm

The head is stylistically different from the royal heads and may be a "trophy head". The casting is thin which suggests an earlier age. (F.H.)
(Girshick, personal communication and Willett, 1994)

Fig. 4
Photograph of the late Ine n'Igun Eronmwon, the
highest ranking titleholder within the brass caster's
guild, who was the main source of information on
casting for R.E. Bradbury, Philip Dark, and William
Fagg in the 1950s. Photograph by Roy Sieber, 1958,
image no. L2,11.

Orhogbua (early sixteenth century), the Ebagua from Oba Ewuakpe (early eighteenth century), and so on (Bradbury 1959: BS218.A).[9] Scholars who spoke only with the senior title-holder, the Ine (fig. 4), collected his family's version of the coming of Igueghae from Ife to Benin and assumed that it referred to the beginnings of brass-casting, as discussed above,[10] rather than to the organization of independent casters into a guild (Dark 1973:47). However, both Philip Dark and I collected accounts—his from Oba Akenzua II and mine from Chief Ihama of Igun Eronmwon—that suggest that, while casting was practiced in Benin from early times, the guild as an organizational unit was not formed until later, during the reign of Oba Esigie, according to Oba Akenzua II, or Oba Ewuare, according to Chief Ihama (Dark 1973:47, Ben-Amos 1995:28). As Garrard points out (1983:18), this tradition makes sense, as it is "not politically motivated . . . , it is consistent with the evidence from Connah's excavations, and it suggests, very reasonably, that from modest origins the Benin school of casting later developed to serve royal needs."

The earliest European description of guild specialization comes from the deposition of a Portuguese ship captain, Lourenço Pinto, who visited the area in 1691: "The artisans have their places carefully allocated in the squares which are divided up in such a manner that in one square [the captain] counted altogether one hundred and twenty goldsmiths' workshops, all working together" (quoted in Ryder 1969:113). Although Pinto may have mistaken gold for golden brass, there are some hints in the literature about the use of gold in Benin.[11]

Because of the prestige attributed to brass, Igun Eronmwon is the highest-ranking craft guild in Benin. It is organized into an age hierarchy, the senior of which constitutes the administrative council. Commissions from the Oba are channeled through the senior members, who distribute the work, handle disputes, and represent the guild to the king. Craftsmen work on order and used to be paid by gifts of food, slaves, and wives. While casting for the Oba, they work in a special room in the palace, *Iwe n'eki*—the room described in the opening quote from Dr. Allen. When they are casting objects for the royal ancestral altars, there appears to be a degree of specialization:

Ine divided the work among the various brass-smiths. Ine himself took the most important piece to be made, and the next object went to Chief Ehanire and so on. . . . The *uhumwelao* [commemorative heads] were made by Chiefs Ehanire, Akenau, and Obodalaye. . . . The *ukhurhe* [rattle staffs] were made by Chief Olague. . . . The bells . . . and

CAT. 102

Head

City of Udo, Benin, Nigeria
Bronze. H. 23.2 cm.
Museum for African Art, Gift of Mala Silson Estate

Twenty miles northwest of Benin City is the town of Udo, a provincial Bini city once a rival of Benin, where the casting of lost-wax figures and heads flourished during the second half of the 16th century. In Udo, the making of heads was influenced by the royal art of Benin. These heads express the desire of the Udo leaders to compete with the *oba*, ruler of Benin, by challenging the mandate that cast heads were solely the prerogative of the King of Benin. (F.H.)
(Willett 1994)

a semicircular plaque (*erara*), if one was to be put on the king's altar, were made by Chief Ihama. Chief Ehanire made the bronze figure in the round (Dark 1973:51–52).

Sumptuary laws regulate the right of those outside the royal family to obtain and display art forms made of brass. Chiefs have the right to wear elaborate brass bracelets, hip pendants, and beaten brass regalia in royal rituals. Occasionally a chief who is bold or powerful enough can display a brass sculpture, as did the eighteenth-century Ezomo, who commissioned an elaborate brass shrine of the hand (see Bradbury 1973:251–70, and Ben-Amos 1999:101, 125, 127, 135). Smaller objects, especially jewelry, are sold in the market by members of Igun Eronmwon. As early as 1600 de Marees noted that women of Benin wore three or four pounds of red copper and tin rings on their arms and legs, often so tightly that it was hard to imagine how they put them on (quoted in Herbert 1984:216).

It was at about the same time, that is, the beginning of the seventeenth century, that the German traveler mentioned earlier noted that in Benin "they value [brass] highly, and also everything red." This statement linking brass and "everything red" reveals an underlying color symbolism that—together with cost and scarcity—explains why brass has had such a hold on the Benin imagination for centuries. Like all metals, brass is associated with Ogun, the deity identified with agriculture, hunting, war, and, nowadays, transport. Metals are imbued with the vital force of Ogun, and their creation and use is ritually charged. But brass differs from iron and other metals in the particular perceptual qualities that give it its special essence and power: redness and shininess. Shininess (*nwananwana*) has both an aesthetic and an apotropaic meaning. As an aesthetic criterion it refers to the rich brocades, velvets, and silks worn by the nobility, the sensual sheen of human hair and skin, and the glossy patina of ivory and brass sculpture. Reflective qualities also allude to the power of rivers, shiny and dangerous abodes of powerful deities who can draw people into their depths. Mirrors—the ultimate in shininess—are used as costumes in rituals; flashing as the dancer moves, they create a protected space. Redness (*ba*) is associated with the aggressive, hot-tempered gods in the Benin pantheon, especially Ogun but also Osun, the power of herbal medicine; Ogiuwu, the god of death; and the Yoruba import Esango, the thunder god. These are the deities with dangerous power to inflict violence and sudden death, but also to protect and open the way. Combined, these qualities of redness and shininess are considered to be "threatening" (*ohan*), that is, fear-provoking, menacing, and, by extension, having the power to drive away evil forces.

Working with brass, then, is a serious process, highly ritualized. The casters sacrifice roosters, goats, and, for the most important pieces, cattle to protect themselves from harm. Prayers are made to the deity Ogun and to the ancestors—particularly the founding ancestor, who also serves as a protective deity (Igueghae in the case of the Ine family)—asking them to preserve the designs and protect the designers. If Ogun or the ancestors are angry, the mold can blow up during pouring and kill the caster (Dark 1973:52).

But brass has another quality, equally important in Edo thought, and that is its association with the capacity to preserve memory. As I have pointed out elsewhere,

In the Edo language, the expression "to commemorate"—*sa-e-y-ama*—literally means to cast a pattern in brass. The verb *sa*, according to Agheyisi (1986:134), means to scoop a liquid into a container, as one does with molten brass into a mold. The notion of commemoration is thus constructed out of the image of a liquid which gets channeled and hardened. In effect, the act of casting freezes history (1999:134).

In the rough-and-tumble of Benin politics, kings were concerned with legitimizing their activities and preserving their memories. It is no surprise, then, that so many of the art forms associated with royalty in Benin have been brass, the most enduring of materials. Indeed brass and other metals are the very symbols of permanence, as expressed in the Benin proverbial saying, "Brass never rusts, lead never rots" (*Eronmwon ei-moton, oze ei-keke*).

1. This observation is essentially accurate except for Allman's "conjecture" that "the mould, after being sufficiently sun-dried, is transferred to the smelting pot and completely submerged in the molten metal, which takes the place of the wax, and the object is accomplished." Instead, the wax was melted or burned out and the space filled with molten metal poured from a crucible. See Fagg 1959, Dark 1966 and 1973, Garrard 1983, and Williams 1974 for descriptions of the process.
2. On the reception of Benin art in England, see Coombes 1994.
3. A different tradition was collected by Captain Roupell and his officials at the time of the 1897 Expedition. They were told (by a group of court officials that did not include members of the casters' guild) that the white men (presumably Portuguese) who came during the reign of Esigie included a man named Ahammangiwa who taught men how to make brasswork (Read and Dalton 1899:6).
4. The radiocarbon dates from the Clerks' Quarters Site Cutting II: A.D. 1180+/-105 and A.D. 1310+/-90.
5. Graham Connah's radiocarbon dates for bronze at Benin are A.D. 1180+/-105 and A.D. 1310+/-90. Compare with the earliest date obtained by Willett and Fleming for Ife (based on thermoluminescence): A.D. 1365+/-70, from Ita Yemoo. Other Ife dates are: A.D. 1420+/-45, at Ita Yemoo, and A.D. 1440+/-64, A.D. 1490+/-85, A.D. 1515+/-45, and A.D. 1535+/-45, at Wunmonije. Willett and Fleming's Benin dates are A.D. 1515+/-55, A.D. 1560+/-40, A.D. 1590+/-45, and A.D. 1600+/-35.
6. Thurston Shaw (1965:92) discusses the earliest attempts at metal analysis in England and Germany.
7. As P. T. Craddock points out (1985), there have been basically two approaches to the question of the provenance of Benin alloys—particularly lead, zinc, and nickel—and their dating. The first analyzes the composition of copper in order to find its source. The major figure in this has been O. Werner, who tested over 200 pieces of sculpture and found that generally speaking the zinc content increases over time. He suggests the Fahlerz of the Harz mountains, southern Germany, as a possible source (1970). The second is the analysis of lead isotopes, first conducted by Goucher et.al. (1976) and later by Willett (1995). Both Goucher and Willett conclude that Benin had a single source of lead for its castings, which differed from that of Ife or Igbo Ukwu. Craddock contends that trying to determine the origin of copper by its composition or that of its lead isotopes is probably a futile exercise because technological factors complicate every step of the way during the casting process. The only fairly safe attribution in his view might well be the copper from the Fahlerz of the Harz mountains in southern Germany, but only for the sixteenth and seventeenth centuries (1985:36).
8. The brass-smiths are one of a series of craft guilds constituting part of the urban population affiliated with the palace and working for the Oba and court. There is a high degree of internal specialization among the smiths; they are subdivided into guilds of brass-casters and blacksmiths who produce ritual weapons (*igun-ematon*), local lamps (*igun ugboha*), and keys, locks, and hinges (*igun eyaenugie*). The guilds are ranked hierarchically, with the brass-casters at the top, reflecting the high prestige of the material with which they worked.
9. These dates are tentatively suggested by R. E. Bradbury (1973: 17–43).
10. The variability of these traditions is illustrated by the fact that when Bradbury had interviewed Ine n'Igun Eronmwon earlier (1951/52 A-18), the Ine had told him that the caster from Ife came during the reign of Esigie, not Oguola, and that his name was Ezohe. Igueghae was his son.
11. Ryder notes that in 1714 the cargo brought from Benin included "20 marks of gold" (1969:138, n.1). A Dutch factor at Ughoton wrote on March 24, 1717, "The King also showed me three gold headbands"—although it is not clear that these were of local manufacture. The Dutch were interested in finding gold, and the director-general of the West India Company came to Benin City and from there went on a two-day journey to a place called Usea (possibly Uzia, in Ishan), where slaves gathered a small and unpromising amount of gold dust (Ryder 1969:163). Henry Ling Roth (1968 [1903]:31, figs. 36–40) illustrates some gold and gold-plated ornaments with typical Benin designs that were collected by R. Allman, the medical officer on the Benin Punitive Expedition. If gold was used at all, it must have been in very small quantities.

Gold

FRANK HERREMAN

Gold is worn and displayed as a status symbol in many cultures. Since the 7th century AD, precious materials were actively traded between West African peoples and Arab merchants across the Sahara to North Africa, Egypt, and Europe. African gold was often exchanged for copper and salt. Among many African peoples, copper was considered to be more valuable than gold. In the 15th century, European seafarers established direct contacts with Ghanaian chiefs and exchanged copper and brass for gold through trading posts along the coast of the Gulf of Guinea, often referred to as the gold coast. Until the discovery of the New World, much of the gold in Europe came from West Africa.

Sub-Saharan Africa has a long established history of metalworking that was preceded by the use of stone tool technology. While the origin of working with copper alloys can be traced back to Europe, or to Mediterranean influences, evidence of iron working and the ability to work with fire suggests that gold working techniques, including lost-wax techniques, were independently developed in Africa. Strong historical connections exist between gold and power in the establishment of pre-colonial states in countries such as Niger, Mali, Ghana, and Ivory Coast. The Akan-speaking peoples, including the Asante and Fante of Ghana, and the Anyi and Baule peoples from Ivory Coast; are particularly well-known producers of gold ornaments.

The Asante peoples of Ghana are perhaps the most prolific makers of gold ornaments. For centuries the Asante nation held important sources of gold, found in rivers or through mining. Since the 17th century, the king, or *Asantehene*, was the main beneficiary of the gold that was produced. Gold plays a major role in the founding myth of the Asante kingdom, whose main symbol and most important emblem of royalty is the Golden Stool. The Asante believe that at the founding of the Kingdom, the priest Komfo Anokye had a vision of the Golden Stool in the sky. A bell and a stool landed on the lap of the first king Osei Tutu. Since then, it is believed that the soul of the Asante kingdom resides in the stool which therefore is accorded a great deal of reverence.

Among the Asante and other Akan peoples, gold is considered the prerogative of kings and chiefs (Blier 1998: 139). It is used to make important status symbols and regalia such as headdresses, jewelry, and additional accoutrements. Asante people consider gold to be the sun's earthly complement. The king, like the Golden Stool, represents the soul and vitality of the nation, an idea that is reinforced by the abundance of gold worn as regalia. Gold has additional associations with the giving and safeguarding of life (Blier 1998:141.)

Mande-speaking peoples introduced lost-wax casting to Akan goldsmiths in Ghana, who transmitted the method to Baule and Lagoon peoples of Ivory Coast. The method of lost-wax casting consists of modeling an ornament in fine wax threads over a charcoal. The mold is heated to melt the wax and molten metal is poured in that takes the form of the wax mold. It is then invested in a clay mold cast (Garrard in Philips 1995: 441). Akan goldsmiths also hammered sheets of gold, a technique known as repoussé. Most known and documented Asante gold objects date from the 19th or early 20th century.

CAT. 103 A AND B

Ceremonial swords and rings
Ashanti peoples, Ghana
Gilded wood, iron, gold, shark skin. H. 76.2 cm. and 71 cm.
Charles and Kent Davis

These state swords have wooden handles covered with gold leaf. They are decorated with gold figural sculptures that were cast using the lost-wax process. The animals and humans represented refer to allegories that emphasize the *Asantahene's* sacred status. (F.H.)

CAT. 104

Lion ornament
Ashanti peoples, Ghana
Gold. L. 19 cm.
Charles and Kent Davis

CAT. 105

Lion ornament
Ashanti peoples, Ghana
Gold. L. 17.8 cm.
Mr. and Mrs. J. Thomas Lewis

CAT. 106

Soul washer disc
Ashanti peoples, Ghana
Gold. D. 15.2 cm.
Mr. and Mrs. J. Thomas Lewis

CAT. 107

Ornament
Akan peoples, Ghana / Ivory Coast
Gold. D. 10.2 cm.
Mr. and Mrs. J. Thomas Lewis

CAT. 108

Ornament
Akan peoples, Ghana / Ivory Coast
Gold. D. 8.9 cm.
Charles and Kent Davis

CAT. 109

Ornament
Akan peoples, Ghana / Ivory Coast
Gold. D. 7.6 cm.
Charles and Kent Davis

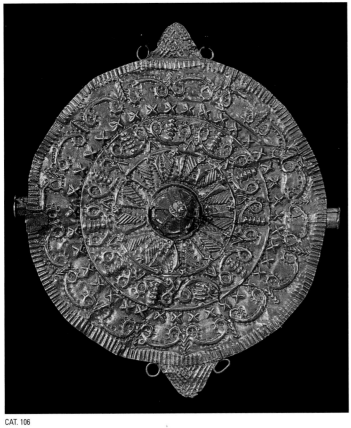

CAT. 106

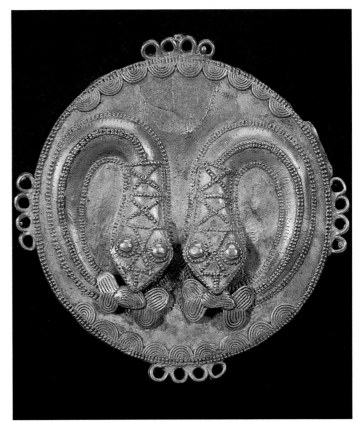

CAT. 107

CAT. 108

CAT. 109

Important Asante gold ornaments include the round soul disks (*akrafomonmu*) that are worn by the ruler, queen mother and members of the court (Cat. 106). These disks function as protective devices. These objects are associated with soul washers *(akrafo)*, officials that conduct the ceremonies to purify the chief's soul. Most soul disks bear abstract patterns while other types of gold ornaments, including royal regalia such as rings and garment attachments, are more figural. Impressive golden ornaments are attached to the ceremonial swords of kings and chiefs (Cat. 103-105). These figural attachments represent animals or anthropomorphic forms and illustrate proverbs and aphorisms that glorify the king and his supernatural capacities.

Gold is also used as a precious material among the Baule, Anyi and the Lagoon peoples of Ivory Coast. Many gold ornaments, including gold hair ornaments, are worn as secular status symbols (Cat. 107-109). However, ornaments may also be attached to regalia such as the crowns and caps of chiefs. Susan Vogel provides valuable information about the symbolic meaning and use of gold among the Baule peoples of Ivory Coast. According to her, the Baule regard gold as a powerful element that is associated with acts of reverence for ancestors. They create solid cast-gold ornaments, carved wooden objects covered with gold foil, and packets of unworked, or raw, gold nuggets or gold dust wrapped in bundles, hidden in the sacred family inheritance. This inheritance symbolizes the family unity and its identity. Each of the bundles represents a specific ancestor and any mishandling of the gold is considered a slight to that ancestor. Altogether, the gold of the different packages is considered a sacred inheritance, symbolizing the "force of the ancestors," and representing the "soul" of the family. Worked gold that is part of the sacred family treasure is brought out and displayed on special occasions, including major funerals. At the end of the funeral, gold ornaments are worn by surviving family members as part of the sacred family inheritance (Vogel 1197:195-202).

The use of gold has universal associations with wealth and prestige. There also are several important African contexts where gold is used to honor ancestor and royal authority.

Material
Differences
Art and Identity
in Africa

The Ephemeral and 'un-Transportable'

Fig. 5a, b.
Spring festival. Ga peoples, Prampram, Ghana, 1967.
The photos show symbolic marks that were painted
with perishable materials during the spring agricultural festival that is celebrated to ensure the coming of
the rains and the success of the crops. The paintings
are made of millet gruel, millet flour, and water.
Photo: Roy Sieber.

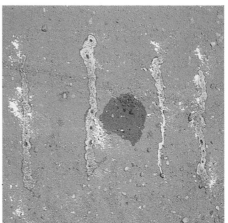

The Ephemeral and 'Un-Transportable'

FRANK HERREMAN

In most sub-Saharan cultures, works of art are created for functional reasons. They may contain the supernatural forces of nature and of ancestor spirits. Many of these works have an extremely limited useful life and are meant to be discarded, or replaced after a single or a few uses (Sieber and Walker 1987: 13).

Some of these ephemeral works have an even shorter life and cannot be reused. At the completion of their ritual use, they are either purposely destroyed by fire, dismantled, or left to decay in nature. In 1967, Roy Sieber attended an annual spring festival at Pram Pram in southeastern Ghana (figures 5a-b). He wrote that:

> "This event is meant to insure agricultural success and has been celebrated for at least a century and a half. The chief priest officiates wearing a costume ensemble that in photographic documentations has remained essentially unchanged for three generations. A critical aspect of the ceremony consists of the priest creating a "painting" on the ground at each of the paths or roads leading to the farms. Four lines of millet gruel refer to the hoed rows, the gruel, and sprinkles of millet flour symbolize the successful millet harvest, and the drops of water, the rains, and the fructifying agent. These "paintings" last only a brief moment before the wind disperses the flour, and the water evaporates. Priest and priestesses later in the ceremony walk over the traces. They have served their purpose. At the conclusion of the ceremony, the priest, a hoe in each hand, mimes planting and empties a vessel of water toward the ocean less than a mile away to attract the early rain clouds that can be seen gathering on the horizon. Clearly the importance of these gestures is not to create a permanent record but, like prayers, to effect or secure a result. Indeed, the test of the efficacy of the ceremony and of the priest lies in the future harvest of grain not yet planted."[1]

Sieber had mentioned the ritual in Pram Pram in an earlier publication, adding the following conclusion with regards to the "paintings":

> "As 'objects' they have no significance, but as events they are a vital but ephemeral part of the call to the spirits for rain and agricultural success" (Sieber and Walker 1987: 24).

The Spring Agricultural Festival at Pram Pram is a striking example of the many rituals that include forms of artistic expression that are short lived and not transferable. It also helps us realize just how limited our knowledge of other forms of artistic expression is, unless they were creat-

CAT. 110

Mask
Angola
Calabash, fabric, fiber, feathers. H. 57.2 cm.
Leonard and Judith Kahan

The exact origin and function of this mask is unknown. The structure consists of a fiber net on which calabash elements representing the eyes, nose, mouth and ears are attached. Another part of a calabash crowns the head. Ropes of fabric represent the hair. (F.H.)

ed in materials that are resistant to decay or were preserved in foreign collections. Over the last decades, art historians like Roy Sieber and cultural anthropologists have become more sensitive to these 'elusive' forms of artistic activities and the importance they take in the ritual activities of many African peoples. Some striking examples of these ephemeral and 'un-transportable' works of art have been assembled in this chapter to suggest the range of events that employ ephemeral materials.

1. Quoted from a note prepared for a manuscript to be included in this publication.

CAT. 111

Mask

Nkporo Ada, subgroup of the Igbo peoples, Nigeria
Bark, wooden framework, pigment, fiber. H. 100 cm.
Private Collection, Belgium

Mask like, made of bark attached to a framework and painted can be more than 6 meters high. Public dances may include more than hundred masks. The dancers' age range from five to the early twenties. (F.H.)
(Cole 1984: 167)

CAT. 112 (PAGE ON THE RIGHT)

Mask

Zombo peoples, Angola
Wood, pigment, feathers, raffia. H. 91 cm.
Pace Primitive Gallery, New York

The painted initiation masks that Zombo initiates wear have a fiber collar and feather crown. The wooden mask is re-used, the fiber attachment and adornments are occasionally replaced. (F.H.)

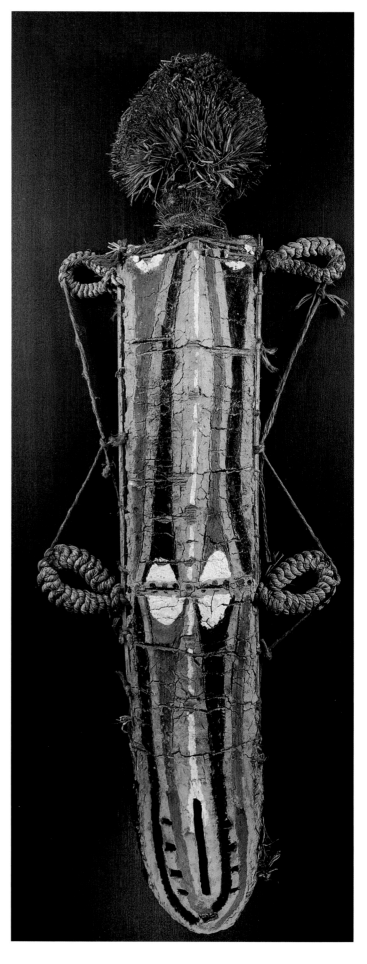

Leaf Masks Among the Bobo and the Bwa

CHRISTOPHER D. ROY

Almost all the peoples who live near the bend of the Niger River after it begins to turn south in east-central Mali, including speakers of languages in both the Voltaic and Mande language families, use masks made of leaves to represent the spiritual power of rebirth and new growth in the springtime. In Burkina Faso, such masks have been described or photographed among the Bwa, Bobo, Marka Dafing, Senufo, and other peoples; and in Mali, among the Bamana, Dogon, and Jula. The Jula people of northern Ivory Coast also use such masks.

Among most of these peoples, the masks represent the spiritual figure named Do (or Dwo, pronounced "Doe"). In Burkina Faso, the religion of Do appears to have originated among Mande speakers, primarily the Bobo, and to have spread to one Voltaic group to the east, the Bwa.[1] The Marka Dafing, a Mande group who penetrated the valley of the Sourou River in the 1600s may have carried the religion of Do with them, and adopted the use of Voltaic mask styles from their new neighbors, the Nunuma and the Winiama. Engravings published with Louis Binger's account of his travels to the great city of Kong in Ivory Coast in 1887–89 record the use of leaf or fiber masks to represent Do a century ago (see fig. 7). The religion continues to flourish, and ceremonies at which leaf and fiber masks representing Do appear are common occurrences in western Burkina each year from March to June.

Do and the masks that embody him among the Bwa are concerned primarily with life and new growth. Leaf masks, considered very sacred, are used most often in initiations and village purification or renewal ceremonies called *loponu*, but may appear briefly in Bwa or Bobo funerals or burials to honor the deceased if he belonged to a clan that uses leaf masks.[2]

The performer wearing the leaf mask becomes Do, and participates in rites that symbolize man's dependence on the forces of nature for survival. In this way "the human community is reintroduced to the cycle of nature, and therefore renews its forces, through the image of the vegetation that is reborn each year" (Capron 1957:104).

Throughout the villages of this region, men pay visits to sanctuaries of Do, sacred ancestral shrines in which the village chief and the priest of Do make numerous sacrifices. At the end of the ceremony, the leaf masks enter the village in a procession that includes all the men and women of the clans that are adherents of Do. Each compound of the eldest man of each clan is visited in turn, before the masks emerge from the village to dance in the fields.

Leaf masks are created in the bush country, early in the morning, when young initiates of the congregation gather wild vines and the leaves of the *karite* tree, a symbol of fertility. Fresh green leaves are taken from the first trees to develop new foliage in the spring, just before the rains begin to fall. The

Fig. 6
A leaf mask for the congregation of Do, at spring *loponu* ceremonies held by the Ye family in the southern Bwa village of Bagassi, March 1983, being used in the performance of a wild, spinning dance in the dry fields that will soon be planted in cotton.

Fig. 7
Leaf masks for the congregation of Do. Engraving by Edouard Riou in Louis Binger's *Voyage au pays de Kong et au mossi* (Paris: Hachette, 1892).

mask attendants (who do not perform) wrap the body of the performer in bundles of these leaves bound together with the vines so that every inch of the human body is concealed, from head to toe, and topped by a crest of dried grasses called *bwosonu* (*Loudetia togoensis*) or of white bird feathers gathered in the bush. The crests of masks in the southern Bwa village of Bagassi are made of feathers from large raptors, including eagles. Young performers have told me that it is very important that the costumes be applied correctly. If the vines to which the bundles of leaves are bound are wound too tightly, they constrict the flow of blood to the limbs and cause numbness or constrain the performer's free and rapid movement in the dance. If they are bound too loosely, they slip down the body during the performance and must be constantly adjusted.

The performer is not permitted to speak during the dance, for speech is a human skill. Similarly, according to the young performers I have spoken to, including Ye Florent, in Bagassi, no man-made objects or materials may be used, for Do is the god of nature, and only natural plant and animal materials may be used. Elsewhere, though, man-made materials are clearly visible in the masks: In other Bwa communities, I have seen masks adorned with small white metal cones attached under the chin; and among the Marka Dafing, strands of brightly colored yarn are woven through the masks' crests. In any case, most of the elements that go into each mask are re-created for every performance, and afterward are promptly destroyed.

The masks appear in the community at dawn, entering the village from the east, with the rising sun. They may perform throughout the day, and are not permitted to drink or eat while wearing the mask. When the sun sets, they leave the west side of the village and hurry as far from the village as possible before night falls. The bundles of leaves are pulled from the body, and the vines that held them in place are cut away. The eagle feathers that form the crests of some masks are saved for the next performance, and the rest of the materials that made up the mask are burned.

Among both the Bobo and the Bwa, the mask performance consists primarily of a rapid spinning that represents the creative power of God.[3] The performance is created around two basic steps: the young male performers leap high into the air and spin in a counterclockwise direction for as many revolutions as possible, re-creating the gesture of Wuro as he molded the earth from a ball of mud at the creation. Then, keeping their feet close together, they move

Fig. 8
Leaf masks (*kore*) at a funeral in the Dafing village of Mana, February 11, 1983. The leaf masks and attendants have arrived from the bush and are entering the courtyard of the dead man's family.

them in small rapid steps while holding their arms up and away from the body. This is the gesture or dance step that is most frequently depicted in the very rare representation of these masks in wooden or brass sculpture.

Although the Bwa and the Bobo are similar in several ways, especially in the lack of central political authority and their worship of Do, they hold different world views.[4] The Bwa are open and receptive to outside influences, and their society is in a constant process of change. They are quick to adopt new ideas or forms that they find useful, and to adapt or transform these discoveries to fit their own specific needs. The Bobo are far more conservative, preferring to preserve the purity of their traditions, and to remain faithful to "the path of the ancestors."

The Bobo creator god is called Wuro. He cannot be described and is not represented by sculpture. Bobo cosmogonic myths (*wuro da fere*) describe the creation of the world by Wuro and the ordering of his creations, which are placed in basic opposing pairs: man/spirits, male/female, village/bush, domesticated/wild, culture/nature, safety/danger, cold/hot, farmer/blacksmith. The balance between forces as they were created by Wuro is precarious, and it is easy for man, through the simplest daily acts, to pollute his world and throw the forces out of balance. Even farming, in which crops are gathered in the bush and brought into the village, can unbalance the precarious equilibrium between culture and nature, village and bush.

Wuro is an otiose creator God, for after creating a perfect world he saw he could not improve upon it; the world was perfect, and its balance ideal but fragile. This balance could be destroyed at any moment by any kind of change.[5] Wuro also sought to avoid confrontations with man, the most difficult of his creatures. He withdrew from the newly created world, leaving behind part of his own vital material, his son Do, the mask, to help mankind. Do is the materialization of one form of Wuro, and his principal manifestation.[6] Do is the major spiritual being through which communication between man and Wuro is possible and desirable in his role as the representative of men to their creator.

Wuro also left behind with man his two other sons, Soxo, the spirit of the bush, of vital force, and Kwere, the spirit that punishes with lightning and thunder. Events that followed the creation by Wuro are explained in a secret language that is taught during initiation.

Wuro is a god of action, whose creations are celebrated in the rapid swirling rotation of masks. Do is usually revealed to man in the form of a mask (in leaves for the original form; in fibers and with a wooden head for later forms), as bull-roarers and other objects that are kept near the congregation shrine. The Bobo use masks of the religion of Do in three major contexts: at harvest time in annual rites called *birewa danga*; in the male initiation (*yele danga*), which is their principal function; and in the burial (*syebi*) and the funeral rites (*syekwe*) of people who have been killed by Do, or of the elder priests of Do.[7] The Bobo have several words for "mask." In the north, masks are called *kore* (sing. *koro*), meaning "something that is old and venerable"; in the center of Bobo country, they may also be called *sowiyera* (sing. *sowiye*), meaning "a disguised man"; and in the south, it is referred to as *siye*, "the shadow man" or "the double." In addition, each mask has its own, personal name.

The most typical Bobo leaf mask is *birewa sowiye*, a mask that appears at the beginning of the performance season to sweep all impurities from the community. The head is made of the leaves of the *saxada* (*Guiera senegalensis*) and of the *nere*. The leaves of the West African mahogany tree form the body, and *saxada* leaves form the arms.

Leaf masks representing the initial and universal form of Do serve to integrate the individual into human society and to link the community of man with the natural world; fiber masks fix the individual in a social grouping, dedicated to one of the later forms of Do. These masks are important agents of socialization. The significance of these lessons is impressed on each new generation during their initiation, which is a major cultural rite.[8]

The Bwa believe that the world was created by God, named Difini or Dobweni, who abandoned man and left the earth when he was wounded by a woman pounding millet with her pestle. To act as his representative among man and as an intermediary between man and the forces of nature, Dobweni sent his son, Do. Although Do is androgynous, it is most frequently represented as male. Do represents the bush and its life-giving force, for the Bwa still depend on the bush for game and gathered food. He shows himself as the source of plant life and the power that gives fruit to man's work in the fields. Do is concerned with all ceremonies that insure the renewal of life.

In the Bwa culture, Do is represented by an iron bull-roarer that is called *aliwe* (meaning "he weeps") or *linyisan* ("he makes a sound"). The man who carries this Do whirls it about his head. The sound that is produced is low and vibrating: it is the voice of Do (*dotanu*). Do is also represented by leaf masks (*bieni*), which, because they must not resemble the creations of man, are made exclusively of wild plants: (vines, leaves, grasses) These leaf masks are used throughout Bwa country (see fig. 6). In the most southern area, called Kademba, near the Nunuma, Winiama, and Lela peoples, the "scarred-Bwa" (*nyaynegay*) people[9] use the wooden masks for which the Bwa are famous. Wooden masks represent spirit characters in family myths and have nothing to do with Do.

Among the Bwa, there is a basic and deeply rooted conflict between the Mande congregation of Do and the use of wooden masks on the Voltaic pattern. Bwa oral traditions make it clear that the use of leaf masks representing Do is a very ancient practice and that originally all Bwa clans were adherents of Do and used leaf masks. Clans that use the *bieni* state emphatically that those who use wooden *nwamba* masks have borrowed the practice from the Nunuma and Winiama to the east. In regions where they exist in the same community, especially in the south, they often comprise rival congregations and never appear together at the same ceremony at the same time, and in some villages never dance on the same day.

In many southern Bwa villages, notably Dossi and Bagassi, clans using each type of mask live side by side. Those who have continued to honor Do with leaf masks regard the adoption of wooden masks as heresy and as an attempt to wrest religious authority from its traditional source, the local earth-priest. They have instituted strict prohibitions that prevent members of wooden-mask clans from participating in rites of Do. Clans that have adopted wooden masks and their magic from the Nunuma and Winiama are aggressive and proselytizing. Songs that accompany the wooden mask performances often insult the clans that persist in using leaf masks, and refer to them as filthy primitives. As a result, fights frequently break out between these clans and have, in the past, resulted in the intervention of the local military police. This has occurred in both Bagassi and Dossi. In Bagassi, the extended Nyumu family (whose lineage extends to Dossi as well) has acquired the use of wooden masks from the east, while the Ye family continues to use leaf masks for the congregation of Do. The members of the two families constitute the two major factions in the village, taunting each other in the streets, engaging in brawls in local bars, and shouting insults from the sidelines during performances of rival families' masks. This conflict between traditions that are, in turn, Mande and Voltaic in origin, reflects the clash of conservative and innovative traditions on the larger scale in central Burkina Faso. The older, more established tradition is Mande (the congregation of Do), while the newer, innovative tradition in the south is the congregation of wooden masks acquired from the Voltaic Nunuma and Winiama.

In contrast, masks in the northern and northwestern areas of Bwa country participate peacefully in the congregation of Do. In the north, the use of wooden masks was acquired from the Bobo to the west, rather than from Voltaic groups in the east, as is the case in the southern Kademba area. Here, leaf masks integrate man into his natural environment in the spring, when farmers leave their villages to work in the fields. Wooden masks, in contrast, reintegrate man into village society following the harvest, when farmers must return to village society and conform to rules for correct social behavior. Wooden masks serve as agents for social control in these villages. Masks of leaves and other materials growing in the wild represent nature, while masks carved of wood with costumes of cultivated fibers represent village culture in the nature/culture balance that is basic to the Bwa worldview.

The original text of this paper was presented at the annual meeting of the African Studies Association in Denver, Colorado, on November 21, 1987, for a panel titled "Exploring the Lands of Do," chaired by Patrick McNaughton, Professor of Art History, Hope School of Fine Arts, Indiana University.

1   There are three groups of people in the region who have been called Bobo: the Bobo-Fing, the Bobo-Oulé, and the Bobo-Nieniégué. The first are the true Bobo and do not recognize any relationship with the Bwa. The latter two comprise the Bwa, and are quite distinct from the Bobo. The Bobo-Oulé (the name given to them by the Jula, and which means "red Bobo") call themselves Bwa. The southern Bwa, who live in the region called Kademba, are called *nyaynegay* or *nieniégué* (meaning "scarred Bwa," because of the elaborate scars applied to their faces and bodies).
    A great deal of confusion on the part of scholars of Voltaic culture has arisen from the practice of early French ethnographers (especially Tauxier) of referring to the Bwa as Bobo or as Bobo-Oulé, with the implication that they are related to the Bobo-Fing.

1   In 1983 Jean Capron told me that Do leaf masks were only used to celebrate new life, not death, among the Bwa. In contrast, Guy Le Moal has written that leaf masks are used for burials and funerals among the Bobo (*Les Bobo: Nature et Fonction des masques*). My own experience is that leaf masks are used for burials and funerals among both the Bobo and the Bwa.

2   During a leaf-mask performance I attended in Bagassi in 1983, the masks of the Ye clan danced beneath a great tamarind tree in the dry dusty fields in which cotton is planted. Each mask spun wildly, leaping and thrusting his arms wide in an athletic pirouette. The feathers that formed the masks' crests were often dislodged by the spinning dance and fluttered to the ground, to be gathered quickly by a young boy wearing a carved wooden pendant representation of Do incarnated as a leaf mask.

3   Both Guy Le Moal and Jean Capron seem to agree that the Bobo and the Bwa should be considered to be distinct ethnic groups, who have drawn on a common pool of religious belief, resulting in many cultural similarities. Among the most important common characteristics is the congregation of Do represented by masks of leaves. See Capron 1973:24–32.

4   It is from this religious basis that Bobo resistance to change of any kind stems. The imposition of colonial rule or of a new military government from Ouagadougou threatened that balance of the Bobo world.

5   During the historic period, Dwo appeared on many occasions, but to individuals and in special places that people remember to this day. These are villages whose locations are known but which no longer exist. Le Moal calls these numerous appearances "subsequent representations." Among these forms, the Bobo distinguish between the oldest, considered to be the most important, and those that appeared afterward. The first of these "subsequent representations" is, in reality, a triple form, comprising Kwele Dwo, Dwosa, and Sibe Dwo. This form is the object of numerous important congregations, and the followers of these congregations are called *sibe*. All other subsequent representations are called *Dwosini*.

6   This is a secondary function, and not all masks of all Bobo clans attend these rites. Masks seem to participate in funerals much more frequently in the Syankoma area in the south, near Bobo-Dioulasso, than in the north.

7   The different levels of knowledge are explained to Bobo boys in several steps spread out over a period of fifteen years. Masks play an essential role in initiation because they reestablish and reinforce the cosmic order created by Wuro, and restore the balance and the rhythms of the natural world and of the community. Each of the new steps in the initiation is punctuated by important ceremonies when the initiates dance with several types of masks.

8   See note 1 above.

Fig. 9
Mbari to Ala at Umugote Orishaeze, with human visitors. This picture shows well the scale of a medium sized *mbari* house that was opened to the public in 1962. Photo: Herbert M. Cole, 1966.

Fig. 10
Partly completed mbari at Umuedi Nnorie. The rough figure in the foreground is called "child of the bad mortar" and is erected before the "yam" figures are started, in a ceremony that draws off any evil that may affect the building process.
Photo: Herbert M. Cole, 1966.

Earth Renews Earth
Igbo *Mbari* Houses

HERBERT M. COLE

An architectural setting of sun-dried mud is populated by seventy-five or a hundred images of people, animals, gods, and imagined creatures, all constructed of sacred clay from termite hills, which are the homes of spirits. The entire edifice is dedicated to an important local deity, usually Ala, who is Earth. Gods normally call for the great sacrifice of building *mbari* houses when things are going wrong, for example when divination reveals that Earth has been wasted, polluted by the blood of war.

Nothing could be more transient than an mbari, especially since once the house is opened it may not be repaired. Were it not for the metal roofs that have been built on these structures since about 1935, they would perish quickly in the heavy rains of the land near Owerri. Even with a good roof, erosion begins nearly as soon as the mbari is opened to an astonished public. The community that builds each new mbari is competing with others recently opened nearby. People want their mbari house to be grander than those of their neighbors—larger, and with more elaborate sculpture, finer painting, and figures never seen before. Their building is the essence of competition.

The sculptured and painted images are many and varied: good and beautiful things, ugly, terrifying, and forbidden things, and things that cause laughter; village scenes and scenes only heard about or hoped for. The "crown" of the house is the goddess or god whom it celebrates, often but not always Ala, Earth. Ala is queen of the gods, an honored, titled woman, font of morality and tradition, mother of the village, of yams and cassava, of all animals. Other figures in the house are her "children": a bicyclist, a woman at a sewing machine, dancers, a goat-headed man, a shameless woman; the ugly half-man-half-ape Okpangu, creature of didactic folktales who attacks foolish or incautious people; a white man emerging from a hole in the ground, a fanciful elephant or ostrich, a hunter, a woman giving birth, an office building, and many others. Then, painted high on an outside wall up under the roof are the sun, the moon, and the rainbow rendered as a double-headed python. These paintings are completed toward the end of a lengthy construction

Fig. 11
Front side of the *mbari* to Ala at Umuedi Nnorie, showing the earth goddess before she was painted. Photo: Herbert M. Cole, 1966.

process during which peace—should there be inter-village fighting as there was frequently in the nineteenth century—is declared and all families must contribute to the building effort. During this period new farms are planted, mock or actual relationships are formed, and multiple sacrifices are made to the ancestors and to all of the local gods. The *mbari* is opened to the public after the specially chosen spirit workers who have built it are purified and return to their families; the unveiling is a grand festival, with dancing and the finest of foods. Villagers are proud of their symbolic new community.

The reasons for transient, ephemeral building materials are clear. Sacred earth is used to model the world anew, and this very transient and friable earth, plus the numinous spirit anthill clay of which the figures are made, must melt back into the ground of being, Earth herself, eternal mother of all. Earth thus replenishes and nurtures Earth, as the community and life itself are also rejuvenated. The cycle of life is complete. From the ashes of a declining old village arises one refreshed and reborn. The painted celestial symbols confirm the *mbari* as not only a revitalized village but as a whole new cosmos.

Fig. 12
"Yam," actually anthill clay, being pounded in a mortar by one of the female spirit workers, just as actual yam is pounded to make the delicacy called fufu. The clay is soaking in the large enamel bowl. Umuedi Nnorie, Imo State, Nigeria. Photo: Herbert M. Cole, 1966.

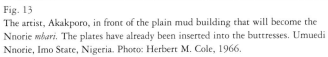

Fig. 13
The artist, Akakporo, in front of the plain mud building that will become the Nnorie *mbari*. The plates have already been inserted into the buttresses. Umuedi Nnorie, Imo State, Nigeria. Photo: Herbert M. Cole, 1966.

Fig. 15
Foreground: pounding "yam" as in fig. 12. Background: Akakporo's assistant, Godwin, modeling one of the *mbari* figures. Umuedi Nnorie, Imo State, Nigeria. Photo: Herbert M. Cole, 1966.

Fig. 14
An artist's assistant, Jasper, holding a stick that will become part of the armature of an *mbari* figure modeled in "yam" (puddle anthill clay). The clay, recently dug from an anthill, lies in a pile behind him. Umuedi Nnorie, Imo State, Nigeria. Photo: Herbert M. Cole, 1966.

Fig. 16
Mbari spirit workers preparing (grinding) pigments from colored riverine clays specially collected for the mbari. Umuedi Nnorie, Imo State, Nigeria. Photo: Herbert M. Cole, 1966.

Fig. 17
The "Big Animal" (*eravwe gangan*) and one of its "children" (*omedjo*) preparing for its entrance, at the festival for the Urhobo water spirit Ohworhu (*Ohworhu Ode*). Photograph by Perkins Foss and Susan C. Moore, September 1972 at Evwreni, Delta State, Nigeria.

Eravwe: An Ephemeral Urhobo Water Spirit Masquerade

PERKINS FOSS

A particularly spectacular masquerade prepared by the Urhobo, of the western fringe of the Niger River Delta in southern Nigeria, appears as an ephemeral art form, one that exists for just a few weeks only to be taken apart and given back to the rivers from which it originally came (fig. 17-18).[1] The Urhobo celebrate the water spirit Ohworhu with a complex display of masks, elaborate costume, especially composed music, and, in the masquerade's most elaborate form, raffia creations that are carried in elaborate danced performances.[2]

A common Urhobo phrase in praise of water spirits is *Edjo n'ame rhe*, which literally means "The spirits come from the water," though a looser translation would be "The spirits are the water" or, conversely, "The waters are the spirits." This circular approach to water spirits is vividly exemplified by the Big Animal (Eravwe Gangan), as it is called in the Urhobo community of Evwreni. The form appears on the final day of Big Ohworhu (Ohworhu Ode), a festival that is fully celebrated only once every ten years. Eighteen feet long, five feet high, and six feet wide, it is constructed out of a frame of split bamboo with an overlay of woven dark and light strips of the split midribs of the oil palm (*Elaesis guineensis*)(Hutchinson and Dalziel 1936: 390), which in turn have been covered with large black spots. Fringes on front and sides are constructed of loose-flowing raffia, emphasizing the undulating motion of the form as it is carried in dance. The facade, peaked as a roof, is decorated with two bold strips of cloth, white over red. Nine bells hang across the front, as well as a live baby chicken.[3] On either side of the peak of the facade are ears and broomlike whiskers. The entire ensemble is borne aloft in dance by three individuals: two inside and a third who follows behind, supporting the creature's elaborate tail. In the four days between the first and second performances for Ohworhu, chosen members of the leaders of Ohworhu, the Unugbedjo ("Mouths of the spirit,"), construct this elaborate creature in secret, and in the moments before sunrise it appears in the open space in front of the central market (*oguan r'afieki*).[4]

Ohworhu is known in most southern Urhobo communities, as well as in those of the neighboring Isoko. In all instances the roots of the water spirit and its associated rituals are closely tied to the populations of the Western Ijo (Izon), who live immediately to the south, in the mangrove swamps that comprise the actual delta of the Niger River. The Urhobo have long had stable relationships with the Ijo.[5] Since at least as far back as the middle of the eighteenth century, Urhobo fishermen have traveled on a seasonal basis south of the Forcados River to establish what are identified on European maps as "Urhobo Fishing Camps" throughout much of the western delta.[6] While working the waters of their hosts, they also had the opportunity to absorb much Ijo lore and culture, especially the dances, music, and performance of the Owu masquerades.[7] While each Urhobo community has its own version of the circumstances of the arrival of Ohworhu, one constant holds: that the water spirit and its dance, music, costume, masquerade forms, and principal musical instruments were brought north by a returning fisherman who had "met Ohworhu" while among the Ijo.

The actual performance of Eravwe begins about one hour into the four-hour festival of

Fig. 18
The "Big Animal" (*eravwe gangan*) greets the musicians and elders, at the festival for the Urhobo water spirit Ohworhu (*Ohworhu Ode*). Photograph by Perkins Foss and Susan C. Moore, September 1972 at Evwreni, Delta State, Nigeria.

Ohworhu Ode (Big Ohworhu). Upon a signal from the drums, the lesser dancers, called *emedjo* or "children of the spirit," shift to the sidelines as the large creature slowly rises from its resting place. As it catches the rhythm of the drums, it undulates forward to the cult leaders at the far end of the arena. When nearly pressing into their faces, it rears up its front and receives blessings of chalk (*oorhe*) and gin (*udi*). Next, in a smooth, quick motion, it reverses its direction, then travels sideways until its fringe brushes up against the tightly packed crowd at the edge of the area. This actual contact with Eravwe is seen as particularly auspicious: at this moment, citizens of Evwreni, say they are receiving special blessing from the waters.

Urhobo lore holds that during day-to-day life the water spirits (*edjo r'ame*) do not stay on land but reside in the waters. On those occasions when a community wants to celebrate the wealth that has come from the waters, or to offer pleas for safety when traveling in often dangerous circumstances, they invite them to land.[8] Festival time is always felt to be potentially difficult and dangerous. One analogy states that if one plays host to extremely powerful, indeed dangerous friends, one goes to great lengths to assure that there are no mishaps. At the end of a festival the rite of Edjenekpo or "Spirits must leave" sends these powerful forces back to their watery abode. In the case of the Big Animal, immediate steps are taken to start the spirit on its way. The festival leaders escort the animal, with its dancers still inside, to a remote piece of water. Here they disassemble the construction, leave the raffia and bamboo at the waterside, and immediately depart. On the fourth day after the festival ends, they quietly return and cast the partially dried vegetation onto the water. It is said that at this point the floodwaters have started to subside, and that they will carry the form away.

1. Initial research on the Urhobo was sponsored in 1966–68 by the Nigerian Department of Antiquities (now the Nigerian Commission for Museums and Monuments). Subsequent study in 1971–72 was supported by a generous grant from the Foreign Area Fellowship Program. I published an initial description of the Ohworhu festival (see Foss 1973). For another perspective, on the Isoko version of the festival, see Peek 1983. For further reading on the Urhobo see Bradbury and International African Institute 1964; Hubbard 1948; and Otite 1980.

2. Thanks go to Oviede Aramuemu Aki (1910–1993), choreographer, artist, dancer, and *Otota* (senior spokesman) of the Ohworhu festival, with whom I spoke at length about Ohworhu. Also of immense help were Julius Itefue, William Okorotete, and Susan C. Moore.

3. The number nine (*rhin-rhin*) is itself of ritual significance, as it is conventionally seen as a pun on the term for "long life" (*rin-rin-rin*)—an appropriate reference for the front of this highly charged, magical form. The Urhobo also allude to the sounds of bells as appropriate for communication with the spirit world.

4. The festival cycle is timed so that the floodwaters that surround much of Evwreni will be at their peak on the day of the final performance. This is seen as a particularly auspicious moment, for it is said that when the Niger Delta peaks, the water spirit forces are nearest.

5. In recent years the dynamic of power-sharing among the Urhobo, Isoko, Itsekiri, and Ijo has been challenged by the petroleum industry, with all groups struggling to receive what they see as their fair share of the new wealth. What once was social and political maneuvering has given way to physical violence and near anarchy.

6. See the maps of the Federal Surveys, Nigeria, in 1960, 1966, and 1970.

7. Ijo performance is studied in Horton 1965, and in Anderson and Peek 2002. A particularly tantalizing but unsubstantiated linguistic relationship seems to exist between the terms "Owu" and "Ohworhu."

8. Horton has written at length about similar beliefs held by the Kalabari Ijo, who live in the far eastern corner of the delta (see Horton 1960).

Kalengula: Ephemeral Masks
Among the Luntu and Neighboring Peoples of the Democratic Republic of the Congo and Angola

CONSTANTINE PETRIDIS

Throughout the southern part of the Democratic Republic of the Congo and adjacent Angola, different peoples have produced and used masks made entirely from perishable materials such as plant fibers, feathers, and hide. Ephemeral mask heads rarely are found in Western collections and generally have not been studied in any depth. Although the adjective "ephemeral" is used here with reference to mask heads in highly fragile materials with a rather short life cycle, it can in fact also be applied to more permanent masks and figure sculptures made of wood. As is generally known, the life span of wood in Africa is limited and ancient sculptures in this material are far and few between.[1]

According to a number of scholars, among certain peoples in Central Africa more temporary fiber, feather, and/or hide mask heads would predate the production and use of more permanent wooden examples.[2] Arthur Bourgeois (1996:405) distinguished between two basically different macro-styles reflecting the diverse ethnic expressions in masking: predominantly wooden helmet-shaped masks found among populations living near the northern edge of the savanna and nearby forests, such as the Suku and the Kwese, and predominantly resin-and-fabric masks made by peoples across the savanna to the south, such as the Yaka and the Chokwe. Both macrostyles are relatively well known, due primarily to the interest scholars have had in the context of the *mukanda* boys' puberty ritual in which they appear.[3] More recently, thanks to art-historical field research conducted by Annemieke Van Damme in the early 1990s, the non-wooden, constructed masks of the Yaka-related Nkanu people have been lifted out of the shadow of their Yaka and Suku peers.[4] A third masking tradition to be associated with the same puberty ritual context, which is not included in Bourgeois's classification, is that of the *minganji* fiber masks of the Pende peoples. Although ample visual documentation on these Pende masks (*minganji*; sing. *munganji*) is available, they have not been treated extensively as yet.[5]

In this short essay, I will shed light on a little-known fiber mask type called *Kalengula*, which has been found among the Luntu and a number of other peoples in the south-central and southeastern part of the Democratic Republic of the Congo. It is striking that this mask type, like many other non-wooden masks in the Kasai River region, appears in many different contexts. Actually, within one and the same culture, the exact same mask type can perform on such varied occasions as a funeral, a chief's investiture ritual, or the entertainment of the community or a visitor. Moreover, *Kalengula* is shared by different neighboring peoples. I have previously discussed the use, function, and iconography of this interethnic mask type at some length in an article in the journal *Arts d'Afrique Noire* (Petridis 2000a).

The name *Kalengula* has been recorded among such diverse peoples as the Luba Katanga (or Shankadi), the Songye, the Mputu, and the Luntu. It is most commonly given to a miter-shaped non-wooden mask, made either from plaited fibers or from a cloth-covered twig armature, although some wooden examples of this type of *Kalengula* have been collected as well.[6] Other characteristics are the tubular eyes and the transversal crest above the forehead, which is often decorated with a rim of feathers. One of the best-known field photographs of a non-wooden *Kalengula* mask is that made by William Burton among the

Fig. 19
Kalengula among the Luba Katanga. Kabongo or Kisengwa village, Democratic Republic of the Congo, 1936. Photo: William Burton, courtesy Africa-Museum, Tervuren [E.PH. 3452]

Luba Katanga in 1936 (fig. 19). A very similar mask, consisting of a fabric-covered miter-shaped armature sporting a rim of long feathers, was photographed in the company of yet another fiber mask by Paul Timmermans among the Nsapo, a division of the Eki Songye subgroup, in the village of Djidu in 1956 (see Petridis 2000b:fig. 6). However, as we will see, the same mask name also was given to two formally quite distinct types of fiber masks. Although the mask type's shape is basically the same among the different cultures mentioned above, it is not sure whether this also holds true for its meaning and function.

Among the Luba Katanga the name *Kalengula* also refers to a society with which the mask would have been associated, but due to lack of any further details the structure and purpose of this society are not known. Among the Songye, at least among the Bala subgroup of the village of Lupupa Ngye as studied in the field in 1960 by Alan Merriam, the name *Kalengula* was given to a mask as well as to the male "cult group" to which it belonged (Merriam 1982:26). Here, the mask was mainly meant for entertainment and described as comical, although he who wore it was supposedly in trance and possessed by his ancestral spirits during the mask performance.[7]

Around 1926, Casimir d'Ostoja Zagourski made a series of photographs showing what seems to be a *Kalengula* masquerader among the (Bakwa) Mputu (fig. 20). Leo Frobenius (in Klein 1988:13) considered the Mputu to be an eastern subgroup of the Luluwa. In fact, the German explorer himself recorded the name *Kalengula* for a mask he saw among the "Bena Kapelle," whom he viewed as another eastern Luluwa subgroup (Frobenius in Klein 1988:26; see also Petridis 1999a:92 n. 6). In Zagourski's photographs the *Kalengula* masquerader is accompanied by women wearing beaded crowns like those called *nkaka* of members of the Mbudye association and adepts of the Bulumbu possession cult among the Luba Katanga and Tabwa. Among the Luntu, members of the Bukalenga bwa Nkashaama _ the so-called leopard society, which also acts as patron and sponsor of a number of mask types, including *Kalengula* _ are always accompanied by a masquerader during their public appearances. However, it cannot be confirmed whether a similar type of leopard society has ever been in vogue among the Mputu. Furthermore, neither the Mbudye association nor the Bulumbu possession cult has ever been reported among the Mputu. As a matter of fact, it also remains an open question whether members of the Mbudye association and Bulumbu

Fig. 20
Kalengula (?) and female dignitaries among the Mputu. Sankuru River region, Democratic Republic of the Congo, 1926. Photo: Casimir d'Ostoja Zagourski (from *L'Afrique qui disparaît!* Series 1, no. 32), courtesy The Metropolitan Museum of Art, New York

mediums among the Luba Katanga and Tabwa have ever made use of masks at all.[8]

In 1955, while on an expedition for the Museum of the Belgian Congo, as the Africa-Museum in Tervuren was then called, Albert Maesen recorded the name *Kalengula* with the names of three other masks among the Luntu subgroup Bakwa Ngula in the village of Beena Tshimbayi.[9] His sketch and photograph of the *Kalengula* masquerader show a man wearing a typical miter-shaped mask head made of plaited fibers with tubular eyes. Masks of this type are preserved in the Anthropology Museum of the University of Zurich and in the Africa-Museum in Tervuren (see Petridis 2000a:fig. 2; 2000b:fig. 5). However, it is unclear whether a similar type of fiber mask has ever been made or even used by the Bindi or the Kongo(-Dinga), as suggested by Marc Felix (1987:12-13 fig. 3, 30-31 fig. 3). Among the Luntu, the *Kalengula* masquerader appears at initiations and funerals of members of the Bukalenga bwa Nkashaama association but may also dance outside the framework of the leopard society for the entertainment of the villagers and occasional visitors or to celebrate the ordination of a Catholic priest.

As I pointed out earlier, Leo Frobenius (in Klein 1988:26) recorded the name *Kalengula* for yet another type of mask made of fibers among the Luluwa. However, Frobenius's Luluwa *Kalengula* is formally similar to a type of fiber mask which later researchers, such as Albert Maesen (1954-55, 43:12-13) and David Binkley (1990:fig. 1), have generally identified as *Munyinga* among the Northern Kete and the Southern Bushoong. In fact, Frobenius (in Klein 1987:43) also recorded the name "*Kalengola*" for a similar mask type among the Northern Kete. The name *Munyinga* was first reported by Hans Himmelheber, who photographed and collected such a mask during his field trip in 1939 in the then Belgian Congo among the Byombo people (fig. 21). The little-known Byombo are generally grouped with the Kuba, but their culture seems to differ in many ways. Aside from

Fig. 21
Munyinga among the Byombo. Ngandu village, Democratic Republic of the Congo, 1939. Photo: Hans Himmelheber, courtesy Museum Rietberg, Zürich

Munyinga _ often with a nose made from the beak of a hornbill _ they also have produced two types of wooden masks: a male character called *Mulwalwa* and a female one called *Cimwana*, rare examples of which are preserved in a number of private and public collections. The *Mulwalwa* mask is sometimes also attributed to the Northern Kete.

Munyinga has been more thoroughly documented by David Binkley, who researched it in the context of the boys' puberty ritual among the Southern Kuba complex, comprising Northern Kete and so-called Southern Bushoong *matoon* villages, in the early 1980s (1990, 1996). "The ascribed purpose of [the boys' initiation ritual] is to transform the novices … into full participating members of the adult community. To remain uninitiated … is to be socially equated with women and children" (Binkley 1996:46). *Munyinga*, which represents a warrior, is one of the male masks to appear during the initiation and coming-out ceremonies among the Northern Kete and Southern Bushoong.

Compared to its female counterpart *Kamakengu*, only one example of *Munyinga* was made per initiation ritual and its construction was entrusted to a skilled elder. During village dances, *Munyinga* as the chief of the forest camp and most important mask was at the head of the line in which masks, titleholders, and novices proceeded from the forest camp to the edge of the village. *Munyinga* was also the first mask to dance with the novices on the village's central dancing square. *Munyinga* may go to the village to beg food for the novices and also acts as a messenger between the forest camp and the village.

Finally, the name *Kalengula* has also been given to a third fiber mask type, an example of which, currently in the National Museum of Ethnology in Lisbon, was exhibited in a previous exhibition of the Museum for African Art (see Herreman 2000:cat. 60). Masks of this type have been field-photographed in Angola by A. de Barros Machado in 1948 and by an unknown photographer before 1958 (fig. 22) (see also Bastin 1961:fig. 2; Herreman 2000:figs. 6-7). Firsthand data by Mesquitela Lima (1967) and by Albert Maesen (1954-55) make it clear that these masks should be attributed to the closely related Kongo(-Dinga), Lwalu, and Mbala _ the last not to be confused with their namesakes of the Kwango River region in southwest Congo _ rather than to the little-known Matapa as suggested by Manuel Jordán (2000:82-84). In Angola they are generally called *Ngongo wa Changa* while in the Congo they bear the name *Shibingidi* (Lima 1967:244, 246; Maesen 1954-55, 33:7).[10] Lima (1967:244) does mention, however, that the Matapa do use a different mask with a similar name. Like among the Kongo(-Dinga) and the Lwalu, this Matapa variant also is danced within the context of the circumcision ritual.

The *Ngongo wa Changa* mask is made of black-colored netting with a beard of fibers from the *punga* plant (*Triumfetta cordifolia*), and the eyes and mouth are made of interlaced fibers from the *kajana* plant (*Eremospatha cuspidata*). A similar skullcap sports a tuft of feathers from birds locally called *kanga* and *kolonvu*. This masquerader plays an important role in the boys' circumcision ritual, called *lubinde* according to Lima (1967:244) and *lubindi* according to Maesen (1954-55, 33:5), leading the initiates, accompanying the ritual specialist in charge, and presiding over a number of rituals. According to Maesen (1954-55, 33:8-9), however, the masquerader begs a present from the initiates' fathers in the village after their sons have been released from their seclusion in the forest.

Considering what has been said in the introductory paragraph, it is very likely that more new traditions of fiber, feather, or hide mask heads will continue to be discovered. Unfortunately, as the case-study of the *Kalengula* mask testifies, because of the lack of a genuine interest by some of the people who observed such masks during their fieldwork, many details about their meanings, uses, and functions have not been recorded and our knowledge remains very superficial. We also know very little about how these masks are made and what kinds of different materials are specifically used. What is clear, however, is that non-wooden masks have a wide geographic distribution and that stylistically they often present an even stronger challenge to the stubborn notion of "one tribe, one style" than some of the equally widely distributed wooden mask traditions. The relationship and interaction between the wooden masks and their non-wooden counterparts in one single ethnic culture is of special interest and deserves further investigation. In the end, the distinction between wooden masks and non-wooden masks will probably prove to be of little relevance from the perspectives of the masks' makers and users.

Fig. 22
Ngongo wa Changa among the Lwalu or the Kongo(-Dinga). Canzar village, Angola, prior to 1958. Photographer unknown (after *Flagrantes da vida na Lunda*, Subsídios para a História, Arqueologia e Etnografia dos Povos da Lunda, Publicações Culturais da Companhia de Diamantes de Angola, 37. [Lisbon: Museu do Dundo, 1958], p. 176).

1. In fact, the two most notable exceptions both originate from Central Africa. One is the repeatedly published ninth-century animal head in the Africa-Museum, Tervuren, Belgium, which was found in central Angola in 1929 (see Van Noten 1972). Recently, the late Marie-Louise Bastin (1997:119) identified this particular object as a container rather than a mask or headdress, as it had long been referred to in the literature. The other archaeological wood carving is the post topped with a human head now in the Museum of Dundo in Angola, which was excavated along the Upper Kwango River in northeastern Angola. This sculpture has attracted much less attention than the Tervuren Museum's animal head, but from an art-historical point of view it is perhaps more interesting since this object type has been produced up to this day and occurs in a wide geographical area in Central Africa (see Petridis 1999b:142-44).

2. This hypothesis has been advanced by Redinha (1956:14) and Bastin (1993:79-80) with reference to the Chokwe. More recently, Marc Felix (1998:358) proposed a "technical and typological" chronology in 11 steps, with "plane face coverings in leaves, skins, and gourds" at the beginning and "wooden face masks without superstructure" at the end of the hypothetical evolution.

3. For more information on Yaka and Suku masks, see especially Bourgeois (1984, 1991). On Chokwe and Chokwe-related masks, see especially Bastin (1982, 1984, 1993) and Jordán (1998). Referring to "wooden and resin-coated polychromed bark-cloth masks supported by a framework of bent branches and associated with the *mukanda* circumcision institution in parts of Zaïre, Angola, Zambia, and Zimbabwe (Rhodesia)," Daniel Crowley (1982:207-8) speaks of a *mukanda* style. This style, "shared by at least 11 ethnic groups," exemplifies what the author calls a "supra-ethnic, institution-connected" art style (1982:215, 217).

4. Aside from a number of shorter articles and chapters, Annemieke Van Damme recently wrote a catalogue published in conjunction with an exhibition of Nkanu art at the National Museum of African Art in Washington, D.C. (Van Damme 2001). The recent Museum for African Art catalogue *In the Presence of Spirits*, devoted to the collection of the National Museum of Ethnology in Lisbon and including an article by Van Damme, contains many examples of constructed, non-wooden masks of various Central African peoples (see Herreman 2000).

5. For more information on the Pende *minganji* masks, see de Sousberghe (1959), Maesen (1975), Ngolo Kibango (1976), and de Sousberghe and Mestach (1981). In passing, I would like to draw attention to yet another *mukanda*-associated masking tradition, about which as good as nothing has been published. During his tenure at the Institute of the National Museums in Kinshasa in the 1980s, Nestor Seeuws made a number of field photographs that show two types of constructed mask among the Kwese. One of these Kwese mask types, which was field-collected by Léon de Sousberghe, is preserved in the Africa-Museum, Tervuren, and was published by Arthur Bourgeois (1991:fig. 18).

6. Thus, Hans Himmelheber (1960:406) recorded the name *Kalengula* for a bixylous mask he collected among the Kalebwe Songye subgroup in 1939 and which is today preserved in the Museum der Kulturen in Basel (see Petridis 2000a:fig. 4). Another wooden mask which could possibly be identified as a Songye variant on the *Kalengula* type is the piece in the collection of Donald and Florence Morris in Detroit (see Petridis 2000a:fig. 5). This latter mask is also somewhat similar to a Konji mask called *Mukonkole*, some examples of which have been collected for the Africa-Museum, Tervuren, by Albert Maesen in 1955 (see also Maesen 1954-55, 54:47-48; Petridis 2000b:figs. 2-3).

7. However, according to unpublished field data of Cynthia Anson, reported by Alan Merriam (1978:96-97), among the Kalebwe Songye subgroup the name *Kalengula* refers to masks used by "the juvenile level of membership of the Kifwebe association."

8. Some scholars have proposed a link between the so-called lion masks of the Luba Katanga, a famous example of which is kept in the Africa-Museum, Tervuren, and the Mbudye association (see Neyt 1993:207-8; Roberts 1995:cat. 156). With regard to the Tabwa, Allen Roberts (1990) has also suggested interesting iconographic connections between the *nkaka* beaded crowns of Mbudye members and Bulumbu adepts and the rare beaded masks which were discovered in the field in the mid-1970s by Marc Felix.

9. Two other non-wooden masks would be used in the context of the Bukalenga bwa Nkashaama association among the Luntu: *Bwadi bwa Mukenge* and *Bwadi bwa Kabwalala*. Formally similar to *Kalengula*, these two masks are also danced with exclusively for the entertainment of the community. Unfortunately, however, I have not been able to find illustrations of either of these mask types and I cannot confirm whether a mask of alleged Luntu origin in the collection of Marc Felix can be related to one of these mask names (see Felix 1992:29-30). Albert Maesen (1954-55, 52:102-3) also made a sketch of a non-wooden miter-shaped mask, called *Bwadi bwa Nkashaama*, not unlike *Kalengula* in the village of Tshiloolo among the Konji, closely related eastern neighbors of the Luntu. However, Maesen is the only author to mention this mask name, literally meaning "the mask of the leopard," and the Bukalenga bwa Nkashaama leopard society of the Luntu does not seem to exist among the Konji.

10. Lima (1967:244) further reports that another Kongo(-Dinga) fiber mask type, called *Byanyansala*, differs little from *Ngongo wa Changa*. Two other similar non-wooden Angolan Kongo(-Dinga) mask types that are discussed and illustrated by Lima (1967:248-49) are called *Ngongo wa Burimbu* and *Ngongo wa Vunyi* (or *Bumputu*). Albert Maesen (1954-55, 33:8) also mentions a second type of non-wooden mask among the Congolese Lwalu and Mbala called *Ngongo wa Manaangu*. The masquerader wearing this mask similar to *Shibingidi* but with a crest of ram's hair runs through the village to announce the initiation of the new candidates into the Ngongo association and its rituals. However, I should point out that Rik Ceyssens has not reported any of the above-mentioned mask names during his field research among the Lwalu and Kongo(-Dinga) in the Democratic Republic of the Congo (personal communication, Jan. 20, 2003; see also Ceyssens 1993a, 1993b, 1995).

Material
Differences
Art and Identity
in Africa

Accumulating Power

Enhancing Spiritual and Secular Power through Accumulating Materials

FRANK HERREMAN

This section brings together objects that are made from a wide range of materials. The chapter opens by presenting examples of objects, including power figures, reliquary figures, emblems and symbols of authority that make use of a wide array of applied mineral, organic, or animal substances. It is followed by two essays; the first by Manuel Jordán discusses metaphorical meanings imbedded in the selection of objects that comprise a Chokwe diviner's (tupele) basket. The essay, by Michele Chadeisson, examines the meaning of the term 'Power Object' and the reasons it has replaced the term 'fetish'.

In Africa, numerous cultures make art works that combine a wide range of materials. The accumulation of materials may add prestige, or function to satisfy purely aesthetic concerns. It is however important to note that certain materials are used because they are believed to contain potent spiritual powers. Ritual specialists combine these different power substances and activate them to diagnose maladies, or seek protection against calamities for a single client or for the entire community. The combination and accumulation of different power substances can be understood through an examination of power figures that occur among different central African peoples. They include include different Kongo groups like the Yombe and Vili peoples; and the Teke, Yaka (Cat. 124, p. 166) Suku and Songye peoples.

Wyatt MacGaffey describes the *nkisi* (pl. *minkisi)*, power figures of the Kongo peoples (Cat. 122-123, p. 164) as containers for empowering medicines (in Verswijver 1995:285). These medicines include white clay, associated with the dead; and other medicines which metaphorically indicate the kind of powers to be invoked. Different medicines are sealed in packets, attached on or inserted in the body of the figure so that if the materials are not effective, they can be removed and replaced by more effective substances. *Minkisi* may function in a judicial capacity, seeking out wrongdoers and punishing them, or as benevolent objects that foster prosperity and fertility among women and crops.

The large power figures from the Songye peoples are among the most impressive sculptures of Central Africa. Similar like the Kongo *minkisi*, the Songye *mankishi* are consulted to solve individual problems, or collective communal issues. Dunja Hersak notes that these figures are not displayed, but rather used privately as protective or therapeutic devices (in Verswijver 1995: 285). The larger figures (Cat. 125-126, p. 168) are used to meet communal needs, whereas the smaller ones are used by individuals (Cat. 127, p. 170). Hersak also mentions that the Songye peoples do not value their statues for visual aspects alone, but rather for the effective nature of the ingredients that are inserted into or attached to the figure. These substances are vegetal, mineral or animal and are activated by the *nganga*, healer and or diviner specialist. D. Hersak divides the power substances that are attached or inserted to the Songye *mankishi* in two groups: those that have an aggressive content, "capable of counteracting the source of malevolent action such as the claws of a leopard, the scales of a venomous snake or the feathers of a hawk"; and a second category that consists of substances that have a positive effect on the client. She also mentions that it is the

CAT. 113

Axe
Teke peoples, Dem. Rep. of the Congo
Iron. L. 41 cm.
Etnografisch Museum, Antwerpen

Figure: Kafigeledio
Senufo peoples, Ivory Coast
Wood, fabric, feathers, earth. H. 55 cm.
Private Collection, Milano, Italy

CAT. 115

Emblem of leopard spirit
Ejagham peoples, Nigeria/Cameroon
Animal skulls, turtle shells, horns, wood, leather, iron,
bamboo, gourd, raffia, woven plant fiber. H. 155 cm.
Charles and Kent Davis

CAT. 116

Mask

Grassland Region, Cameroon
Wood covered with copper, hair, fabric. D. 38 cm.
Mr. and Mrs. J. Thomas Lewis

nganga who defines the "power and value" of the statue. The Songye believe that the ritual specialist is the true creator of the power figure, while the sculptor is the provider of the "figural receptacle."

Outside of Central Africa, the use of power figures also occurs among different groups of the Republic of Benin and Togo, including the Fon and Ewe peoples. They create figures that carry medicinal substances, and are mostly used as household devices against different kinds of maladies (Cat. 117).

Among the Senufo peoples of Ivory Coast, the *kafigeledio* figure (Cat. 114) incarnates a spirit capable of rendering verdicts, performing divination, applying sanctions, and inciting powerful forces that range from helpful to destructive (Bouttiaux-Ndiaye in Nicolas 1997: 251). The *kafigeledio* consists of a wooden figure that is entirely covered by a fabric costume. A hood that covers the head is often crowned with feathers. The figure holds small twigs, attached to the hands. These can be moved separately to designate the person who will fall victim to its powers. *Kafigeledio* statues are often covered with sacrificial substances.

The accumulation of materials also occurs in another category of objects that function as secular emblems of closed societies or make the social position of its owner visible. Among the Ejagham peoples of the Cross River region, border of Nigeria and Cameroon, men are expected to become members of an all-male leopard spirit society called *ngbe*. Some of the *ngbe* sub-associations have their own emblem named *nkpa* (Cat. 115) (Nicklin in Philips 1995: 373). This emblem usually takes the form of a panel that is displayed in the association's lodge. The rectangular emblem consists of a mat, strengthened at the edges with lengths of palm midrib and decorated with raffia tufts. Attached to the mat are skulls and horns of beasts like goats, a cow and other animals consumed at the foundation feast. Most important is the presence of one or more membrane drums. Such drums are used by the society's crier in making announcements. A baton-like staff and a palm-fiber broom are also attached. The brooms are carried in procession as devices to sweep away hostile 'medicines'.

CAT. 117

Two attached power figures with gourd in between
Ewe peoples, Togo
Wood, gourds, cowry shells, beads, fibers. H. 25.4 cm.
Private Collection

Copper: A Material for Kings, Chiefs and Ancestors

Materials that are rare and valuable are often used in the creation of important ritual objects. Perhaps the most precious of all imported materials was copper. It was applied on status symbols like fly-whisks and axes. Because of its capacity to reflect light it also may cover parts of ancestor and power figures, and give them a more dramatic presence.

Chiefs among the Teke peoples of the Malebo Pool, Democratic Republic of the Congo, make use of richly decorated ceremonial axes, named *imbo*, as symbols of authority. Figural axes are used to (Cat. 113), represent an ancestor. The blade that emerges from his lips illustrates the power of the chief's word, intervening at the conclusion of a palaver (Gwete in Verswijver 1995: 301). Teke axes may combine different techniques of metal working. The forged blade is decorated with chiseled geometric motifs. Copper sheet, covering the top of the handle, is hammered to model the ancestor's head with the representation of the striated facial scarifications and tags are used to model the coiffure. The wooden handle is entirely covered with copper tags, hammered sheet and wire. The precious nature of copper to embellish the axe is used to emphasize the importance of its owner.

Among the Bamun and neighboring peoples in the Western Province of Cameroon the most precious masks are covered with fine sheets of copper that are pinned all over the face (Cat. 116). The application of iron to model the eyes, lips and open mouth, enhances the

CAT. 118

Reliquary figure
Kota peoples, Gabon
Wood, plant fiber, metal strips, shell. H. 42 cm.
Galerie Jacques Germain, Montreal

CAT. 119

Reliquary figure
Kota peoples, Gabon
Wood, metal sheets, ivory, nails. H. 58.4 cm.
Corice Canton Arman and Arman

CAT. 120

Reliquary figure
Bembe peoples, Congo
Wood, fabric, ivory. H. 52 cm.
Private Collection

realism of the fully modeled face. Masks such as these are said to be owned by the *Fon*, king.

While the ceremonial axes of the Teke peoples are intended to be used by living chiefs, copper and brass is also applied to the making of reliquary and ancestor figures. Different peoples, including the Kota, Obamba, Mahongwe and Massango of Gabon (Cat. 118-119) make abstracted anthropomorphic figures that serve as protectors of the relics of important village ancestors. The reliquaries lower ends are stuck into the relic container, with the head and openwork lozenge shape below protruding from the basket's top. Together, the reliquary figure, the basket, and its content or relics, should be seen as a full figure (Herreman in Philips 1995: 236). The head and upper part of the reliquary figure are mostly covered with metal, including iron, brass and red copper. A combination of brass, copper or iron plate, decorated with hammered repoussé motifs, or strips from the same materials, are attached with iron nails to the wooden structure of the figure. The eyes are represented by shell, porcelain, or bone. One of the main reasons to make use of copper and brass is that it reflects light, which is believed to deter unwelcome visitors to the shrine where the relics are kept.

The Bembe peoples of the Democratic Republic of Congo, make use of European fabrics to create effigies that function as recipients of ancestral relics. The body of the figure (Cat. 120) with spread legs and arms is made of two fabrics that are wrapped and stitched around the body. A checkered fabric covers the torso and the other fabric with abstract design covers the arms and legs. On top of the head a topi is modeled and ivory is used to represent the eyes. The Bembe insert relics into the torso of these figures. Just like the application of important brass or copper among the Teke, Kota and their neighboring peoples, exotic fabrics are considered as precious material among the Bembe peoples.

Many materials that are used in ritual practices to alleviate suffering are believed to contain spiritual forces. In a more secular context, the addition of precious materials enhances the prestige of its owner.

Tupele Divination Materials and Their Relative Symbolic Attributes

MANUEL A. JORDÁN

Introduction

The efficacy of Central African figurative sculpture is often hinted at in its compelling forms and visually expressive qualities. From the generally calm and dignified sculptural idioms of the Luba to the audacious aesthetics of Songye *mankishi* and Kongo *minkisi* figures, characteristic poses, gestures, and overall physical demeanor accord a sense of agency, an indication that a sculptural creation may be the embodiment of an animate force.[1] A figure, however, is just an object until it is activated by a ritual expert through invocations and with the aid of propitious medicines, substances, and additive materials. These cumulative materials, including animal, human, vegetal, mineral, and manufactured parts, help induce a spiritual entity to reside, embody, or manifest itself through a sculptural form. Specific types of addenda may further enhance the entity's supernatural powers or strategically direct it toward a desired goal. Choice materials may be added to petition a spirit for specific favors, ranging from health and good fortune to the active pursuit of retribution on one's enemies.[2] Without these powerful and symbolic additive parts, many figurative forms are practically devoid of their directive, their essence, and their identity. This is most apparent when one considers the so-called "power figures" of the Kongo, Teke, Yaka, Songye, and their related neighbors, many of which look incomplete when stripped of their ritual ingredients—an action that would render them deficient in their original contexts.

Whereas these materials may be considered additive parts to figurative sculpture, they take center stage in divination arts. The *mboko* divination gourds of the Luba and Songye, and the *ngombo ya chisuka* divination baskets of Chokwe and related peoples, contain a myriad of objects that symbolically represent a microcosm of life.[3] In these containers, natural items such as earth substances, stones, shells, vegetal matters, and animal and insect remains are combined with manufactured objects including ceramic shards, glass, beads, metal rings, coins, plastic pieces, and carved or constructed artifacts, including multiple figurines. After tossing or repeatedly shaking these symbolic objects within a divination container, a diviner is able to draw meaning from the configuration they take in relation to each other. The diviner uses this information to seek cause and resolution for a variety of problems (theft, bad luck, illness, infertility, or other calamity) brought forth by a client or clients.[4]

These articles of divination, called *tupele* (sing. *kapele*) by the Chokwe, are semantically flexible: their meaning and significance vary according to both the physical orientation of the objects within the container (up, upside down, sideways) and which objects are adjacent to one another. Additionally, their meaning changes in relation to the particularities of the case brought to the diviner.[5] Where these modes of divination are practiced, moreover, there is no strict classification system in which all objects are understood as materials with definite ascribed meanings. Even diviners working as associates may identify or define a divination piece differently. Certain general associations do seem to exist, however, and some definitions may be shared by diviners outside the context of a divination session.

CAT. 121

Divination basket: *ngombo*
Chokwe peoples, Angola
Wood, fiber, fur, metal, horn, seed pods, bones, quills, leather, rattan. D. 35.6 cm.
Museum for African Art, Gift of Cecilia S. Smiley

This *ngombo* still retains a variety of materials that once made it an efficient instrument of divination. The double-rattle with bells was used at the beginning of divination sessions by the *nganga* to call or get the attention of his tutelary ancestral spirit, *hamba kayongo*. The pieces of cloth attached to what actually is the front of the basket (facing a client), served to add a dynamic quality to it when the diviner tossed the *tupele* objects on the air before letting them settle on the front rim for his interpretation. The pieces of cloth may have served as backing material for additional animal pelts. Present is the fur of a genet, a nocturnal animal that is considered agile and evasive. Symbolically, genet furs relate to invisibility and the diviner's ability to reveal that which is hidden (like the truth behind a case); also his talent in evading evil or negative forces. The bundle with pointed sticks is made from either weasel or mongoose skin, with the same symbolic associations. A diviner may use a stick to mark his basket with red clay or white chalk; or hand it to a client at the end of a divination session to indicate guilt or innocence. For this, the diviner holds one end of the stick and the client the other. Then the diviner proceeds to mark the stick with a white (innocent) or red (guilty) line. Last, the stick is broken in two and the client bites the half-stick, then circles it around his/her head, and tosses towards the back. Additional pieces include an antelope horn that is plugged with another horn and with potent medicines or *vitumbo*. This is an important item that the diviner stuck in the ground as a "screen of truth" to filter false information from clients. Diviners often add water in the cavity of such horns so they can "see images" related to the cases they mediate. The glass or mirror embedded on the basket's front rim, also associated with water, serves a similar purpose as an additional revelatory implement. The red seeds around the glass are commonly described as the "eyes of witchcraft," indicating the diviner's constant battle with antisocial forces. This glutinous element marks one of four cardinal points around the basket's rim.

This *ngombo* includes carved wooden representations of the Chihongo (male) and Pwo (female) mask ancestral characters. Among several other possibilities, these *tupele* may indicate an affliction where the mask characters persistently harass a victim in his or her dreams. This affliction could be considered ancestral and it may be resolved if the afflicted individual follows the wish-

The rest of this essay will focus on some tupele definitions provided by two Zambian diviners, Mr. Chipoya (Chokwe/Luchazi) and Mr. Sasombo (Luvale), based on the contents of their divination baskets. Some additional information comes from explanations provided by Lunda diviner Mr. Chitofu Sampoko and Chokwe ritual expert Mr. Bernard Mukuta Samukinji. This information is presented in the interest of recording firsthand accounts on the diversity and significance of divination materials in thought and practice.[6]

Animal Parts

Jimbo and Nkaka: The Aardvark's Hoof and the Pangolin Scale

Mr. Chipoya identifies an aardvark's hoof (*jimbo*) as one of the most important tupele in his divination basket. He explains that if it shows at the front rim of the basket after the objects are tossed, this means that the client has been suffering from an affliction for a long time. The diviner adds that aardvarks act like witches in that they dig holes in graveyards, move at night, live underground, and are very difficult to see (a metaphor for invisibility).[7]

A related kapele is a scale from a pangolin; both the animal and its scale are called *nkaka*. Both Mr. Sampoko and Mr. Samukinji explain nkaka as a symbol representing ancestral influence. The pangolin, like the aardvark, also digs, moves at night, lives underground, is hard to see; in this case these qualities are equated with the nature of ancestors or the animal's ability to access the ancestral realm (below ground). It is significant that the word "nkaka" also means "grandparent," suggesting that language (pangolin/grandfather/ancestor) as well as the animal's behavior help to define this symbol in its association with the ancestral world.

Antelope Horns and a Warthog's Tooth

Horns from different-sized antelopes appear in divination baskets. Mr. Chipoya explains that a duiker-horn kapele called *lusende lua kahi*, obtained from an animal captured with a trap, indicates that the client has been ambushed by witches or evildoers. A related piece, also a duiker horn, reveals that an individual has died of natural causes rather than through the premeditated acts of his or her enemies. The latter horn is collected from an antelope who has died from natural causes rather than being trapped or hunted in any way. In this case the way the antelope died is associated with the details of the client's problem.

Mr. Chipoya mentions that an additional duiker horn with small perforations (*likuma*) around its open side suggests that a client is ill as a result of his or her own actions. Every hole in the horn represents an instance when the client has insulted a neighbor. In such a case the client is considered responsible for his or her own condition; nobody else is at fault. Mr. Sasombo mirrors this explanation in discussing a similar horn with holes in his own basket: he calls it *mazu vituvituvi* and equates the holes with "piercing words," meaning "there is too much talking and too many insults."

According to Mr. Chipoya, the fact that antelopes stay in groups, with one "leader" who looks out for danger, is relevant for all of these horn tupele, which apply to cases involving groups of people. They bear on cases, for example, where one individual is unable to get along with family or neighbors, endangering the social balance.

Mr. Sasombo explains that the social behavior of warthogs is also observed in relation to group human actions. A kapele in the form of a warthog tooth (*chihenge*) reveals that an individual who has confessed his or her guilt did not act alone in causing harm. The diviner explained that just as warthogs always travel in groups, so do some evildoers.

es of the deceased relative who is upset. Correlated with *tupele* that suggest witchcraft, the masks may be interpreted as "creatures" sent by evildoers to harm their victims. The carved figurine that seems to be in a seated position, with elbows resting on the knees and both hands on its chin, represents the influence of a male ancestor. The smaller one in a standing position with one hand on the chin is the female ancestor. A figurine with one raised arm is a unique anthropomorphic representation. One figurine with two raised arms, and holding its head on the sides is interpreted as a "crying hypocrite." The piece with two figurines, one behind the other, indicates a procession to a funeral. The *kapele* suggests the imminent death of a victim. Miniature representations of a penis and a vagina relate to gender, infertility or impotence. A one-legged figurine may represent a "violent death." The miniature drum or mortar may suggest the mode of ritual healing to be followed, or need for specific medicines to redress a client's affliction. An X-shaped piece is probably the representation of a currency copper cross and it may be associated with jealousy, theft, and material wealth. Two miniature rifles are included in this ngombo, one probably addresses hunting problems, and the other may be a representation of a "night gun" or supernatural weapon of witchcraft. A miniature dog relates to hunting and/or the diviner's ability to see invisible things as dogs are attributed with those qualities. A canoe representation relates to an "extraordinary journey through a consequential path." A small ring-like piece is a bracelet and indicates inheritance. The small bird is a kapele that relates to infertility; birds eat seeds after they are planted, not allowing them to germinate. Other natural and found objects included in this basket are discussed in the article. (Manuel Jordán)

The Monitor Lizard

For Mr. Sasombo the dried jaws of a monitor lizard (*musevu*) represent a person who makes promises but changes his or her mind. The kapele has to do with distrusting someone because he or she is inconsistent in behavior and therefore suspicious. This reflects the monitor's "inconsistency": it sometimes walks on land, sometimes swims in rivers, sometimes climbs in trees.

The Invisible Genet

Mr. Sasombo and Mr. Chipoya explain the common occurrence of genet pelts and parts (such as paws) in divination baskets in relation to invisibility. Genets are considered evasive, tricky creatures with the ability to hide from sight. The metaphor extends to humans who "cover up" their true intentions. Both diviners accordingly "lift" the skins to reveal the secrets or evil intentions that others hide. The reverse side of this is that they also use genet pelts to conceal their materials (or make them invisible) from evildoers.

The Feather Bullet and the Night Gun

Red feathers from the head of a touraco bird, or *ndua nganga*, were "caught in the air" by Mr. Chipoya after evildoers shot him with a "night gun." The supernatural bullet was disguised as the bird's head. The diviner includes the feathers in the basket to illustrate his prowess in combating evil, and as kapele revealing that such a weapon has been employed against one of his clients.

A miniature rifle, carved or manufactured, in divination baskets is identified as a "night gun" (*uta wa ufuku* or *kaliloze*). Combined, the touraco feathers and gun kapele assert a diviner's suspicions that a client is under attack through powerful supernatural weapons. Mr. Chipoya mentions that the uta wa ufuku is made with material from human bones collected at the graveyard. To treat a patient who has been shot by such a bullet, the diviner uses an antelope horn as a suction cup to extract each bullet from the body of the afflicted individual.

Plant/Vegetal Matters

Seed of the World and Seed of the Heart

According to Mr. Chipoya, a large, round, flat seed that is dark in color, called *lifuchi*, represents "the whole world." The lifuchi relates to the power of chiefs over all things and to the ability of diviners to "see it all." In divination this seed tells the diviner whether "things are in order" (in balance) in a larger-than-local context. Mr. Sasombo similarly describes lifuchi as representing "the world," and mentions that this kapele helps him ot "see things far away."

A different seed, *chindawa*, looks like a miniature bicycle seat. Mr. Chipoya explains that the midline of this bifurcated seed relates to two sides of something, so that the seed is used as a metaphor for conflicts or "quarrels" that divide families into opposing sides of an argument.

Another seed, called *muchima*, is small and reddish in color. To Mr. Chipoya it represents a heart—specifically the rooster's heart he had to swallow during his initiation as a diviner. The rooster heart is the same as his tutelary ancestor's heart. When divining, Mr. Chipoya sporadically makes deep grave sounds that seem to originate from his solar plexus. He explains that these sounds occur when his *hamba kayongo* (ancestor that guides him in divination) communicates with him through the rooster's heart he swallowed.

Fig. 23
Chokwe/Luchazi diviner, Mr. Chipoya, with his divination basket.
Photo: Manuel Jordán, northwestern Zambia, 1991.

Fig. 24
Detail of Mr. Chipoya's divination basket, including multiple tupele symbols.
Photo: Manuel Jordán, northwestern Zambia, 1991.

Fig. 25
Mr. Chipoya tossing objects within his basket during a divination session.
Photo: Manuel Jordán, northwestern Zambia, 1991.

Fig. 26
Tupele materials rest at the front of Mr. Chipoya's basket for his interpretation. Photo: Manuel Jordán, northwestern Zambia, 1991.

The Seed That Breathes

A strobile, or the seed or fruit of a coniferous tree, represents the diviner's hamba kayongo, his protective or tutelary spirit. For Mr. Chipoya the shell represents the diviner himself while the seed inside, "which shakes like a rattle," signifies the spirit that aids him to "see" in divination. He identifies the spirit as that of his late father (actually his maternal uncle), Sakanengo. A hole atop the piece allows the spirit to "breathe."

Mr. Sasombo provides a contrasting explanation for an identical piece in his basket, saying that the strobile, called *livale*, "tells him" that somebody is "hiding something." The rattling seed inside means there is something concealed that the diviner needs to define. Mr. Sasombo's hamba kayongo is represented in his basket by the tip of a gourd with incised striations. He explains that this kapele could mean that a client is suffering from an ancestral affliction requiring that the client become a diviner. He adds that this means that beer must be brewed as part of the healing process and it must be served in a gourd container (this honors the ancestor).

Awkward Roots

Mr. Chipoya identifies two plant roots with zoomorphic shapes as the hyena (*munguli*) and "an animal that walks upside down" (*kahwehwe*). These, he explains, are creatures of witchcraft. The hyena specifically walks strangely, moving in one direction but looking in the other, as if the animal were going two ways at the same time. For Mr. Chipoya evildoers mimic this "trick" of hyenas by sending hyenalike creatures to harm their victims by confusing them. To look back while walking is also considered a gesture of distrust, and is associated with wrongdoing.

Another root that derives symbolism from its morphology is a small, spiral one described by Mr. Sasombo as an indication that the client is keeping thoughts to him- or herself. The spiral is perceived as turning inward, and tells the diviner that the client is hiding information. The diviner must make the spiral turn outward to bring the truth to the surface.

Gourd Piece and Problems That Multiply

A round flat segment from the bottom of a gourd with wartlike protrusions is a kapele that for Mr. Chipoya uses scabies as a metaphor. He notes that those suffering from the disease first have a spot that multiplies when it is scratched. Similarly, the kapele indicates that a particular problem may have unforeseen ramifications unless properly addressed.

Mr. Sasombo includes a similar round gourd fragment, without the warts, in his divination basket. In relation to some anthropomorphic tupele, this kapele may indicate problems with pregnancy that may be reversed with proper treatment.

Corncob and More Insults

A piece of a corncob without kernels, called *chihungu*, tells Mr. Sasombo that a client's whole family is against him or her, because of insults the client has made toward them. Every hole in the corncob is an insult. Unlike the antelope horn with holes described by both Mr. Chipoya and Mr. Sasombo (see above), this piece does not necessarily mean that the client is at fault. If the corncob and the horn with holes appear together in the basket, however, the client is definitely suspect.

Honeycomb and Basketry Piece

Mr. Sasombo explains that a piece of honeycomb (*chinyingi*) allows the diviner to tell whether a client's statements are true or false. If the diviner makes an assertion that the client refutes, the diviner may toss the objects in the basket to see if chinyingi shows. If it

Fig. 27
Luvale diviner, Mr. Chitonji Chinyama Sasombo,
with his divination ensemble. Photo: Manuel Jordán,
northwestern Zambia, 1991.

Fig. 28
Detail showing Mr. Sasombo's divination basket and
the double rattle he uses to call his tutelary ancestor to
aid him in divination. Photo: Manuel Jordán,
northwestern Zambia, 1991.

does, the diviner knows that the client is lying or trying to confuse him. A related kapele called *mandamba* takes the form of a miniature fiber basketry piece. It indicates that a client may be complaining of problems that he or she has actually caused.

In the cases of both the holed antelope horn and the corncob, the cavities they feature are associated with words uttered (insults). The small cavities in the honeycomb and in the surface of the tightly woven basketry piece similarly relate to words, this time those that represent misinformation.

Found or Manufactured Items

Shells and Material Wealth

Mr. Chipoya explains that a small ball of glutinous materials with an embedded shell, called *chimbi ya kusemuka*, indicates jealousy between brothers and sisters. A shell itself (*pashi*) relates to something beautiful, valuable, or symbolic of status and wealth. This kapele indicates that a sibling is attempting to harm another in order to obtain what rightfully belongs to the other. Similarly, Mr. Sasombo says that tupele made from shells indicate jealousy or theft between relatives. He mentions that shells are shiny and are treated like money. Both diviners explain that beads in their baskets represent currency, value, or wealth as well.

Glass Tears and Darkness

A piece of clear glass called *masoji*, or "tears," indicates that a person is crying because of somebody else's death. Mr. Chipoya says that appearing with an anthropomorphic figurine whose arms are to the sides of its head (a figure interpreted as a crying hypocrite), this glass would indicate the client is actually at fault for someone's death, but it can also refer to another individual named through the divination session. Both Mr. Chipoya and Mr. Sasombo identify a piece of dark glass as *ufuku*, meaning "night" or "evening time." The night gun uta wa ufuku shows what can happen in the darkness of night, but ufuku, according to Mr. Chipoya, may relate to an eventual healing process that must be pursued at midnight or from one evening until sunrise the next day.[viii]

The Bundle of Death

Kufwa—the word means "death"—is also a miniature bundle of earth, cloth, fibers, and roots collected in a graveyard. The bundle resembles a corpse, wrapped in cloth and hung on a pole for carrying at the time of burial. According to Mr. Chipoya and Mr. Sasombo, this kapele usually relates to a death that has already occurred, but it may also suggest someone's imminent death.

Basketry Spiral and Time

Mr. Sasombo explains that a small spiral made using a basketry technique imitates the beginning of the construction of the divination basket. Called *kaputu kambango*, it means "the beginning of something." This kapele relates to concepts of time, from a precise start to the current state of some condition or event. It may tell the diviner that an illness is at an advanced stage.

The Sun Button

A common shirt button included in a divination basket indicates the specific time when an affliction started. Whereas a fragment of dark glass indicates night, Mr. Sasombo calls the button *likumbi*, a name also used to refer to the sun, daytime, or a day's time. The button must be white, and its four holes (for the thread to attach it to a shirt) are symbolically associated with the cardinal points and the cycle of the sun, which in turn reflects the cyle of time.

Conclusion

The explanations of tupele above are not intended to provide monolithic definitions for divination materials or symbols. A danger of a list of even a few of these items is that it may suggest some form of functional categorization, but one always comes back to the realization that the randomness and apparent chaos of throwing them all within a basket is more consistent with their multireferential, often ambiguous symbolic nature.[ix] The idea of a kind of symbolic "cookbook" also rubs against the grain of these divination ensembles. Perhaps the best notion is to see the explanations above as working definitions provided by diviners outside a ritual context.

It is worth noting how these materials gain meaning through factors such as visual correlation and metaphor (a root looks like a hyena, whose behavior is equated with human distrust and wrongdoing), language and semantic associations (the name for the pangolin and its scale, nkaka, is also the name for "grandparent" or "ancestor"), and metonymy (the kufwa bundle, made with grave-collected materials, imitates a corpse and is associated with death). Wyatt MacGaffey (1991) presents information critical to our understanding of similar materials and symbols in well-documented Kongo minkisi. These pervasive materials, whether part of a divination ensemble or configured as addenda to figurative sculpture, are not peripheral in Central African thought systems; rather they are crucial to an articulation of meaning that is intertwined with human experience. Through such materials the brokerage of symbolic knowledge by outstanding individuals is made tangible, actively addressing ordinary human conflict through extraordinary means.

1. For examples, see Nooter Roberts and Roberts (1996), Hersak (1986), Félix (1987, 1995), and Lehuard (1989).
2. See MacGaffey (1991) for documented information on related materials in the context of Kongo *minkisi*.
3. See Nooter Roberts and Roberts (1996) for a discussion of divination items in relation to memory and history, and Jordán (2002) for an essay on diverse divination implements used in Central Africa.
4. See Peek (1991), Pemberton III, ed. (2000), and LaGamma (2000) for insight into a number of divination art forms used throughout Africa. See Rodrigues de Areia (1985), Martins (1993), Fontina (1997), and Jordán (1996, 2000), for divination practices among Chokwe and related groups.
5. See Rodrigues de Areia (1985) for the most thorough and comprehensive publication on *tupele* to date.
6. The information presented here was documented between 1991 and 1993 while I was working with Mr. Chipoya and Mr. Sasombo in Zambia. For a more thorough discussion of these symbols and accounts provided by other diviners see Jordán (1996, 2000). I have opted not to include carved figurative tupele in this essay in order to focus on lesser-known materials. See Rodrigues de Areia (1985) or Jordán (1996, 2000, 2002) for information on those.
7. For related definitions and a throrough study of animal symbolism in African art, see Roberts (1995). For a theoretical approach to symbolic thought in divination among the Lunda-Ndembu see Turner (1967, 1975).
8. All the diviners I worked with in Zambia would ritually treat cases of ancestral affliction in the evening. Cases of witchcraft required rituals that lasted through the night into daylight.
9. See Turner (1967) for a discussion of the multireferential nature of symbols.

CAT. 123

Power figure: *nkisi*

Kongo peoples, Dem. Rep. of the Congo
Wood, clay, feathers, fibers, glass beads, seeds,
pigment. H. 25.4 cm.
Cecilia S. Smiley

CAT. 122 (LEFT)

Power figure: *nkondi*

Kongo peoples, Dem. Rep. of the Congo
Wood, iron, mirror, fiber, fabric. H. 73.7 cm.
Corice Canton Arman and Arman

The figure is spiked with nails and iron blades. They
testify to the oaths and promises exchanged between
the *nganga*, diviner or healer, and his client. Large figures are often associated with leaders. They serve as
guardians and protectors of the village. The *nganga*
continually modifies the figure through inserting the
nails and blades into the figure. The abundance of
blades and nails testifies that this power figure handled
a great number of cases. (F.H.)
(Boutiaux-Ndiaye in Nicolas 1997: 223).

A French Perspective on African "Power Objects": Travel, Philosophical and Anthropological Accounts

MICHELE CHADEISSON

Is there a better illustration of Western misconceptions about religious imagery than the word "fetish"? The historical foundation of this neologism[1] and its use in anthropological discourse in French texts (or in texts translated into French)—where it has undergone various transformations both in form and meaning—reveal much about this construction of religious and aesthetic otherness.

During the fifteenth and sixteenth centuries, when Portugal was establishing trading routes to East Asia and expanding its colonial empire there and in parts of Africa and America, some Portuguese sailors explored the Guinea coast in hopes of finding gold and converting its people. Although they probably did not expect to encounter any indigenous people schooled in the Christian faith, they thought they would be able to recognize and classify African religious beliefs. Such was not the case: Africans seemed to submit their actions to the magical power of objects that travelers were unable to identify, much less name. The foreigners' accounts describe a multitude of "things" that appeared to be considered sacred or worshiped as "gods," but failed to recognize them as idols.[2] The causes of this terminological deficit are mainly of a cultural nature. At the heart of this problem is the Wisdom of Solomon (the pre-Christian writing included in the Apocrypha), which contains a lengthy catalogue of paganisms and is thus a significant reference work for any reflection on idolatry. According to Wisdom of Solomon, there are three great idolatries: the cult of the stars, the cult of the animals, and the cult of the heroes. The idol, at once an emblematic figure and a sign of these idolatries, can be either natural or man-made. Natural idols comprise all of God's creations that are worshipped: stars, animals, men. Deified images of these (i.e., sculptures) constitute the second category of idols.

However, the three types of natural idols specified in Wisdom of Solomon represent only a fraction of the various objects that form the basis of African religious practices. Travelers related that the peoples of Africa paid more significant homage to some objects and materials not mentioned in that text: small objects (such as twigs, bones, teeth, feathers, horns), and also stones, plants, mountains, seas, amalgams of different materials, and finally "anything that comes to their mind' or "the first thing they bump into." Each of these objects, plants, geographic settings, etc. seemed to have inspired its own cult.

As to the second category of idols, fifteenth- and sixteenth-century travelers in Africa seemed never to have seen such objects, or, if they did, usually ignored them, regarding them as insignificant—a disturbing manifestation of cultural blindness. Here, this shortcoming was undoubtedly related to an inability to accept a different way of representing things: by not corresponding to Western aesthetic standards, the African god could not be perceived as representing an idol in the traditional sense of the term.

Thus, Western chroniclers were confronted by a profusion of sacred natural objects not identified in Wisdom of Solomon and man-made objects that, to their eyes, were not worthy of being called sculptures. As they lacked a concept or an expression to identify and categorize these objects, there gradually appeared in their writings a new category of religious figure, which at first they called *feitiço* (in English, "fetish"), a term originally connected to

Portuguese witchcraft (*feitiçaria*) and that here referred exclusively to natural objects and materials. Exit statuary.

"Fetish" was not an innocent term. This terminological choice and the theory that was soon to supplement it determined the Westerners' attitude toward African religions. By reducing the African sacred object to an organic "thing," these travelers ended up presuming that the fetish represented nothing but itself, referred to nothing but itself. And if that were so, perhaps it was because there was nothing to represent or to refer to—an assumption easily made, since they thought that prayers, offerings, sacrifices were being directly addressed to the fetish. And if the fetish had no mediating function, one could then conclude that there was no supernatural world involved—no "beyond."

The cult object was the object of the cult, the material god. A correlation was thus drawn between untamed nature and absence of religion, the lack of sculptures and the immanent power of things. Africans were therefore, at the very most, fetish-makers or sorcerers, but under no circumstances could they be considered religious peoples.

However, it should be noted that although this spiritual exclusion had its roots in cultural causes, one must not underestimate the economic motivations underlying such attitudes, such as the fortunes to be made in the slave trade. If African peoples had no conception of the beyond (i.e., had not been enlightened by divine revelation), this proved their lack of humanity. This conclusion, we now know, furthered Western interests.

At the beginning of the seventeenth century, the Dutch renamed the African ritual object *fetisso*, a term they borrowed from the mercantile jargon of the coast (Pietz 1987:39). French historian-geographer Pierre Davity changed it into *fetisse* in the 1630s (Davity 1637:404), and in 1669 Nicolas Villault de Bellefond gave it its definitive French name, *fétiche* (Villault de Bellefond 1669:55). This object of ritual devotion assumed many forms and functions but remained, as before, a natural material or an assemblage of natural materials.

However, chroniclers seemed to have had some difficulty figuring out whom the worshippers addressed their prayers to. There are many reasons for Westerners to have interpreted the rituals they saw as being directly addressed to objects. Among other things, fetishes, following the example of living beings, had feelings (anger, kindness, jealousy, and so on). They drank, they ate, received presents, were revered and feared. Prayers and requests were unquestionably directed to them.

But a careful reading reveals something more complex, having to do with the emanation of power. Peter de Marees, in his *Description et récit historial du riche Royaume d'Or de Guinée*, published in 1605, described an African king's visit to a *fetisso* tree to perform a sacrifice when his country was short of money. As soon as the sacrifice was done, "a voice arose that undoubtedly came from the Devil" (de Marees 1605:27). Although the tree was here in accordance with the physical value the author generally assigned to the *fetisso*, it was transformed into a place where a spirit revealed itself. The object was here devoid of potential value, becoming the vector of a force that transcended it. Villault de Bellefond, appropriating this passage from de Marees in 1669, no longer designated the tree's material substance as *fétiche*, but just what transcended, what acted, what manifested itself through that tree (Villault de Bellefond 1669:284). Dethroned by an intangible fetish, the object was here only a vector of power.

CAT. 124

Power Figure
Yaka peoples, Dem. Rep. of the Congo
Wood, iron. H. 45 cm.
Private Collection

166

In another example of this semantic wandering, de Marees recounted how villagers of the Gold Coast assuaged their *fetisso* by bringing some food up to the mountains when lightning and thunder struck (de Marees 1605:28). The text is ambiguous, perhaps due to the poor translation into French: who or what was the *fetisso*? who or what received the homage of the faithful? In their own accounts of this same scene, Davity identified the mountains as the *fetisso* (Davity 1637:404), while Villault de Bellefond declared that the mountains were their *fetiches'* homes (Villault de Bellefond 1669:268). Thus, the term *fétiche* could refer to a physical, terrestrial god or to something more ethereal, supernatural. This remarkable conceptual disjunction would reach its peak in the next century.

Throughout the eighteenth century, those who wrote about this subject emphasized the fetishes' natural aspects and hardly ever spoke about them as sculptures. It was widely believed that "images [were] not worshipped" on the Guinea coast (Bosman 1705:164), in accordance with the idea that the act of creation was the mark of evolved societies. This weakness in appreciation on the part of Westerners, this blindness about African artefacts, reveals just how dominated they were by their own commercial interests, which could not justify, for example, the massive deportation of slaves other than by obliterating their civilized character.

Thus, the natural fetishes were the "true divinities," and were not represented by images or statues (Bosman 1705:153). Prayers, offerings, and sacrifices were directly addressed to them. The most convinced advocate of this notion of a cult directly addressed to natural objects was undoubtedly Charles de Brosses, who, by the way, coined the term *fétichisme* in 1760 (de Brosses 1988 [1760]:11). According to him, the African fetish represented nothing; it was "divine of its own divinity" (ibid.:82) and must therefore be considered a sign of a society in its infancy. In so saying, de Brosses reiterated the terrible correlation between a lack of man-made idols and an absence of spiritual mediation. Conforming to the earlier chroniclers' perception, de Brosses's *fétiche* was the object of the cult, a veritable god.

Nevertheless, this idea had little or no impact on de Brosses's contemporary theorists. Some writers referred to the fact that, despite their material cults, Africans paid some homage to immaterial entities. The power of the fetish, from this point of view, was not inherent in the object itself but arose from and was transcended by these entities. Along with their new awareness of "genies" and other "spirits," which was almost entirely missing in former travel writings, Westerners discovered a subtle world of invisible entities exerting their power on human beings concurrently with the terrestrial gods. Surprisingly, the word *fétiche* would also apply to these supernatural powers. This was too many senses for one word. By this time, it could successively—or simultaneously—refer to a spirit, an image of a spirit, an object invested by an immanent power, or an object invested by a supernatural power. This semantic and conceptual jumble reflects the imprecision of foreign chroniclers when relating religious beliefs that were alien to them.

At the beginning of the nineteenth century, travelers, philosophers, and chroniclers of foreign cultures recounted in turn how they perceived otherness. However, conventional Western notions about Africans remained largely unchanged from the preceding century. But the question of whether Africans regarded their fetishes as gods or as symbols of gods became crucial. In 1830, Auguste Comte, for example, refused to accept that Africans lacked religious beliefs (Comte 1830), but subscribed to the notion that they lacked metaphysics. The axiom that the fetish was mainly a material god was still supported thirty years later, as is apparent, for example, in a statement by an eminent member of the Societé d'Anthropologie, Charles Letourneau: "They have no concept of immaterial beings; everything is usually tangible, visible." (Letourneau 1865:595–96).

By the 1860s, the multitude of foreign travelers in Africa led to a new appreciation of otherness, and particularly of religious otherness, thus finally overturning one of the major

CAT. 125

Power figure
Songye peoples, Dem. Rep. of the Congo
Wood, metal, beads, studs, horn, shell. H. 89 cm.
Adam M. Lindemann

CAT. 126

Power figure
Songye peoples, Dem. Rep. of the Congo
Wood, horn, fiber, oil. H. 70.5 cm.
Adam M. Lindemann

168

misconceptions about Africa: its supposed absence of religion. By the same token, the idea that African religious worship subsisted in a cult directly addressed to natural objects was contested: this cult was in fact addressed to spirits, genies, and souls present in those objects—or transmitting their power to them—but from whom they were quite distinct. This incarnation theory consequently dominated the anthropological discourse on African religions at the end of the nineteenth century. By recognizing the existence of these genies, spirits, and other divinities, writers on the subject corrected mistaken ideas about both the status and the aspect of the fetish.

With regard to its status, the fetish was no longer that terrestrial god invested with an immanent power, but rather an incarnation of a supernatural entity. Former nationwide fetishes (such as epidemics or elements) were relegated to the rank of instruments through which the gods manifested their anger and their power. Geographic settings (seas, rivers, mountains) turned into deities' shelters. Smaller organic fetishes (trees, rocks) turned into altars. Former little fetishes were converted into propitiatory substances. Lastly, wild animals were transformed into incarnations or messengers of the Gods.

In terms of fetishes' aspect, the growing acceptance of the theory of incarnation brought with it a corresponding rise in the discussion of anthropomorphic or zoomorphic sculptures in French accounts. They probably corresponded much better to this new theory of embodiment than natural substances.

This partial correction of the French perception of African woodcarvings was accompanied by a new notion—representation—which anthropological discourse imposed on the fetish at the beginning of the twentieth century. Like the theory of incarnation, representation suggested that Africans conceived a world of spirits different in nature from the tangible, material world. However, unlike the idea of embodiment, this idea of representation supposed the spirits somewhere above instead of inside the material object. The two forms of power—immanent and transcendent—were thus challenged. Westerners had once more reoriented their interpretation of African images, and in so doing restored to them some of their dignity. Exit power.

The chain reaction set off by the theory of representation put an end to the now-discredited concept of fetishism, which was replaced by different concepts and terms: "witchcraft" or "sorcery" (for utilitarian procedures) and "animism" (for religious activities). Anthropologists stopped using the term "fetishism" and began avoiding the term "fetish" in their discourse because of its evolutionist connotation (i.e., helping perpetuate the notion that African civilizations were still in their infancy), but it didn't completely disappear. "Fetish" was still used to designate assemblages of natural materials as well as sculptures that are physically altered by the addition of certain organic substances. Complex and extremely powerful, these objects would remain specifically associated with defensive "witchcraft" rather than with the (newly) religious "animism."

Because of this incipient re-evaluation of African cultures by Western anthropologists at the beginning of the twentieth century, it seemed as if there would be no more changes in the concept of the fetish. But then, in 1910, came the publication of *L'âme d'un peuple africain: les Bambara*, by abbot Joseph Henry. His conclusions disrupted the inexorable progression in the meaning of the term "fetish" from a godless cult object to a legimate representation or incarnation of the spirit world. According to the abbot, the Bamana conceived of two separate spirit worlds: the *gnena* and the *gna*. Whereas the *gnena* was clearly distinct from the object it inhabited, the *gna* never left the object it chose to live in. The spirit and its material container were so bound together that the Bamana had a special term for this perfect, holy union: *boli*. Men were thus compelled to regard the spirit and its shelter as a single entity. Seventeen years later, Charles Monteil added that this union was so intense that destroying the object would lead to the end of its cult (Monteil 1977

CAT. 126 (DETAIL)

[1924]:254). If a *boli* was so essential that its physical destruction brought about the collapse of its cult, we may wonder just how valid was anthropologists' notion of African sacred objects, at the time, as merely shelters or representations, and furthermore, what exactly was these objects' relationship to the spirits that were supposedly represented by them or incarnated in them. How much truth was there to this view of the object as subordinated by the spirit, restricted to an image or a container? Despite the important questions raised by Henry's "symbiotic pair" thesis, it would have no effect on subsequent writings about these objects: French anthropology would redirect the line of thinking toward the spirits "represented by" physical objects.

But modern scholars have in recent decades revived the discourse that had nearly disappeared a century ago. By about 1900, the word *fétiche* no longer referred to the "classical" sculptures supposedly representing the gods and the ancestor spirits. These sculptures now received recognition and acceptance by Western commentators and were finally regarded as conforming to Western criteria for religious imagery: dignity of the pose, meticulous modeling of forms and motifs, etc. But Western visual conformism has clearly made a distinction between these forms and the ones altered with ritual accumulations. Those, which were still considered aesthetically "incorrect," would be relegated to the rank of magical devices and would stay under their old category, "fetishes." In other words, the form defined the function.

Nevertheless, there is much ethnographical data that contradicts this view of a correspondence between form and function in these religious objects. American scholar Leon Siroto, in his remarkable analysis of African images (Siroto 1976), has strongly criticized this correlation.

Another view, which presumes an opposition between religion and magic, holds that there are, on the one hand, "noble" religious activities dealing with a world of supernatural entities and, on the other hand, "obscure" magical activities dealing with the earthly power of physical substances. This opposition is now refuted by a number of scholars, who would like to end this conceptual schism between the two sometimes disparate, but often complementary, practices. Both are grounded on the belief in spirits, and in acting on them through objects invested with energy that force, attract, seduce, and lure these spirits to make them serve the community.

But then, what should these objects be called? Scholars have admitted that it was not easy to get rid of such a concept and term as "fetish," since it seemed clear that some objects effectively functioned as fetishes. After many attempts to replace "fetish" with other terms, they decided that the substitutes, all of which maintained the distinction between "magical objects" and "religious or symbolic objects," did not clarify the issue. Finally, though, Arnold Rubin came up with a term that avoids the false opposition between magic and religion and thus solves this lexical dilemma: "power object."[3]

Although the term "power object" resolves many issues, there is still a fundamental problem inherent in the concept itself. At the beginning of the twentieth century, the re-evaluation of African religions turned the power object into a sanitized representation, purging it of any kind of power. This approach, imposed by a Western way of thinking, resulted in an extremely narrow interpretation of sacred images that is not universally accepted.

In Africa, the cultural object assumes many forms: in some cases representations, but more often altars, intermediaries between men and spirits, concentrations of earthly and supernatural powers, fixed places for an entity to inhabit, and so on. Sometimes, the identification between the entity and the object is virtually total. In Benin, for instance, the *vodù*, as described by ethnologist Marc Augé, is "entirely present in each one of its figures." (Augé 1986:121). That is, the object made to serve as a means for the supernatural entity to manifest itself becomes indistinguishable from the spirit it gives form to; they both constitute the god. This has been termed the "actualization" (*actualisation*) or "materialization" (*presentification*) of supernatural powers, which Hellenic scholar Jean-Pierre Vernant defined in

CAT. 127

Power figure
Songye peoples, Dem. Rep. of the Congo
Wood, fiber, metal studs. H. 19.7 cm.
Dr. and Mrs. James Christensen

170

1985 as follows: assigning to an otherwise invisible entity "a physical place in our world, thus enabling humans one way or another to communicate with it, make true contact with it"; its aim is "to present this entity here and now in order to put it at their service, in ritually required ways" (Vernant 1985:27). A few years later, Lucien Stephan added a clarification: Once "the invisible being manifests itself in the object," it becomes "alive and, in the most logical way, the user behaves toward it as a living being" (Stephan 1988:151). Nonetheless, this definition of the power object holds that an entity already exists before the object that manifests it is created or chosen, even if there is, in the end, no distinction between the spirit and the object.

The most audacious theory about the identity of power objects was proposed by Jean Bazin in his study of the hieratic, powerful *boli* of the Bamana people. According to Bazin, the *boli* is not the materialization of a pre-existing religious power or spirit; instead, he believes that this power is created at the same time as the object—that they are inseparable, not only physically but conceptually. Each *boli* has its own history, its individual reputation, and its own cult. When the Master of the cult creates a boli by making a sacrifice involving blood, it is not an offering to some ethereal divinity but a means of activating the power and of feeding and giving form to the power object (Bazin 1986). Indeed, no divinity is invoked by the Master of the cult when the sacrifice is performed.

Each *boli* takes its name not from a god but from its own lineage, itself determined by the basic material it is made of, which distinguishes it from all other *boli*. The uniqueness of each one is valued so highly that its destruction would entail the end of its cult (here, Bazin makes the same point as Monteil, discussed above). Thus, the *boli* is not simply one of numerous effigies or merely the shelter for an ethereal entity, it is "this particular thing that nothing can replace" (Bazin 1986:260).It would therefore be vain to try to discover who it represents or materializes, because it represents or materializes nothing but itself. What we are confronted with here is "a religion not of mediation but of presence": "The god, if there is a god, is entirely present in the enigmatic appearance of these things tinged with blood" (ibid.:258). Its materialization is to be considered a pure act of creation. The sacrificer sculpts—and goes on sculpting—the god's body with blood. What we might have taken here for a sacrifice is nothing but "an act of re-engendering" through a kind of "transfusion" that gives it a high dose of energy and "transforms the inert into the divine." In this case, blood is not the meal of the gods, but rather "what makes the divine present in the thing"(ibid.:270). The *boli* must be understood as a "material-individual," a "person-thing" (ibid.:266).

Bazin's interpretation of the *boli* is contradicted by two specialists who deal with this same cultural area, Jean-Paul Colleyn (Colleyn 1985 and 1988) and Danielle Jonckers (Jonckers 1993), who claim that there is an invisible power pre-existent to the making of the object and to whom the sacrifice is addressed. All three scholars do agree on the fact that the object is the manifestation of a power. What they disagree on, essentially, is the nature of this power. Nevertheless, Bazin's interpretation remains extremely innovative and appealing in many respects. It would allow, among other things, a redirecting of the investigation toward some power objects whose identity has not yet been specified.

Nobody would now contest that the object is a main component of the power. To negate it and give importance only to the invisible world would leave some (huge) stones unturned.

1 The origin of the term and its inscription in the Christian discourse has been discussed by William Pietz (Pietz 1987).
2 The words "things" and "gods" are the words used by the writers discussed in this essay (in French as *choses* and *dieux*), and thus appear within quotation marks.
3 Rubin first used this term in the catalogue to his 1974 Pace Gallery exhibition; see Rubin 1974.

Bibliography

Adams, Robert McCormick
1989 "Smithsonian Horizons." *Smithsonian* 19b(12):14.

Agheyisi, Rebecca N.
1986 *An Edo-English Dictionary*. Nigeria: Ethiope Publishing Corporation.

Allison, Philip
1968 *African Stone Sculpture*. London: Lund Humphries.

Allman, R.
1987 "With the Punitive Expedition to Benin City." *The Lancet*, 2(July 3): 43-4.

Alpers, Edward A.
1992 "The Ivory Trade in Africa: a Historical Overview." In *Elephant. The Animal and its Ivory in African Culture*, Doran H. Ross, (Ed.) Los Angeles: UCLA, Fowler Museum of Cultural History. pp. 349-363.

Anderson, Martha and Philip Peek
2002 *Ways of the Rivers: Arts and Environment of the Niger Delta*. Los Angeles: University of California, Los Angeles.

Antubam, Kofi.
1963 *Ghana's Heritage of Culture*. Leipzig: Koehler & Amelang.

Aquina, Sister Mary (A. K. H. Weinrich)
1968 "Mutimwi- A Note on the waist belt of the Karanga." *NADA* 11(5): 3, 4.

Augé, Marc
1986 "Le fétiche et le corps pluriel." In *Corps des Dieux*. Paris: Gallimard, Le Temps de la Réflexion VII. pp. 121-37.

Barley, Nigel
1983 "Placing the West African Potter. " In *Earthenware in Asia and Africa*, John Picton (ed.). Colloquia on Art and Archaeology in Asia: no. 12. London: University of London, School of Oriental and African Studies. pp. 93-105.
1994 *Smashing Pots*. London: British Museum Press.

Barnes, Sandra
1980 "Ogun: An Old God for a New Age." *ISHI Occasional Papers*.
1989 *Africa's Ogun: Old World and New*. Bloomington: Indiana University Press.

Bassani, Enzio
2000 *African Art and Artifacts in European Collections 1400-1800*. London: British Museum Press.

Bastin, Marie-Louise
1961 "Un masque en cuivre martelé des Kongo du nord-est de l'Angola." *Africa-Tervuren* 7(2): 29-40.
1982 *La Sculpture Tshokwe*. Meudon: Alain et Françoise Chaffin.
1984 "Ritual Masks of the Chokwe." *African Arts* 17(4): 40-45, 92-93, 95-96.
1993 "The *Akishi* Spirits of the Chokwe." In *Face of the Spirits: Masks from the Zaire Basin*, Frank Herreman and Constantine Petridis (eds.). Ghent: Martial and Snoeck. pp. 79-95.
1997 "Le réceptacle au pays des Tshokwe: Utilitaire, rituel ou de prestige." In *Réceptacles*, Christiane Falgayrettes-Leveau, (ed.). Paris: Editions Dapper. pp. 117-38.

Bazin, Jean
1986 "Retour aux Choses-Dieux." In *Corps des dieux*. Paris: Gallimard, Le Temps de la Réflexion VII. pp. 253-73.

Ben-Amos, Paula
1980 *The Art of Benin*. New York: Thames and Hudson.
1999 *Art, Innovation, and Politics in 18th Century Benin*. Bloomington: Indiana University Press.

Bent, James Theodore
1892 *The Ruined Cities of Mashonaland*. London: Longmans, Green.

Berns, Marla
1989 "Ceramic Arts in Africa". *African Arts* 22(2): 32-37.
1995 *Ceramic Gestures: New Vessels by Magdalene Odundo*. Santa Barbara: University Art Museum, UC, Santa Barbara.

Biebuyck, Daniël P.
1973 *Lega Culture: Art, Initiation, and Moral Philosophy among a Central African People*. Berkely: University of California Press.
1986 *The Arts of Zaire. Vol. II. Eastern Zaire: the Ritual and Artistic Context of Voluntary Associations*. Berkely: University of California Press.
2002 *Lega. Ethics and Beauty in the Heart of Africa*. Gent: KBC Banking & Insurance, Snoeck-Ducaju en Zoon.

Binger, Louis
1892 *Voyage au pays de Kong et au mossi*. Paris: Hachette.

Binkley, David A.
1990 "Masks, Space and Gender in Southern Kuba Initiation Ritual." *Iowa Studies in African Art* 3:157-70.
1992 "The Teeth of Nyim: The Elephant and Ivory in Kuba Art." In *Elephant. The Animal and its Ivory in African Culture*, Doran H. Ross, (Ed.) Los Angeles: UCLA, Fowler Museum of Cultural History. pp. 277-291.
1996 "'Bounce the Baby': Masks, Fertility, and the Authority of Esoteric Knowledge in Northern Kete Initiation Rituals." *Bulletin of the Elvehjem Museum of Art*, pp. 45-56.

Blackmun, Barbara Winston
1992 "The Elephant and its Ivory in Benin." In *Elephant. The Animal and its Ivory in African Culture*, Doran H. Ross, (Ed.) Los Angeles: UCLA, Fowler Museum of Cultural History. pp. 163-183.

Bosman, W.
1705 *Voyage de Guinée*, [1704]. Utrecht: A. Schouten.

Bourgeois, Arthur P.
1981 "Kakungu among the Yaka and the Suku." *African Arts*, 14(1): 42-4; 88.
1984 *Art of the Yaka and Suku*. Meudon: Alain et Françoise Chaffin.
1991 "Mbawa-Pakasa: L'image du buffle chez les Yaka et leurs voisins." *Arts d'Afrique Noire* 77:19-32.
1996 "Central Africa." In *The Dictionary of Art*, Jane Turner, (ed.). London: Macmillan. 1: 400-6.

Bradbury, R.E.
_____ Notes on file at the University of Birmingham Library. A series: Field notes, Benin City and surroundings, 1951/52; BS series: Benin Scheme Field notes, 1957-61.
1973 *Benin Studies*. London: Oxford University Press.

Bradbury, R. E. and International African Institute
1964 *The Benin Kingdom and the Edo-Speaking Peoples of Southwestern Nigeria*. London: International African Institute.

Brain, Robert and Adam Pollock
1971 *Bangwa Funerary Sculpture*. London: Gerald Duckworth & Co.

Brincard. Marie-Thérèse
1989 *Sounding Forms: African Musical Instruments*. New York: The American federation of the Arts.

Buchner, M.
1908 "Benin und die Portuguiesen." *Zeitschrift furEthnologie* 11: 981-2.

Burssens, Herman
1962 "Yanda-beelden en Mani-sekte bij de Azande (Centraal-Afrika)." (with summary in French) (*Annalen – Nieuwe reeks in 4°- Wetenschappen van de mens – n° 4*). Tervuren: Koninklijk Museum voor Midden-Afrika.
1988 "Le sculpteur sur bois." In *Utotombo. L'art d'Afrique noire dans les collections privées belges*. Bruxelles: Société des Expositions du Palais des Beaux-Arts. pp 19-36
1992 *Mangbetu: art de cour de collections privées belges*. Bruxelles: Kredietbank.

Cameron, Elisabeth
1992 "The Stampeding of Elephants: Elephant Imprints on Lega Thoughts." In *Elephant. The Animal and its Ivory in African Culture*, Doran H. Ross, (ed.). Los Angeles: UCLA, Fowler Museum of Cultural History. pp. 295-305.

Ceyssens, Rik
1993a "Material and Formal Aspects of Copper Masks from the Upper Kasai." In *Face of the Spirits: Masks from the Zaire Basin*, Frank Herreman and Constantine Petridis, (eds.). Ghent: Martial & Snoeck. pp. 97-113.
1993b "Sens du 'Grand Masque' dans le Haut-Kasayi." *Baessler-Archiv* 41(2):355-81.
1995 Cat. nos. 57-61. In *The Tervuren Museum Masterpieces from Central Africa*, Gustaaf Verswijver et al., (eds.). Munich: Prestel and Tervuren: Royal Museum for Central Africa. pp. 163-66.

Chikwendu, V.E. and A.C. Umeji
1979 "Local sources of raw materials for the Nigerian bronze/brass industry." *West African Journal of Archaeology* 9: 151-65.

Childs, Terry
1991 "Style, Technology, and Iron Smelting Furnaces in Bantu-Speaking Africa." *Journal of Anthropological Archæology* 10: 332-59.

Claerhout, Adriaan
1976 "Two Kuba Wrought-Iron Statuettes." *African Arts* 9(4): 60-64, 92.

Cline, Walter
1937 *Mining and Metallurgy in Negro Africa.* Menasha: George Banta.

Cole, Herbert M.
1992 "The Igbo: Prestige Ivory and Elephant Spirit Power." In *Elephant. The Animal and its Ivory in African Culture*, Doran H. Ross, (ed.). Los Angeles: UCLA, Fowler Museum of Cultural History. pp. 211-225.

Cole, Herbert M. and Chike C. Aniankor
1984 *Igbo Arts.Community and Cosmos.* Los Angeles: UCLA, Museum of Cultural History.

Colleyn, Jean Paul
1985 "Objets forts et rapports sociaux le cas des Yapere Minyanka." In *Fétiches, Objets enchantés, Mots realizes.* E.P.H.E., Systèmes de pensée en Afrique noire, cahier n° 8. pp. 221-61.
1988 *Les Chemins de Nya.* Paris: Editions de l'Ecole des Hautes Etudes en Sciences Sociales.

Comte, Auguste
1830 *Cours de philosophie positive.* 52ème leçon [1830]. Paris: Editions Schleicher.

Connah, Graham
1975 *The Archaeology of Benin.* Oxford: Clarendon Press.

Coombes, Annie E.
1994 *Reinventing Africa: Museums, Material Culture and Popular Imagination.* New Haven: Yale University Press.

Cordwell, Justine M.
1952 *Some Aesthetic Aspects of Yoruba and Benin Cultures.* Unpublished Ph.D. Dissertation. Northwestern University, Evanston, Ill.

Cornet, Joseph
1978 *Pierres sculptées du Bas-Zaire (Kinshasa).* Kinshasa: Institut des Musées Nationaux.

Cosentino, Donald J. (ed.)
1995 *Sacred Arts of Haitian Vodou.* Los Angeles: UCLA Fowler Museum of Cultural History.

Craddock, P.T.
1985 "Medieval Copper Alloy Production and West African Bronze Analysis - Part I." *Archaeometry* 27(1): 17-41.

Craddock, P.T. and John Picton
1986 "Medieval Copper Alloy Production and West

African Bronze Analyses - Part II." *Archaeometry* 28(16): 3-32.

Crahmer,W.
1909 "Uber den indoportugiesischen Ursprung der Beninkunst." *Globus* 95(23): 345-9, 360-5.

Crowley, Daniel J.
1982 "Mukanda: Religion, Art, and Ethnicity in West Central Africa." In *African Religious Groups and Beliefs*, Simon Ottenberg, (ed.). Meerut: Archana Publications for the Folklore Institute. pp. 206-21.

Czekanowski, Jan
1924 *Forschungen im Nil-Kongo Zwischengebiet.* Band VI. Zweiter Band. Ethnographie. Uele/Ituri/Nilländer. Leipzig: Klinhardt und Biermann.

Darish, Patricia
1990 *Fired Brilliance: Ceramic Vessels From Zaire.* Kansas City: Kansas City Gallery of Art.

Dark, Philip J.C.
1962 *The Art of Benin.* A Catalogue of an Exhibition of the A.F.W. Fuller and the Chicago Naturall History Museum. Chicago: Chicago Natural History Museum.
1966 "Cire-perdue Casting: Some Technological and Aesthetic Considerations." *Ethnologica*, n.s. 3: 222-30.
1973 *An Introduction to Benin Art and Technology.* Oxford: Clarendon Press.

Dawson, Douglas
2001 *Of the Earth Ancient and Historic African Ceramics.* Chicago: Douglas Dawson Gallery.

Devisse, Jean
1993 *Vallees Du Niger.* Paris: Reunion des Musees Nationaux.

d'Avity, Pierre, sieur de Montmartin
1637 *Le Monde ou la Description Générale de ses 4 Parties.* Paris: Claude Sonnius. Revised ed., with corrections and additions by Jean-Baptiste de Rocoles. Paris: Denys Bechet et Louis Billaine, 1660.

d'Azevedo, Warren L.(ed.)
1973 *The Traditional Artist in African Societies.* London & Bloomington: Indiana University Press.

de Brosses, Charles
1988 *Du culte des dieux fétiches*, [1760]. Paris: Fayard.

de Grunne, Bernard
1998 *The Birth of Art in Black Africa.* Luxemburg: Banque Generale du Luxembourg.

de Marees, Peter
1605 *Description et récit historial du riche Royaume d'Or de Guinée.* [1602]. Amsterdam: Claeffon.

de Maret Pierre
1985 "The Smith's Myth and the Origin of Leadership in Central Africa." In *African Iron Working, Ancient and Traditional*, R. Haaland and P. Shinnie (eds.). Oslo: Norwegian University Press. pp. 73-87.

de Sousberghe, Léon
1959 *L'Art Pende.* Mémoires, Beaux-Arts, IX, 2. Brussels: Académie Royale de Belgique.

de Sousberghe, Léon and Jean Willy Mestach
1981 "'Gitenga': Un masque des Pende." *Arts d'Afrique Noire* 37:18-29.

Dechamps, R.
1970 Première note concernant l'identification anatomique des bois utilisés pour des sculptures en Afrique. *Africa-Tervuren* 17(3-4): 77-82.

Dewey, William J.
1986 "Shona Male and Female Artistry." *African Arts* 19(3): 64-7.
1990 *Weapons for the Ancestors.* (video) Iowa City: University of Iowa Video Production Unit.

Dewey, William J. and S. Terry Childs
1996 "Forging Memory." In *Memory: Luba Art and the Making of History*, Mary Nooter Roberts and Allen F. Roberts (eds.). New York: The Museum for African Art. pp. 61-84.

Dewey, William J. and Allen F. Roberts
1993 *Iron, Master of Them All.* Iowa City: The University of Iowa Museum of Art and The Project for Advanced Study of Art and Life in Africa.

DjeDje, Jacqueline C. (ed.)
1999 *TurnUp the Volume! A Celebration of African Music.* Los Angeles: UCLA Fowler Museum of Cultural History.

Dobbelman, A. H. M.
1976 *Het Geheime Ogboni Genootschap; een Bronscultuur uit Zuidwest Nigeria.* Berg en Dal.

Drewal, Henry John
1992 "Image and Indeterminacy: Elephants and Ivory." In *Elephant. The Animal and its Ivory in African Culture.* Doran H. Ross (ed.). Los Angeles: UCLA, Fowler Museum of Cultural History. pp. 187-207.

Duchateau, Armand
1990 *Benin.Hofkunst uit Wenen.* Brussel: Gemeentekrediet.

Egharevba, Jacob U.
1968 *Short History of Benin.* 4th edition, [1934]. Ibadan: Ibadan University Press.

Elsen, Jan
1996 *The Sickle Weapons: Part I.* Tribal Arms Monographs, vol. I, no.1. Brussels: Tribal Arts.
2000 *The Sickle Weapons: Part III.* Tribal Arms Monographs, vol. I, no.3. Brussels: Tribal Arts.

Ezra, Kate
1986 *A Human Ideal in African Art: Bamana Figurative Sculpture.* Washington D.C.: Smithsonian Institution Press.
1988 *Art of the Dogon: Selections of the Lester Wunderman Collection.* New York: The Metropolitan Museum of Art.
1992 *Royal Art of Benin: The Perls Collection in the Metropolitan Museum of Art.* New York

Fagg, Bernard.
1977 *Nok Terra Cottas*. Lagos: National Museum.

Fagg, William
1959 "Cire-Perdue Casting." In *7 Metals of Africa [a traveling exhibition, the Cleveland Museum of Art, the City Art Museum of St. Louis, the University Museum]*, Margaret Plass (ed). Philadelphia.
1960 *Nigerian Images*. London: Lund Humphries.
1963 *Nigerian Images*. London: Lund Humphries.

Félix, Marc Leo
1987 *100 Peoples of Zaire and their Sculpture: The Handbook*. Brussels and Bukavu: Tribal Arts Press.
1991 *Kipinga, Throwing-Blades of Central Africa*. Munich: Fred Jahn.
1992 *Luba Zoo: Kifwebe and Other Striped Masks*. Brussels: Zaïre Basin Art History Research Center.
1995 *Art & Kongos*. Brussels: Zaire Basin Art History Research Center.
1998 "Hypotheses." In *Makishi lya Zambia: Mask Characters of the Upper Zambezi Peoples*, Marc Leo Felix and Manuel Jordán. Munich: Fred Jahn. pp. 336-65.

Fischer, Eberhard und Hans Himmelheber
1975 *Das Gold in der Kunst Westafrikas*. Zürich: Museum Rietberg.
1976 *Die Kunst der Dan*. Feldforschung in Zusammenarbeit, mit Georg W. Tahmen e.a. Zürich: Museum Rietberg.

Fontina, Mário
1997 *Ngombo: Tradições no Nordeste de Angola*. Portugal: Câmara Municipal de Oeiras.

Förster, Till
1997 *Zerrissene Entfaltung: Alltag, Ritual und künstlerische Ausdruckformen im Norden der Côte d'Ivoire*. Studien zur Kulturkunde. Band 107. Köln: Rüdiger Köppen Verlag.

Foss, Perkins
1973 "Festival of Ohworu at Evwreni." *African Arts* 6(4) (Summer): 20–27, 94.

Frank, Barbara E.
1998 *Mande Potters and Leatherworkers*. Washington, D.C.: Smithsonian Institution Press.

Garlake, Peter S.
1973 *Great Zimbabwe*. London: Thames and Hudson.

Garrard, Timothy F.
1983 "Benin Metal-Casting Technology." In *The Art of Power/The Power of Art: Essays in Benin Iconography*. Los Angeles: Museum of Cultural History, UCLA. pp. 17-20.

Geary, Christaud M.
1992 "Elephants, Ivory and Chiefs: The Elephant and the Art of the Cameroon Grassfield." In *Elephant. The Animal and its Ivory in African Culture*. Doran H. Ross (ed.). Los Angeles: UCLA, Fowler Museum of Cultural History. pp. 229-257.

Gebauer, Paul
1979 *Art of Cameroon*. Portand: The Portland Art Museum in Association with the Metropolitan

Museum of Art, New York, N.Y.

Girschick, Paula Ben-Amos
1995 *The Art of Benin*. Washington, DC: The Smithsonian Institution Press.

Goucher, Candice L, Jehanne H. Teilhet, Kent R. Wilson and Tsai Hwa J. Chow.
1976 "Lead isotope studies of metal sources for ancient Nigerian `bronzes.'" *Nature* 262(5564) (July 8): 130-1.

Griaule, Marcel
1938 *Masques Dogon*. Paris: Institut d'Ethnologie.

Harter, Pierre
1973 Les pipes ceremonielles de l'ouest camerounais. Arnouville: Arts d'Afrique Noire
1986 *Arts anciens du Cameroun*. Arnouville: Arts d'Afrique Noire.

Henry, Joseph,
1910 *L'âme d'un peuple africain: les Bambara*. Bibliothèque Anthropos.

Herbert, Eugenia W.
1984 *Red Gold of Africa*. Madison: University of Wisconsin Press.
1993 *Iron, Gender and Power: Rituals of Transformation in African Societies*. Bloomington: Indiana University Press.

Herreman, Frank (ed.).
2000 *In the Presence of Spirits: African Art from the National Museum of Ethnology, Lisbon*. New York: The Museum for African Art and Ghent: Snoeck-Ducaju & Zoon.

Hersak, Dunja
1985 *Songye. Mask and Figures*. London: Ethnographica Ltd.
1986 *Songye Masks and Figure Sculpture*. London: Ethnographica Ltd.

Himmelheber, Hans
1960 Negerkunst und *Negerkünstler*. Braunschweig: Klinkhardt & Biermann.

Hodgkin, T.
1975 Nigerian Perspectives: An Historical Anthology. London

Horton, Robin
1960 "The Gods as Guests: An Aspect of Kalabari Religious Life." Lagos: Nigeria Magazine.
1965 *Kalabari Sculpture*. Lagos: Department of Antiquities. Federal Republic of Nigeria.

Hubbard, Rev. John Waddington
1948 *The Sobo of the Niger Delta: A Work Dealing with the History and Languages of the People Inhabiting the Sobo (Urhobo) Division, Warri Province*. Zaria: Gaskiya Corp.

Hutchinson, J. and J. M. Dalziel

Hutchinson, J. and J. M. Dalziel
1936 *Flora or West Tropical Africa*. London.

Jacob, Alain
1977 *Poteries, ivoires de l'Afrique noire*. Paris. ABC décor.

Jeffries, M.D.W.
1951 "The Origins of the Benin Bronzes." *African Studies* 10(2): 87-92.

Jeremine, E.
1945 "Etudes des statuettes Kissiniens au point de vue minéralogique et pétrographique." *Journal de la Société des Africanistes* 15: 3-14.

Johnson, Marion
1983 "Two Pottery Traditions in Southern Ghana." In *Earthenware in Asia and Africa*, John Picton (ed.). Colloquia on Art and Archaeology in Asia: no. 12. London: University of London, School of Oriental and African Studies. pp. 208-218.

Jonckers, Danielle
1993 "Autels sacrificiels et puissances religieuses. Le Manyan." In *Fétiches II. Puissance des objets, Charme des mots*, E.P.H.E., Systèmes de pensée en Afrique noire, cahier n°12, pp. 65-101.

Jones, Adam (tr. and ed.)
1983 "Andreas Josua Ulsheimer's Voyage of 1603-4." In *German Sources for West African History 1599-1669*. Wiesbadan: F. Steiner.

Jordán, Manuel A.
1996 "Tossing Life in a Basket: Art and Divination among Chokwe, Lunda, Luvale and Related Peoples of Northwestern Zambia." Unpublished Ph.D. dissertation, The University of Iowa, Iowa City.
2000a "Art and Divination among Chokwe, Lunda, Luvale, and Other Related Peoples of Northwestern Zambia." In *Insight and Artistry in African Divination*. Ed. John Pemberton III. Washington, D.C., and London: Smithsonian Institution Press.
2000b "The Matapa and Kongo Kasai or Kongo-Dinga Peoples." In *In the Presence of Spirits: African Art from the National Museum of Ethnology, Lisbon*, ed. Frank Herreman. New York: The Museum for African Art; Ghent: Snoeck-Ducaju & Zoon. , pp. 77-84
2002 *Ngombo: Divination Arts of Central Africa*. Munich: Fred Jahn.

Jordán, Manuel (ed.)
1998 *Chokwe! Art and Initiation among Chokwe and Related Peoples*. Munich: Prestel.

Kasfir, Sidney Littlefield
1992 "Ivory from Zambia Country to the Land of Zinj." In *Elephant. The Animal and its Ivory in African Culture*. Doran H. Ross (ed.). Los Angeles: UCLA, Fowler Museum of Cultural History. pp. 309-327.

Kense, Francois J.
1983 *Traditional African Iron Working*. Calgary: Department of Archaeology, University of Calgary.
1985 "The Initial Diffusion Of Iron to Africa." In *African Iron Working*, R. Haaland and P. Shinnie (eds.). Oslo: University of Oslo Press. pp. 11-27.

Klein, Hildegard (ed.)
1987 *Leo Frobenius: Ethnographische Notizen aus den*

Jahren 1905 und 1906. II: Kuba, Leele, Nord-Kete. Wiesbaden: Franz Steiner (Studien zur Kulturkunde, 84).
1988 *Leo Frobenius: Ethnographische Notizen aus den Jahren 1905 und 1906. III: Luluwa, Süd-Kete, Bena Mai, Pende, Cokwe.* Wiesbaden: Franz Steiner (Studien zur Kulturkunde, 87).

Kriger, Colleen E.
1999 *Pride of men: Ironworking in 19th Century West Central Africa.* Portsmouth , NH: Heinemann.

LaGamma, Alisa
2000 *Art and Oracle: African Art and Rituals of Divination.* New York: The Metropolitan Museum of Art and Harry N. Abrams, Inc.

Lang, Herbert
1924 "Famous Treasures of a Negro King."
The American Museum Journal 18(7): 527-552.

Lecoq, Raymond
1953 *Les Bamiléké.* Paris: Présence Africaine.

Lehuard, Raoul
1989 *Art Bakongo. Les centres de style.* 2 Vol. Arnouville: Arts d'Afrique Noire.

Lehuard, Raoul and Louis Perrois (eds.)
1999 *Ni anonyme ni impersonel.* 3e Colloque Européen sur les arts d'Afrique noire. Vanves, 23 octobre 1999. Arnouville: Arts d'Afrique Noire.

Letourneau,Charles
1865 "Sur la Religiosité." *Bulletins et mémoires de la Société d'Anthropologie de Paris.* pp. 595-96.

Levinsohn, Rhoda
1984 *Art And Craft Insouthern Africa.* Johannesburg: Delta Books.

Lima, Mesquitela
1967 *Os akixi (mascarados) do Nordeste de Angola.* Lisbon: Museu do Dundo (Subsídios para a História, Arqueologia e Etnografia dos Povos da Lunda, Publicações Culturais da Companhia de Diamantes de Angola [Diamang], 70).

MacGaffey, Wyatt
1991 *Art and Healing of the Bakongo Commented by Themselves: Minkisi from the Laman Collection.* Stockholm: Folkens Museum.

Maesen, Albert
1954-55 Unpublished field notebooks nos. 33, 43, 52, 53, and 54. Royal Museum for Central Africa, Ethnography Section, Tervuren.

Maesen, Albert
1975 "Un masque de type gitenga des Pende occidentaux du Zaïre." *Africa-Tervuren* 21(3/4):115-16.

Marshall, H.F.
1939 *Intelligence Report on Benin City.* Benin City, Nigeria: Ministry of Local Government.

Martinez-Constantin, Nadine
1999 "Tellem et Dogon: problème d'identité. " In *Ni anonyme ni impersonel.* 3e Colloque Européen sur les arts d'Afrique noire. Vanves, 23 octobre 1999, Raoul

Lehuard and Louis Perrois (eds.). pp. 99- 111

Martins, João Vicente.
1993 *Crenças, Adivinação e Medicina Tradicionais dos Tutchokwe do Nordeste de Angola.* Lisbon: Instituto de Investigação Científica Tropical.

McIntosh, Roderick J.
1989 "Middle Niger Terra Cottas before the Symplegades Gateway". *African Arts* 22(2): 74-83.

McNaughton, Patrick R.
1988 *The Mande Blacksmiths: Knowledge, Power and Art in West Africa.* Bloomington, IN: Indiana University Press.

Merriam, Alan P.
1978 "Kifwebe and Other Masks among the Basongye." *Africa-Tervuren* 24(3):57-73; 24, 4:89-101.
1982 "Kifwebe and Other Cult Groups among the Bala (Basongye)," In *African Religious Groups and Beliefs,* ed. Simon Ottenberg. Meerut: Archana Publications for the Folklore Institute, pp. 19-34.

Meyer, Piet
1981 *Kunst und Religion der Lobi.* Zürich: Museum Rietberg.

Monteil, Charles
1977 *Les Bambara du Ségou et du Kaarta,* [1924]. Paris: Maisonneuve & Larose.

Murray, K.C.
1941 "Nigerian Bronzes: Work from Ife." *Antiquity* 15(57): 71-80.

Mveng, Englebert.
1975 "Problématique d'une esthétique Negro-africaine." *Ethiopiques* Juillet(3): 68-88.

Neyt, François
1993 *Luba: Aux sources du Zaïre.* Paris: Dapper.

Ngolo Kibango
1976 *Minganji, danseurs de masques Pende.* Bandundu: Centre d'Etudes Ethnologiques (Ceeba), II, 35.

Nooter, Mary H.
1990 Catalogue entries. In *Art of Central Africa. Masterpieces from the Berlin Museum fur Volkerkunde,* Hans Joachim Koloss (ed.). New York: The Metropolitan Museum of Art.

Nooter Roberts, Mary, and Allen F. Roberts
1996 *Memory: Luba Art and the Making of History.* New York: Museum for African Art, and Munich: Prestel.

Otite, Onigu
1971 "Totemism in Orogun, Midwestern Nigeria." *African Notes* 6(2): SIEBER, Roy – 1973 Approaches to non-Western Art, pp. 425-432 in W.L. D'AZEVEDO 1973, q.v.
47-52.

Otite, Onigu (ed.)
1980 *The Urhobo People.* Ibadan: Heinemann Educational Books (Nig.) Limited.

Ottenberg, Simon
1975 "Masked Rituals of Afikpo." In *The Context of African Art.* Seattle & London: University of Washington Press.

Peek, Philip
1983 "The Celebration of Oworu among the Isoko." *African Arts* 20(1): 34–41, 98.

Peek, Philip M., ed.
1991 *African Divination Systems: Ways of Knowing.* Bloomington and Indianapolis: Indiana University Press.

Pemberton III, John, ed.
1989 "The Oyo Empire." In *Yoruba: Nine Centuries of African Art and Thought,* Henry John Drewal , John Pemberton III, Rowland Abiodun. New York: The Center for African Art. pp. 147-188.
2000 *Insight and Artistry in African Divination.* Washington, D.C., and London: Smithsonian Institution Press.

Petridis, Constantine
1999a "Luluwa Masks." *African Arts* 32(3):32-47, 91-94.
1999b "Tree Altars, Spirit-Trees, and 'Ghost-Posts' among the Luluwa and Neighboring Peoples." *Baessler-Archiv* 47(1):115-50.
2000a "Notes succinctes sur les masques kalengula des Luntu et des peuples voisins (République Démocratique du Congo)." *Arts d'Afrique Noire* 115:17-25; 116:19-27.
2000b "Beknopte aantekeningen over een luipaardgenootschap en een rammasker bij de Luntu." *Mededelingen der Zittingen van de Koninklijke Academie voor Overzeese Wetenschappen* 46(2):113-32.

Picton, John, ed.
1983 *Earthenware in Asia and Africa.* Colloquia on Art and Archaeology in Asia: no. 12. London: University of London, School of Oriental and African Studies.

Pietz, William
1987 "The problem of the fetish. 2: The origin of the fetish." *RES* 13: 24-45.

Phillips, Tom.
1995 *Africa. The Art of a Continent.* New York: Prestel.

Puccinelli, Lydia
2000 *The Artistry of African Currency.* Washington D.C.: Smithsonian National Museum of African Art.

Read, C.H. and O.M. Dalton
1899 *Antiquities from the City of Benin in the British Museum.* London: British Museum.

Redinha, José
1956 *Máscaras de madeira da Lunda e Alto Zambeze.* Lisbon: Museu do Dundo (Subsídios para a História, Arqueologia e Etnografia dos Povos da Lunda, Publicações Culturais da Companhia de Diamantes de Angola [Diamang], 31).

Richards, Audrey I.
1935 "Bow Stand or Trident?" *Man* 35:390-2.

Roberts, Allen F.
1988. "Of Dogon Crooks and Thieves." *African Arts* 21(4): 70-75, 91.
1990 "Tabwa Masks: An Old Trick of the Human Race." *African Arts* 23(3): 36-47, 101-3.
1995a *Animals in African Art: From the Familiar to the Marvelous*. New York: Museum for African Art, and Munich: Prestel.
1995b Cat. no. 156. In *Treasures from the Africa-Museum, Tervuren*, eds. Gustaaf Verswijver et al. Tervuren: Royal Museum for Central Africa. p. 351.
1996 "The Ironies of System D." In *Recycled, Reseen: Folk Art from the Global Scrap Heap*, C. Cerny and S. Seriff (eds.). Santa Fe: Abrams for the Museum of International Folk Art.

Rodrigues de Areia, Manuel L.
1985 *Les Symboles divinatoires: Analyse socio-culturelle d'une technique de divination des Cokwe de l'Angola*. Coimbra: Centro de estudos Africanos.

Ross, Doran H. (ed.)
1992 *Elephant. The Animal and its Ivory in African Culture*. Los Angeles: UCLA, Fowler Museum of Cultural History.

Roth, Henry Ling
1968a *Great Benin: Its Customs, Art and Horrors*. London: Routledge and Kegan Paul, [1903].
1968b Halifax: A. King and Sons. Reprinted London: Routledge and Kegan Paul. [1903]

Rubin, Arnold
1974 *Accumulation: Power and Display in African Sculpture*. New York: Pace Gallery.

Ryder, A.F.C.
1969 *Benin and the Europeans 1485-1897*. London: Longmans, Green and Co Ltd.

Sassoon, Hamo
1983 "Kings, Cattle and Blacksmiths: Royal Insignia and Religious Symbolism in the Interlacutrine States." *Azania* 18(1983): 93-106.
1995 "Omusinga holder." In *Africa. The Art of a Continent*, Tom Phillips, (ed.). New York: Prestel p.157.

Schildkraut, Enid
1989 "Mangbetu Pottery: Tradition and Innovation in Northwest Zaire". African Arts 22(2): 38-47.

Schweeger-Hefel, Annemarie
1981 *Steinskulptur der Nyonyosi aus Ober-Volta*. München: Fred Jahn.

Schweeger-Hefel, Annemarie und Wilhelm Staude
1972 *Die Kurumba von Lurum*. Monographie eines Volkes aus Ober-Volta (West-Afrika) Wien: Verlag A. Schendl.

Shaw, Thurstan
1965 "Spectrographic Analyses of the Igbo and other Nigerian Bronzes." *Archaeometry* 8: 86-95.
1970 *Igbo Ukwu*. London: Faber and Faber. 2 vols.

Shayt, David A.
1992 "The Material Culture of Ivory outside Africa." In *Elephant. The Animal and its Ivory in African Culture*. Doran H. Ross, (ed.). Los Angeles: UCLA,

Fowler Museum of Cultural History. pp. 367-381.

Sieber, Roy
1973 "Approaches to non-Western Art." In *The Traditional Artist in African Societies*, Warren L. d'Azevedo (ed.). pp. 425-432
1980 *African Furniture And Household Objects*. Bloomington: Indiana University Press.

Siroto, Leon
1976 *African Spirit Images and Identities*. New York: Pace Gallery.

Smith, Fred T.
1989 "Vessels and Harmony among the Guruns." *African Arts* 22(2): 60-65.

Spindel, Carol
1989 "Kpeenebele Senufo Potters." *African Arts* 22(2): 65-73.

Spring, Christopher
1993 *African Arms and Armor*. Washington DC: Smithsonian Institution Press.

Stephan, Lucien
1988 "La sculpture africaine: essai d'esthétique comparée." In *L'Art Africain*. Paris: Mazenod. pp. 31-358.

Stevens, Philips, Jr.
1978 *The Stone Images of Esie, Nigeria*. Ibadan: Ibadan University Press, and Lagos: Federal Department of Antiquities.

Stossel, Arnult
1984 *Africanische Keramik*. Munich: Harmer.

Thompson, Robert Farris
1971 *Black Gods and Kings*. Los Angeles: the Regents of the University of California.

Thompson, Robert Farris and Joseph Cornet
1981 *The Four Moments of the Sun*. Washington D.C.: National Gallery of Art.

Turner, Victor.
1967 *The Forest of Symbols*. Ithaca: Cornell University Press.
1975 *Revelation and Divination in Ndembu Ritual*. Ithaca: Cornell University Press.

Underwood, Leon
1949 *Bronzes of West Africa*. London, Alec Tiranti.

Van Damme, Annemieke
2001 *Spectacular Display: The Art of Nkanu Initiation Rituals*. Washington, D.C.: National Museum of African Art, Philip Wilson Publishers.

Van Noten, Francis
1972 "La plus ancienne sculpture sur bois de l'Afrique Centrale?" *Africa-Tervuren*, 18(3-4): 133-136.

Vandenhoute, Jan P.
1945 *Het masker in de cultuur en de kunst van het Boven-Cavally gebied*. Unpublished Ph.D. dissertation, University of Ghent.

Vansina, Jan
1969 "The Bells of Kings." *Journal of African History* 10(2): 189-97.
1978 *The Children of Woot: A History of the Kuba Peoples*. Madison: the University of Wisconsin Press.

Verly, Robert
1955 "La statuaire de pierre du Bas-Congo (Bamboma-Musurongo)." *Zaire* 9(5): 451-528.

Vernant, Jean-Pierre
1985 "De la présentification de l'invisible à l'imitation de l'apparence." In *Image et signification*. La Documentation Française, Rencontres de l'Ecole du Louvre. pp. 25-27.

Villault de Bellefond, Nicolas
1669 *Relation des Costes d'Afrique appelées Guinée*. Paris: Denys Thierry.

Werner, O.
1970 "Metallurgische Untersuchungen der Benin-Bronzen der Museums fur Volkerkunde Berlin." *Baessler-Archiv* 17: 71-153.

Werner, O and Frank Willett
1975 "The composition of brasses from Ife and Benin." *Archaeometry* 17(2): 141-56.

Wilcox, Rosalinde G.
1992 "Elephants, Ivory, and Art : Duala Objects of Persuasion." In *Elephant. The Animal and its Ivory in African Culture*, Doran H. Ross, (Ed.) Los Angeles: UCLA, Fowler Museum of Cultural History. pp. 261-273.

Willett, Frank
1967 *Ife in the History of West African Sculpture*. London: Thames and Hudson.
1981 "The Analysis of Nigerian Copper Alloys Retrospect and Prospect." *Critica d'Arte Africana* n.s., fasc. 96(178): 35-49.

Willett, Frank and S.J. Fleming
1976 "A Catalogue of Important Nigerian Copper-Alloy Castings Dated by Thermoluminescence." *Archaeometry* 18(2): 135-146.

Willet, Frank, B. Tornsey and M. Ritchie
1994 "Composition and style: an examination of the Benin bronze heads." *African Arts* 27(3):60-67,102.

Williams, Deirdre
1968 "The Dance of the Bedu Moon." *African Arts* 2(1):18-21.

Williams, Denis
1974 *Icon and Image*. London: Allen Lane.

Womersley, Harold
1984 *Legends and History of the Luba*. Los Angeles: Crossroads Press.

MUSEUM FOR AFRICAN ART

Donors

Foundation, Corporate & Government Donations

Altria Group, Inc.
Carnegie Corporation of New York
Equal Foundation, Inc.
The Hearst Foundation
The Andrew W. Mellon Foundation
Mitsui, USA Foundation
National Recreation Foundation

Colgate-Palmolive Company
Edison Schools, Inc.
Entrust Capital, Inc.
The GE Fund
J.P. Morgan Chase Foundation
Time, Inc.
Toyota Motor North America, Inc.
United Way of New York City
Andy Warhol Foundation for the Visual Arts
The Oprah Winfrey Foundation

ABC, Inc. and The Walt Disney Company
American Express
Bloomberg
The Citigroup Private Bank
Consolidated Edison Company of New York, Inc.
Credit Suisse First Boston
Credit Suisse First Boston, Private Client Services
Debevoise & Plimpton
Deloitte & Touche
The Irene Diamond Fund
Empire BlueCross Blue Shield
Étant donnés: the French-American Fund for
Contemporary Art
Goya Foods
Keyspan Foundation
Marsh & McLennan Companies
Mitsui Steel Development Co.
Motown Records Company, L.P.
NBC 4
The New York Community Trust
Helena Rubinstein Foundation
May and Samuel Rudin Family Foundation
UBS Paine Webber, Inc.
Vanity Fair
Volvo Cars of North America
Washington Mutual Bank

Bcom3 Group
de Coizart Charitable Trust u/w S.K. de Coizart
Fast Company and Inc. Magazines
The Fund for the City of New York
Gibson, Dunn & Crutcher LLP
Goldman, Sachs & Co.
Merrill Lynch & Co., Inc.
Mitsui Foods, Inc.
North General Hospital
Rockefeller Group Development Corporation
William H. Kearns Foundation

Ambac Financial Group
Carlson Companies, Inc.
Guiness UDV
Hearst Entertainment, Inc.

Hines
Hinman, Straub, Pigors & Manning
La Bernadin
Mitsui Plastics
Mitsui Textile Corporation
NBA
NFL
The New York Times Co. Foundation
New York State United Teachers
Piaget
Schieffelin & Somerset
SKYAUCTION.com
Tonio Burgos & Associates
Warner Bros.

Individual Donors

Corice Canton Arman and Arman
Mr. and Mrs. Charles B. Benenson
Ms. Sherry Bronfman
Mr. Henry Buhl
Mr. and Mrs. Louis Capozzi
Dorothy and Lewis B. Cullman
Drs. Jean and Nobel Endicott
Mr. Richard Faletti
Mr. and Mrs. Jacques Germain
Mr. Irwin Ginsburg
Mr. Jonathan D. Green
Ms. Marion Greene
Mr. Lawrence Gussman
Jane and Gerald Katcher
Helen and Martin Kimmel
Ms. Elizabeth Krupnick
Caral and Joe Lebworth
Mrs. Jo Levitt
Drs. Marian and Daniel Malcolm
Jennifer and Art Mbanefo
Kathryn McAuliffe and Jay Kriegel
Mr. Robert Neimeth
Mr. Onuoha Odim
Mr. and Mrs. James J. Ross
Lynne and Robert Rubin
Merton D. Simpson
Mrs. Cecilia Smiley
Mr. John Tishman
Mr. Jason H. Wright
Harold and Maureen Zarember
Mr. Daniel M. Ziff

Ms. Peg Alston
Ms. Joan Barist
Anna and Carlo Bella
Mr. and Mrs. Daniel L. Black
Ms. Diahann Carroll
Mr. David Christensen
Dr. and Mrs. Sidney Clyman
Mr. Charles Davis
Mr. Kent Davis
Mr. Lance Entwistle
Michael and Nancy Feller
Ms. Vianna Finch
Ms. Jean Fritts
Dr. Suzanne Frye
Denyse and Marc Ginzberg

Myrna and Stephen Greenberg
Gail Gregg and Arthur Salzberger, Jr.
Mr. and Mrs. Gerdalio Grinberg
Mrs. Elinor Guggenheimer

Mr. and Mrs. Jack Hartog
Lesley and Evan Heller
Geoffrey Holder
Ellen Kaplowitz
Guy and Roxanne Lanquetot
Diane and Brian Leyden
Mrs. Dorothy Lichtenstein
Mr. Adam Lindemann
Ms. Elsie McCabe
Robert Lyons
Mary Jane Marcasiano
Mrs. Kendall A. Mix
Jeanne Moutoussamy-Ashe
Janet and Daniel Murnick
Amyas Naegle
Mr. Michael Oliver
Ms. Maria Patterson
Mr. and Mrs. Peter O. Price
Beatrice Riese
Leonardo and Louise Riggio
Mr. David Rockefeller
Mr. and Mrs. Richard Rothman
Mr. Howard Rubenstein
Mrs. Harry Rubin
Ann and Dick Solomon
Ann and Paul Sperry
Jerome and Ellen Stern
Mr. Dennis Swanson
Ms. Julie Taymor
Mr. Eugene Thompson
Judith and Michael Thoyer
Mr. Jonathan M. Tisch
Ms. Helen Tucker
Mr. Bernard Tschumi
Mr. Lucien Van de Velde
Mr. Jerome Vogel
Ms. Claudia Wagner
George and Joyce Wein
Ruth Weiss
Janice Savin Williams and Christopher J. Williams
Mr. William Wright

Lynn and Samuel Berkowitz
Mrs. Patti Cadby Birch
Ronald and Linda Blatt
Mr. Zachary W. Carter
Mrs. Katherine Cline
Dr. and Mrs. Oliver E. Cobb
Ms. Martha Cotter
Ms. Gail Yvette Davis
The Honorable David N. Dinkins
Dr. and Mrs. Gilbert Graham
Mr. and Mrs. John Herrmann
Mr. and Mrs. Peter Klosowicz
Mr. Luciano Lanfranchi
Mr. and Mrs. Jay Last
Mr. Matthew Li
Ms. Bella Meyer
Mr. Steven Morris
Mr. and Mrs. Ronald Nicholson
Dr. and Mrs. Emanuel Papper
Mr. and Mrs. Fred M. Richman
Mr. Eric Robertson
Mr. Richard Robinson
Ms. Elizabeth Seidman
Mr. and Mrs. Eliot Slade
Mr. and Mrs. Howard Tanenbaum
Mr. and Mrs. William Taubman
Mr. Victor Teicher
Ms. Kathy van der Pas

Volunteers

Jennifer Goldberg
Volunteer Coordinator

Ruth Antrich
Jacqueline Beckels
Sandra Black
David Brown
Ethel Brown
Margaret Burbidge
Peter Chamedes
Cheick Cisse
Nancy Clipper
Brenda Colling
Jay Cooke
Aiesha Cousins
Pamela Crowley
Gail Yvette Davis
Sandra Dickerson
Dallas Fuentes
Delinda Harrison
Valerie Horowitz
Hope Hyder
Stephanie Johnson
Kari Kipper
Jennifer Lee
Shalewa Mackall
Eileen McGinn
LewEleanor McNeely
Margarita Mesa
Antoinette Moss
Laura Nurse
Yvonne Rabsatt
Terry-Ann Samuel
Armand Samgare
Sandra Schofield
Tanya Serdiuk
Temitayo Shajuyigbe
Anthony Snowden
Pamela St. Cyr
Aiesha Turman
Wendy Urquhart
Harriet Walker
Paul Weidner
Claude L. Winfield
Cynthia Wood
Lisa Yancowski
Judy G. Young

Lenders List

Buffalo Museum of Science
Corice Canton Arman and Arman
Myrna and Ira Brind
Mr. and Mrs. Carrie-Vacher
Dr. and Mrs. James Christensen
John Crawford
Gerald and Lila Dannenberg
Charles and Kent Davis
Walt Disney Imagineering
Drs. Jean and Noble Endicott
Etnografisch Museum, Antwerpen
Galerie Jacques Germain, Montreal
Marc and Denyse Ginzberg
Toby and Barry Hecht
W. and U. Horstmann
William Itter
Leonard and Judith Kahan
Mr. and Mrs. J. Thomas Lewis
Adam M. Lindemann
Drs. Daniel and Marian Malcolm
Charles D. Miller III
Noguchi Foundation
Michael Oliver
Pace Primitive Gallery, New York
Françoise Billion Richardson
Laura and James J. Ross
Richard H. Scheller
Simmons Collection
Anthony Slayter-Ralph
Cecilia S. Smiley
Gary van Wyk and Lisa Brittan/ Axis Gallery, New York
Jerome Vogel
Stewart J. Warkow
James Willis Tribal Arts
and those who wish to remain anonymous